KENTUCKY IN THE NEW REPUBLIC

KENTUCKY IN THE NEW REPUBLIC

The Process of Constitution Making

JOAN WELLS COWARD

THE UNIVERSITY PRESS OF KENTUCKY

Publication of this book has been supported by a
grant from the Organization of American Historians.

Library of Congress Cataloging in Publication Data

Coward, Joan Wells, 1936-
 Kentucky in the new republic.

 Bibliography: p.
 Includes index.
  1. Kentucky—Politics and government—To 1792.
 2. Kentucky—Politics and government—1792-1865.
 I. Title.
 F454.C86   320.9'769'03   77-92920
 ISBN 0-8131-1380-6

Scholarly publisher for the Commonwealth,
serving Berea College, Centre College of Kentucky,
Eastern Kentucky University, The Filson Club,
Georgetown College, Kentucky Historical Society,
Kentucky State University, Morehead State University,
Murray State University, Northern Kentucky University,
Transylvania University, University of Kentucky,
University of Louisville, and Western Kentucky University.

Editorial and Sales Offices: Lexington, Kentucky 40506

For my Mother and Father

CONTENTS

ACKNOWLEDGMENTS

THE MANUSCRIPT SOURCES upon which this book is based were so widely scattered that I sometimes felt like a detective rather than a historian while I was doing the initial research. My quest could not have been undertaken without a fellowship grant from the American Association of University Women. It would not have been successful without the generous and sympathetic assistance of the librarians in all the research centers I visited. I owe particular thanks to Dr. Jacqueline Bull and the Special Collections staff at the University of Kentucky, who brought together and organized resources to study Kentucky history and provided a hospitable environment in which to use them.

During the writing and revision of this manuscript, several people have helped to clarify my thinking and simplify my prose. Clarence L. Ver Steeg has given unceasing encouragement and guidance since the inception of this project as a doctoral dissertation at Northwestern University. Elinor Bowen and John Holm provided guidance with the computer programming and interpretation. John Schutz, Allen Woll, Patricia Watlington, Robert Horowitz, and Richard Jensen have read and criticized part or all of the manuscript. The Family and Community History Center at the Newberry Library has twice offered me respite and an opportunity to retool intellectually. Finally, my husband Bob, by his consistent impatience with methodological imprecision, has challenged me to sharpen my analysis. My manuscript has been improved by their efforts, but the final responsibility is mine alone.

1

THE ORIGINS OF KENTUCKY CONSTITUTIONALISM

"On the emigration to America,
and peopling the western Country"

To western woods and lonely plains.
Palemon from the crowd departs,
Where nature's wildest genius reigns,
To tame the soil, and plant the arts.
What wonders there shall freedom show!
What mighty states successive grow.
. . . .

What charming scenes attract the eye
On wild Ohio's savage stream!
. . . .

Here reason shall new laws devise,
And order from confusion rise.

Philip Freneau[1]

THE INITIAL STAGE in the fulfillment of Freneau's romantic prophecy was reached with the formation of the first western state. Virginia and its western district of Kentucky agreed in 1790 upon the terms of their separation, and Kentucky's admission into the Union was scheduled for June 1792, after a constitutional convention to be held in April of that year.[2] The emergence of such new states excited much interest because it fused two enterprises, each of which had been unleashed by the Revolution and in which Americans believed they had a special destiny. "Peopling the western Country" by itself reflected the exuberant expansionism of the new nation, perhaps to fill the continent. At the same time, Americans were actively engaged in studying the "science of government," seeking the legal and constitutional principles which ought to govern free peoples. It was anticipated that new states would put those true principles into practice.

Of course, the shift of the population westward was not new, but it was vastly accelerated by the Revolutionary War and independence. Roots were loosened by the dislocations of the war at the same time the British ban on trans-Appalachian settlement was eliminated. Individuals and families, most of them seeking personal improvement rather than planning a grandiose new society, braved danger and discomfort to move. Although the Appalachian Mountains were breached along their entire length, it was the fertile soil of Kentucky, reputedly so rich it afforded "all the necessities of life spontaneously," which proved initially most attractive. By 1790 the population of the Kentucky district had reached 73,677.[3]

American exploration into political principles was more directly a product of the Revolution. Confrontation with England had focused upon constitutional relationships, and independence required its proponents to codify their understanding of proper governance. Starting in 1776, each state drafted a constitution, tested its operation, and in several cases rewrote it. The climax of this constitutional inquiry came with the drafting of the United States Constitution in 1787 and the prolonged debate on ratification in 1787-1788. The deliberation concentrated upon the structure and function of government. Where should the locus of power be placed to curb potential tyranny? Who should be entrusted with the responsibility of electing or appointing officials, either at the local or central level? What powers should be given or denied to government? What was the proper relationship between the branches of government? In 1776 and 1777, caught up in the antimonarchical reactions against England and George III, Americans feared executive abuse of power. The first constitutions reduced the governor to a cipher and vested most power in the legislature. But state legislatures during the 1780s often seemed large and unruly; further, they sometimes passed laws which, however popular, violated conservative belief in property rights. Increasingly, the "democratical" branch of the legislature was regarded as a serious threat to republican government, and constitutions in the late 1780s built in a greater separation of powers to check excesses in any and all branches of government.[4]

This debate over constitutional structure sometimes obscured deeper concerns. Supporters of independence discovered that the Revolution had done more than displace British authority; it had given impetus to challenges of existing institutions. In ways that many revolutionaries could not have foreseen, the whole nexus of politics, the relationship between citizen and government, was disrupted. Traditionally and ideally, suffrage was limited to those with a stake in society – land or, at minimum, the payment of taxes. Voters chose the best man, measured by family connections, status, and personal qualities. Each representative then expected to use his own independent judgment, to lead rather than simply represent constituents. In theory, he, together with his fellow delegates in the assembly, enacted legislation designed for the benefit of the whole community rather than for individual or particularistic purposes.[5]

Such a politics of deference, with the passive role it prescribed for ordinary citizens, had never been as secure in the colonies as in England, but the Revolution accentuated even further the insecurity. Popular participation had been invited and encouraged during and after the Stamp Act crisis, and the rhetoric of independence directed against the British also extended to equality among Americans. As a consequence, politics operated somewhat differently after the Revolution. Candidates were more often forced to canvass the voters for election and to solicit their opinion. Citizens presumed to grill candidates upon the issues and to instruct those elected upon how they should cast their vote. Legislatures contained men from the middling and lower ranks. By no means had deferential politics disappeared, but in some places at least it was on the defensive.[6]

Kentucky became something of a testing ground, a focus, for the debate upon constitutional ideas, assumptions, and structure. Accident of timing rather than any maturation of political society produced this result. Poets and romantics could anticipate the growth of mighty states, but more prosaically minded men could see signs that Kentuckians were not equipped for independence. An independent social system had not yet developed, partly because of the speed with which Kentucky was settled and partly because of the heterogeneity of its population. Not a single adult had been born within its boundaries, a fact contemporary historian Humphrey Marshall thought "a singularity worth a passing notice." The condition was not so singular as Marshall thought – every frontier passed through a similar phase – but Kentuckians were an unusually mixed lot. Despite Virginia's jurisdiction, probably one-half of the white population migrated from other states, especially Pennsylvania, Maryland, and the Carolinas. German and Scotch-Irish migration was substantial. Religious affiliations were important on the frontier, but they were fragmented and at odds. The dominant religious groups, Baptists and Presbyterians, differed upon points of theology and upon the proper relationship between church and state. Residents of Kentucky identified each other by religion and origin and made "Distinctions and Particions" on those bases.[7]

Land legislation had created other rifts in the Kentucky population. Virginia's first priority, when it established authority over Kentucky in 1776, was to guarantee the loyalty of western settlers. By laws passed in 1777 and 1779, pioneers who had settled or improved lands before 1779 were given or allowed to preempt up to 1,400 acres. In 1779, however, Virginia began to use western lands to repay war debts. The legislature authorized military land warrants to veterans, ranging from 100 acres for common soldiers to 5,000 acres for colonels, and sold treasury warrants at forty pounds per hundred acres, cash or credit.[8]

The land program caused endless confusion, controversy, and competition. Virginia issued warrants without prior survey, leaving location of land to the owners and insuring overlapping claims and title disputes. It issued warrants for more land than was available, provoking the comment that states ought "to be just, before they are generous." Soldiers, fearful that all land would be claimed before they could get west, pressured the assembly into reserving a large part of southern Kentucky – the Green River Military District – for settlement of their claims.[9]

Virginia opened the door to extremely unequal land ownership with its military and treasury warrants. Speculators – resident and nonresident alike – acquired title to hundreds of thousands of acres. Generous military bounties to officers, in Virginia nearly always gentlemen, provided for the transplantation of eastern genteel families onto large plantations. Some poor but enterprising pioneers succeeded in joining the ranks of land accumulators by hiring out as "land jobbers" and deputy surveyors, locating land for warrant holders and obtaining a proportion of the surveyed acreage as payment. The earliest arrivals who had been in Kentucky before 1779 had title to as much as 1,400 acres, a comfortable estate if well located. But those who came later, hoping to receive the same preemption rights, were disappointed, and many became tenants. By the early 1790s, probably a majority of Kentucky householders were landless; data are sparse, but only 35 percent in Madison and Lincoln counties owned land.[10]

Upon this ill-formed and quarrelsome conglomeration of Virginians and non-Virginians, frontier pioneers and eastern gentlemen, tenant farmers and land speculators, the state of Virginia imposed its own political institutions. By creating counties in Kentucky (nine by 1790), Virginia extended its own county court system to the west and gave Kentuckians representation in the Virginia House of Delegates (two seats per county).[11] The intention of the parent state was to govern in its own way, but even this limited goal was not fully realized. The political system in the stable eastern part of the state, where gentry control was unchallenged, did not transplant readily to a diverse community built upon rapid expansion of population and property acquisition. More important for Kentuckians, the system did no more than govern; it had not developed political institutions and leadership prepared for self-government before 1792.

At the heart of the stability and continuity of Virginia politics was the county court. By law and custom, the justices of the peace dominated every aspect of local life, serving as legislature, executive, and judiciary. They controlled the nominating process for local officers – sheriff, surveyor, county lieutenant, militia officers, as well as additional justices of the peace – and the governor rarely dared reject their nominations. In eastern Virginia the justices could be drawn from an established planter group, but in Kentucky there were not always such gentlemen available. Furthermore, frontier conditions encouraged respect for skills having nothing to do with birth or breeding: militia leadership or ingenuity and cunning in land acquisition. The Kentucky county courts necessarily included these elements, commencing the development of an indigenous political leadership founded partly upon eastern connections and partly upon western accomplishments.[12]

Foundations were laid, but in 1790 the courts still lacked the stability of membership and common outlook necessary for local control. Courts met irregularly, especially during the early years. The fluidity of the population was reflected by the bewildering frequency with which justices moved on and off the courts. They had not achieved the self-confident domination over the appointive process which Virginia county courts maintained. Even when Kentucky counties insisted that the governor follow court recommendations to the letter, he felt free to ignore them and even to commission justices not nominated. The names of well-qualified easterners who moved west were sometimes placed above more senior justices.[13]

With these courts, Virginia did at least give its western district local governmental institutions, however shaky and weak they remained before statehood. For the rest, Kentucky was less fortunate. It was one of only two states (Maine was the other) before 1850 to enter the Union without a period of self-government as a colony, independent state, or territory. It never possessed its own executive or legislature, and representation in Virginia's assembly provided no meaningful participation in an elective political system. Kentucky voters were forced to limit their choice of legislators to men willing to make the seven-hundred-mile journey. Most of the delegates were gentlemen from Virginia, combining legislative and personal reasons for the trip. In social standing, they were similar to the justices of the peace usually selected in eastern counties, but the impact upon political development was quite different. In Virginia, a high proportion of legislators was reelected year after year, but Kentucky gentlemen eschewed yearly trips, so continuity of service was entirely lacking. Sixteen percent (131 men) of Virginia representatives served five or more years in the House of Delegates since independence; of those from Kentucky counties, 63 percent served only once, with no man serving more than four years. Few Kentuckians, then, had legislative experience; none had gained skills and recognition enough to move into the legislative leadership group which held most effective power.[14]

The only districtwide political institutions were the nine statehood conventions held from 1784 to 1790 in Danville, located in the center of Kentucky. These meetings were genuinely representative and attracted potential political leaders; with more than a dozen men attending at least five conventions, there was a measure of continuity. But however faithfully attended, the conventions provided no experience equivalent to regular participation in the legislative sessions, since the agendas were limited to issues related to statehood and the meetings quite brief. Furthermore, the conventions which had originated in an effort to unify support for statehood instead exacerbated enmities within Kentucky society. The conflict over statehood distorted politics and the political process long after the issue was actually resolved.[15]

Divisions were not over the desirability of statehood – all Kentuckians agreed that there were legitimate grievances against Virginia rule and that the district would eventually separate – but upon its timing, method, and terms. Questions relating to land were central: Would Virginia titles be honored by the new state? Might absentee speculators be subject to discriminatory legislation or large landholdings be broken up? Another important concern was the kind of government which would be formed. Upon these issues, Kentuckians broke into three groups, designated at the time "partisans," the "country party," and the "court party." Although too ill defined and ill organized to warrant a modern designation as parties, these groupings can be identified and their relationships described.[16]

The partisans, denigrated as the "rabble," sought statehood through congressional enactment in 1780, hoping to bypass Virginia's jurisdiction, annul old land grants, and open the way for a new land distribution. They had believed they would control the new government and that it would be "constructed on free liberal and democratical principles." By the mid-1780s they shifted to opposition, now believing that the influx of genteel families had made the "aristocratic spirit dominant" and that the expenses of a new government would be too great a burden for the poor. In their efforts to delay statehood, partisan leaders appealed for popular support, soliciting signatures for instructions to the conventions and for anti-statehood petitions carried east to Richmond.[17]

Such activity alarmed and aroused the gentry. They believed the partisans opposed separation because taxes would be collected more vigorously under a new government than under Virginia. Partisans, they thought, "plainly wish to avoid the Burdens of Government, and it is to be feared the Restraints of Government also." But they were more deeply concerned with opposition tactics than with motive. Accustomed to the deferential politics of Virginia, they found public activity distressing. They organized the series of conventions and encouraged the establishment of a district newspaper – the *Kentucky Gazette* – in 1787, in order to muster popular support for statehood. They asked the citizens to elect "enlightened men" who would make the wisest decision in convention and were discomfited when the partisans denounced that as a "*common place stile of aristocratic advocates.*" Alarmed by the use of instructions to the fifth convention, they refused even to accept them; and, distressed that petitions to the Virginia assembly disturbed the solid facade they wanted to present, they assured eastern correspondents that the petitions had received more attention than the obscure signers warranted.[18]

Although most gentlemen were distressed by partisan activity and most eventually supported statehood, they were by no means united. Indeed, by 1787, the statehood terms specified by Virginia had divided supporters into two groups. The country party, composed of planters and surveyors, found the guarantees of Virginia land titles satisfactory and urged a legal separation with Virginia based upon those terms. But the court party, so-called because at its center were lawyers and judges of the Kentucky district court, was unhappy. Although some members were planters, they had not come to Kentucky early enough to hold title to much land under Virginia and may have hoped for more under the new state. Well educated and ambitious, they were interested in the economic, commercial, and political development of Kentucky and were frustrated by the district's inability to act independently. Since their plans for Kentucky depended upon access to Mississippi navigation, they were infuriated when they learned in early 1787 that Congress was negotiating a twenty-five-year surrender of the Mississippi to Spain. Under the leadership of one of the most ambitious adventurers in United States history, James Wilkinson, court party members began to toy with the idea of a unilateral separation from Virginia.[19]

Precisely how they wanted the maneuverings to end is unclear. Wilkinson hoped to detach Kentucky from the United States and ally it with Spain, a goal which others may have shared. But threats of secession could also be used to pressure a slow and reluctant Congress to admit Kentucky into the Union or to bargain for more favorable terms of admission. Quite possibly the men themselves did not know where these plans would lead, but they were prepared to take any steps they believed would benefit the people of Kentucky. In a climactic convention in November 1788, Wilkinson attempted to obtain a declaration of independence, but his own court party partners backed down, apparently in the face of popular disapproval. Subsequently, the convention petitioned Virginia for a legal separation and asked Congress to renew efforts to obtain Mississippi navigation. It required two more years and two more conventions, but Kentucky moved toward an orderly separation.[20]

This convention and the court party's so-called Spanish Conspiracy marked a turning point in Kentucky colonial politics. Personal antagonisms cut deep, but more significant was the rift among gentlemen who traditionally expected to govern with the consent and acquiescence of ordinary citizens. Suspicions of court party treason could not easily be calmed. For a time court party members almost completely disappeared from the local political scene, most not attending the next two conventions. Perhaps popular disapproval forced political retrenchment, perhaps party members decided to maintain a low profile, but for whatever cause, at the time when statehood was an accomplished fact, the individuals who had been most active in planning for statehood and most interested in the future government were eclipsed.[21]

In contrast the partisans were organized and active. Industrious and shrewd leaders developed techniques for mobilizing popular support. An increased number of partisans attended the eighth and ninth conventions, filling the political void left by the court party's withdrawal. One gentleman described the eighth convention despairingly, "the folly of the District was fully represented. Dullness the off spring of ignorance presided." The representatives of the ninth, it was said, "are so far from being the most enlightened Characters that on the contrary they are frequently from the lowest order of the people." Partisans continued to resist statehood, sending a petition with over four hundred signatures to Richmond in 1789. The final vote in the ninth convention was only 24 to 18. They had not averted separation, but their strength was impressive.[22]

Although most of their efforts were directed toward avoiding statehood, some partisans began somewhat tentatively to consider what an appropriate government ought to be. "A Farmer" told *Gazette* readers in 1788 that "OUR GREATEST POLITICIANS" had imposed separation; if the people were forced to submit, they should contemplate the future government. He then posed queries suggesting the outlines of a radical program: How should the institution of slavery be treated? Should there be more than one house? Should clerks, attorneys, and surveyors be excluded from the legislature? What was the best mode of electing local officials? Several others joined in the inquiry, though not all shared his radical perspective.[23]

Although Kentucky gentlemen did not participate in the newspaper debate, some – particularly court party members – had been participants in the nationwide discussions upon law and politics, both among themselves and with friends elsewhere. A small group formed a Political Club, patterned upon the Phi Beta Kappa Society of Williamsburg, to discuss problems of government and political economics. Particularly interested in constitutional inquiry, they debated and rewrote the United States Constitution in 1788 and named a committee of six to write a suitable constitution for Kentucky.[24] In their debates and in correspondence with the east, Kentuckians sometimes pondered general principles, but their focus was upon Kentucky and what they believed its peculiar circumstances.

At the heart of the problem was the perception these gentlemen had of their own society. Much more than outsiders, who tended to assume Kentucky's readiness for independence, Kentuckians recognized the inadequacy of preparation. Ironically, the court party members who most strongly supported separation were the most aware of its dangers. Their motives for such support of statehood were all negative, stemming from frustration at the colonial status: The United States was unable or unwilling to obtain Mississippi navigation; Virginia provided no executive to secure protection against Indian attack; distant government was unaware of or indifferent to western problems. They did not deny opponents' charges that the population was unready, unassimilated, unused to effective government; they simply expressed hope that differences would disappear and government closer to home would be effective. But the political inclination of the people at the time of statehood, as described by a perceptive observer, did not encourage much immediate optimism.

The peculiar character which belongs to our citizens in general will contribute for a time at least to our unhappiness. They were formerly citizens of other countries, and a great proportion of them have been induced to come here by a spirit of discontent or adventure; Citizens generally consisting of such men must make a very different mass from one which is composed of men born and raised on the same spot. Our people are all wise and *ought to be* great men; they see none about them to whom or to whose families they [have] been accustomed to think themselves inferior.

Relocation, he thought, had broken the ties of traditional deferential politics and had aroused individual ambition in every man.[25]

Fears about the governability of the population were matched by apprehension about the sufficiency of appropriate leadership. Possessed of an elitist sense of the qualities needed for judges, executives, and legislators, court party observers found too few in the conventions and county courts of Kentucky to fill the necessary slots. In the future, they hoped more qualified people would move in, but meanwhile the government ought to be tailored to present circumstances by being smaller or simpler.[26]

Their intractable dilemma of wanting statehood when they considered Kentucky unready was compounded by the task of writing the first state constitution. They believed this constitution was critically important in establishing the proper development of the state and in attracting the kind of people needed to govern it. Yet they thought themselves and other Kentuckians lacking the knowledge and skill to write it. Their first solution was to engage in an almost frantic search for assistance from outside. Starting in 1785, Kentucky gentlemen sent letter after letter to the east. Advice was solicited from Thomas Jefferson, jurist Edmund Pendleton, and lawyer George Nicholas. However, James Madison, who had close blood and personal ties with Kentuckians and whose constitutional abilities were well understood before 1787, was most persistently sought. No less than four men importuned him, including one man who told Madison, fifteen months after being named to a Political Club committee to write the constitution, "I fear that few will be found in that Body who have sufficiently attended to political Subjects to quallify them for the task of framing a good System of Government. . . . [if] you could be prevailed upon to draw up a plan of Government . . . there is every reason to believe that it would be adopted in toto."[27]

Others continued to look for outside help almost to the eve of the convention, believing that "in our infant Country we have very few characters, who have turned their attention to these important subjects." In return they received letters of advice, but no more. Madison declined to send a draft as he had been requested, because of press of time and "Ignorance of many local circumstances & opinions which must be consulted in such a work." Instead he recommended a reading of a recently published volume of state constitutions for material upon which to draw. Despite their self-doubts, Kentuckians were on their own.[28]

2

KENTUCKY'S FIRST CONSTITUTION

AS THE CONSTITUTIONAL debate began in 1790, Kentucky remained an inchoate society. There had been no long period of seasoning in which people of different origins might form social and political networks. Political institutions were weak, political experience scanty. Bitter divisions had submerged the political fortunes of the few gentlemen who had engaged in any constitutional explorations. There was a void, and one man, recently arrived in the west, aspired to fill it.

District Court Judge Caleb Wallace reported in 1785, "Money is scarce and Disputes for Land Numerous so that Gentlemen of the Law may have sufficient Employment if like the antient Romans they would appear for their Clients Gratis." The quantity of business did indeed lure lawyers to Kentucky, although they fully intended to make the undertaking profitable. Among them was Virginian George Nicholas who had every reason to be optimistic about his prospects. Son of a one-time state treasurer and tied to some of the state's most influential families, his own career was already well under way. He had attended the College of William and Mary, studied law under George Wythe, and fought in the Revolution, advancing to lieutenant colonel while still in his mid-twenties. While in the Virginia assembly in 1778 and 1781, he demonstrated a willingness to modify accepted principles and practices when necessary. Frustrated by the ineffective war effort, he proposed the appointment of a dictator during the emergency. Further, he moved that the assembly investigate the conduct of Governor Thomas Jefferson. With deep public discontent after the invasion of Virginia, such a motion may have seemed a good political step to young Nicholas, and the resolution passed in the assembly. Jefferson and his friends were embarrassed and annoyed, but Nicholas seemingly backed off, answering Jefferson's appeal for particulars with a diffident letter and not attending when Jefferson replied to the charges in the assembly. Perhaps he retracted, as Jefferson later claimed, for a cordial friendship developed between him and James Madison, and Nicholas supported Jefferson's political party in the 1790s.[1]

After the war, Nicholas practiced law in Charlottesville. In the House of Delegates, he allied himself with Madison in the fight to establish religious freedom. In 1788, when he had already decided to move to Kentucky, he was elected to the Virginia ratifying convention, which fourteen Kentucky delegates also attended. The westerners were almost completely silent during the proceedings, but they must have observed their future compatriot with great interest.[2]

George Nicholas was scarcely a prepossessing figure. Short, with a large bald head, he was so obese that he had once been caricatured as "a plum pudding with legs to it." Yet, for all his ungainly appearance, he was a highly respected member of the faction supporting the constitution. He had prepared carefully, evaluating the arguments that might be most persuasive. In convention, he was considered the best match for the formidable Patrick Henry. Speaking in a monotone, with no witticisms, no humor, no movement except a gesturing of one finger and one hand, he picked out the inconsistencies of the anti-Federalist arguments. For example, in response to Henry's expressed apprehension that the new government would have insufficient representation, Nicholas suggested that, by the course Henry proposed, "Virginia would relinquish the number we are entitled to, and have none at all."[3]

Nicholas reserved his best efforts for converting Kentucky delegates from their anti-Federalist predilections. "That country contains all my wishes and prospects," he assured them. "There is my property and there I intend to reside. I should be averse to the establishment of any system which would be injurious to it." Kentuckians feared a strong national government might yield the westerners' precious right to navigate the Mississippi, and the anti-Federalists played upon such fears. Nicholas contended that Kentucky rights, including those of navigation, were more likely to be protected by a strong national government than a weak one. He failed to convince the delegates, who voted 10 to 3 against ratification, but his own avowed commitment to the west was not lost upon the Kentuckians present.[4]

Nicholas moved within the year and built an elegant plantation near the court center of Danville. He commenced a career combining planting with the law, also joining other Kentuckians in efforts to promote manufactures and develop a well-balanced economy. Widely considered the best lawyer in the district, an appraisal in which he concurred, Nicholas obtained "a great run of business" and became so prosperous that a friend joked that he might forget his republican principles.[5] In financial position, in social status, and at the bar, Nicholas retained absolute confidence in his preeminence. Considering the humility with which other Kentucky leaders sought advice, his self-assurance was rare.

While still in Virginia, Nicholas had forsworn politics in his new residence, believing that he was making "a sufficient sacrifice when I bury myself there without giving up my happiness and content by engaging in a new state of warfare with knaves and fools." He enjoyed political maneuvering from the background but was disdainful of an increasingly assertive electorate. In politics, he thought, "you would spend your time and money to no purpose, in serving people who think they confer a favor on you by permitting you to do so." But his constant reiteration never to "offer for or accept of any post under government" had always excepted the Kentucky constitutional convention. His interest in such matters was well established and, he declared, "I never intend to have any hand in the game of government but wish to know how the *hands* are managed." In fact, his planned withdrawal from government made his participation in the convention particularly crucial, since only there would he be able to shape the future government. Thus it was as a candidate that he watched the election campaign heat up.[6]

Nicholas reported at the end of 1790 that those who had opposed statehood were silent, "most of them convinced and well satisfied that it should take place." He no doubt hoped that the divisive politics of the previous years would end and that the population would return to a more passive role. But such hopes were ill founded, as widespread interest in the constitution emerged during 1791. Public activity became so great that one gentleman reported in August that "the People of Kentucky are mere Fanatics in Politics – Constitutions are forming in every Neighbourhood." The gentry were particularly distressed, as the December 1791 election neared, by the emergence and spread of county committees, local irregular groups composed of representatives from each militia company. At least four or five county groups formed, and three sent representatives to a meeting in Harrodsburg. Other locales were reported stirring, preparing to join the movement. One infuriated justice of the peace threatened physical punishment for those abetting the committee activity. Although the Kentucky elite had attracted opposition before, such formal organization and coordination were apparently new.[7]

The institution of local committees and associations originated in the Revolutionary experience. First serving as pressure groups in the 1760s and early 1770s, they eventually took on governmental functions as the royal authority collapsed, gaining a quasi-legitimacy in the process. They had generally not been radical in membership or function, often including gentry and middling elements. In Virginia, the committees had indeed often been identical in membership to the county courts whose authority they replaced or supplemented. Although there was some feeling that committees were no longer needed once royal authority was replaced by local governments based upon popular consent, they remained a useful means of organizing the citizenry. In Kentucky, during the 1780s, the statehood conventions represented continuing efforts by Kentucky leaders to muster popular support. The first convention in 1784 had consisted of men elected from each militia district. Furthermore, in 1787, western settlements concerned about Mississippi navigation had formed committees of correspondence. Unquestionably the organizers intended the customary leaders to direct committee activity, just as the Virginia gentry had during the Revolution.[8]

The committees of 1791 differed sharply from previous models. Instead of functioning as tools of the gentry, the new groups were rooted in the popular ferment within Kentucky and included men not previously active in politics. Perhaps the committees originated in the anti-statehood fight of the 1780s. Some committee expressions of dissatisfaction with statehood suggest such a connection, but scanty membership records preclude a definitive judgment. Committee proposals, particularly those of the Bourbon County group, did contain the same anti-elitist sentiments some statehood opponents had expressed earlier.[9]

The Bourbon County committee, under the chairmanship of an obscure figure, William Henry, demanded the continuing use of committees in order to assure democratic control of government. Henry and his supporters traced the legitimacy of such groups both to Revolutionary antecedents and to democratic principles. They described committees, composed of two from each militia company, as the best means of establishing the true will of the people; annual elections, while desirable, were liable to corruption through flattery and grog. During the statehood process itself, county committees first should choose slates of delegates to the convention, then draw up instructions containing important governmental principles to direct convention deliberations, and finally submit the draft constitution to the voters.[10]

The government proposed in the Bourbon committee instructions was local, democratic, simple, and cheap. Elections by ballot would be conducted in districts convenient to voters rather than at one spot in the county. Freemen would elect justices of the peace, sheriffs, and all militia officers of the rank of colonel or lower; a one-house legislature would choose all other government officers, who would be paid in country produce. County committees would continue to deliberate, to assemble the people when necessary, and to instruct their representatives upon pending legislation. Instruction was the key element, since it guaranteed continuing control over state governmental activity. The Bourbon County plan maintained that the legislature should not repeat past error by merely copying the laws of other states. Instead the state code should be "adapted to the weakest capacity" and thus "happily supercede the necessity of attorneys." Kentucky's government should be one in which "the farmer, the mechanic, and even the common labouring man have a voice . . . equal to the lawyer, the colonel or the general."[11]

Educated Kentuckians found this program appalling, one summing it up derisively, "The exclusion not from the Legislature only, but from the barr, of Lawyers, the abolition of Slavery, and low Salaries to the Officers of Government, and that to be paid in produce, The committees it is expected, will insist much upon. It will be a new scene to see a Chief Judge at the end of a term, riding upon a bag of Corn, & driving home the Cows & Calves, he has receiv'd for his quarters Salary, And the Governor trudging home with a baskett of Eggs upon his Arm."[12] Even more frightening than the proposals was the possibility of their widespread acceptance. The *Kentucky Gazette* provided a free forum for the Bourbon County committee spokesmen. Consequently, the newspaper report that a number of committees had formed and were attempting coordinated action provoked strong reaction.

The most direct response – engaging in public debate upon constitutional issues – was also the most limited. Only one writer, "The disinterested Citizen," discussed substantive alternatives to the committee proposals, and he was clearly writing a defense of particular constitutional principles which he thought ought not require explication because they were "so universally admitted." "The disinterested Citizen" was quite possibly Nicholas himself, since the arguments were the same that he later employed in convention. The columns stressed the necessity for absolute separation of powers between three branches, for a Senate, and for a Bill of Rights. Some suggested that a Senate was unnecessary, expensive, and an unacceptable check upon popular control; since there was but one interest in society, better a one-house legislature. "The disinterested Citizen" avoided sharp criticism of the lower house but suggested tactfully that house members might be "good" but "ignorant" and that unintended mistakes which resulted from the "passion and hurry so incident to a multitude" would be corrected by the wise action of an upper house. Three times he insisted that a separate and specific Bill of Rights was necessary to protect minority rights, especially property rights. He feared its omission would endanger slaveholding.[13]

Other writers declined to attack the committee program or offer alternatives, pointedly insisting that was the "province of the convention." Instead, energy and ink were employed in denying both the legitimacy of the committees and their right to nominate slates of candidates and to instruct their elected delegates. The vehement assault was on the whole committee process which violated and threatened expectations about the convention. Opponents stressed the importance and delicacy of the convention task and the necessary skills, which were not likely to be found in committee choices. Essential qualities were integrity and wisdom, the latter defined as political intelligence, a native genius tempered by education and experience. Committees were arousing prejudices against "men of Fortune, learned men, the Judiciary & Barr" and insisting that "*plain honest Farmers*" ought to write the constitution. If the committees prevailed, only the most ignorant and unworthy members of the community would be elected, and the outcome of the proceedings would be disastrous. Committeemen were "utter strangers to the fundamental principles of free government"; if such "a set of novices should find means to push themselves forward, they will only be able to establish, under the name of a constitution, a collection of absurdities."[14]

At the same time that they defined a set of criteria for convention delegates, opponents attacked committee activity. Such institutions were extralegal, they thought, since no laws sanctioned them. More important, committees encouraged faction and destroyed what the writers claimed was the unanimity of the community. By presenting a slate of candidates, committees insulted the voter's intelligence by urging him to submit to the electoral choice of the group rather than exercise his independent judgment. "A Citizen" asked on the eve of the election, "Have you my fellow Country men, resigned your rights as Free men and Electors?" The thrust of the argument was plain: if no factions existed and voters acted independently, using criteria of education and experience, the gentry would be elected.[15]

Finally and most persistently, before and after the election, attacks focused upon the committee plan to employ instructions to guide convention deliberation. "A.B.C.," the committees' most articulate and persistent critic, thought it negated the true meaning of representation and tried to convince "the good people of Kentucky" that, although "all power derives from the community, the community should exercise none except in choosing representatives." If the representatives were bound by instructions from their constituents, it mattered little how well qualified they were. The proper function of a convention – an assembly of men gathered to learn from each other – would not be accomplished, and the delegates would instead be mere clerks. Instead of a good constitution produced by free debate and consensus among independent delegates, there might be no constitution at all, since committee instructions from different counties would not agree.[16]

While publicly attacking committees and criticizing committee activity, some gentlemen were impelled by the mobilized opposition to engage in electioneering themselves. As one reported, "thinking men" were alarmed and were "determined to watch and court the temper of the people." A wealthy candidate apologized for his failure to attend a previous convention. A committee critic believed that, except in Bourbon County, men were engaging in committee activity because they wanted to moderate the popular temper rather than because they approved. "Torismond," a defender of the Bourbon County committee, implicitly corroborated his opponent when he conceded that "rich designing men . . . procure themselves to be elected into county committees." Even George Nicholas, however disdainful of the electorate and of the political arena in private, was compelled to campaign and to participate in a Mercer County political meeting. Faced with strong opposition to lawyers, he forced one critic to concede that he was the one lawyer who should be sent to the convention.[17]

The topic of slavery was raised at that same meeting, whereupon one candidate denounced it as shameful and Nicholas supported it, saying that Negroes were only good for bondage. Essentially the only substantive issue raised in the campaign, slavery was being controverted nationally and had previously been vented in some Kentucky churches as well as occasionally in the *Kentucky Gazette* during the 1780s. It later became a central topic in the convention but did not emerge so strongly before the election; only a few references and one real dialogue on the subject can be found in the newspaper. More disputation apparently occurred in August and September issues no longer extant, but probably not a really heated newspaper debate.[18]

The explanation for the reticence of proslavery Kentuckians unquestionably related to the general effort to avoid issues and reestablish traditional deferential politics. Gentlemen genuinely believed that the convention was the proper place to settle delicate questions, and proslavery advocates could assume that a triumph of deference would prevent any serious antislavery challenge in the convention. On the other hand, antislavery writing was also limited. Some people thought the county committees were emancipationist and, in fact, at least four committeemen were at one time or another active in antislavery. But if there was a real bond between the emancipation movement and the county committees, it was not stressed at the time. The committees did not include emancipation among their published goals, and their critics did not, with rare exception, attack them on that basis. Even in one case when committee spokesman "H.S.B.M." was accused of favoring emancipation, he denied the charge, claiming that his "principal design, is to endeavour to obtain the freedom of the whites"; only when this liberty prevailed was there any hope for a plan of gradual emancipation.[19]

Probably the uncertain state of public opinion in Kentucky contributed to the reticence. Some certainly held strong proslavery or antislavery views – as the Mercer County debate demonstrated – but others were as yet undecided upon the moral and political implications of slavery and emancipation. Even if resolute themselves, they could not know surely how others stood within the diverse population of Kentucky. It was apparent that positions on slavery did not cut cleanly along class lines or even lines of slaveholding. Some gentlemen and slaveholders, in Kentucky as in Virginia, considered slavery an evil to be somehow eradicated. And support of the radical democracy of the committees by no means required sympathy for slaves or support of emancipation. Slaves were useful on the frontier, upon farms of any size, for purposes of clearing the land, and nonslaveholders continued to move into the ranks of those owning slaves.[20]

When the election results were published, it was not apparent what the most important determinants had been, but, in retrospect, it is absolutely certain that the election had not become a referendum on slavery. The sixteen elected delegates who voted for emancipation in the convention were chosen from seven of the nine Kentucky counties, with no more than three from any five-man delegation. Mercer County voters elected the two men who had spoken so strongly on opposite sides of that question. Instead, some thought that county committees had triumphed, one fearing the convention would "committ many blunders" because "County Committees, composed of very many ignorant & some bad men, have borne the sway in our elections." Some other newspaper comment seems to corroborate this opinion, although historian Humphrey Marshall denied such success, "as most of the electors, thought themselves qualified to choose their representatives without the assistance of the committees."[21]

Whether or not entire slates of committee delegates were elected, the groups had certainly mobilized popular opinion against "great men," and the gentry were heartsick at the results. Congressman John Brown expressed "serious·apprehensions, that the result of their labours will fall greatly short of the public expectation." Marshall thought the voters had rejected "the best talents from each county" and chosen "those who had taken the most pains to please, or who happened at the time, to be, the greatest favorites with – the people." There were, he thought, practically no "qualified constitution makers." But George Nicholas, one of the few he did consider qualified, was elected – though "hard pushed" – because of efforts to cultivate the voters.[22]

A survey of the forty-five elected delegates suggests no definitive victory for elite or committee. The committee efforts, if successful, turned up no more than a half-dozen newcomers, men with small land portions and no prior officeholding who presumably could have succeeded only with committee support. Other delegates may well have participated in committee activity and canvassed for election, but, by any measure of social, economic, or political standing, they were solid citizens, known and respected within their communities. Seven were ministers – three Baptists, three Presbyterians, and one Methodist – illustrating the religious diversity of Kentucky as well as the importance of churches in a frontier society. Since no minister had previously served in the statehood conventions and because Baptist preachers ordinarily avoided political involvement, their presence provoked comment. The traditional assumption that the seven were elected as emancipators may be accurate, since slavery was a question upon which churches were deliberating.[23]

The remaining thirty-odd delegates represented the amalgam that was the emerging Kentucky gentry, an admixture of pioneers and newcomers. Over half from Virginia, many had served in the Revolution and had established themselves in Kentucky with their military land warrants. Most had attended one or more of the previous statehood conventions and, of those eligible (thus excepting lawyers, judges, and ministers), had received a commission as a justice of the peace. Preponderantly planters, whose tax lists included sizable herds of cattle and a number of stud horses, two-thirds owned five or more slaves.[24]

Political unknowns or Kentucky gentlemen, the convention delegates shared a remarkable lack of preparation for the task before them. Only eleven members had served more than one term in the Virginia legislature. Probably no more than six, including two ministers, had attended college. Others had possibly received private education of some kind, but for most there is little evidence of more than an ordinary English education. Educational deficiencies of the group were most glaringly demonstrated by the election of only two lawyers in a convention of forty-five. Only George Nicholas and Anglican minister-turned-lawyer, Benjamin Sebastian, had legal training, despite a district bar of three dozen men containing veterans of the statehood conventions and some whose future careers would be distinguished.[25]

The lack of experienced legislators resulted partly from Kentucky's isolated frontier situation, but popular opinion extending through much of the United States was a major factor in the exclusion of lawyers. Kentuckians were expressing widely shared opinions when they denounced lawyers as self-seeking villains and declared that "the fewer Lawyers and Pick pockets there are in a country, the better chance honest people have." In Kentucky, the fiasco of the Spanish Conspiracy may also have contributed. Most of the well-educated gentlemen associated with the court party were not among the elected delegates: James Wilkinson, who had left Kentucky permanently; Congressman John Brown; his lawyer brother, James; and Federal District Court Judge Harry Innes. Thus the convention delegates were largely novices. Humphrey Marshall thought Kentuckians had reversed the usual expectation that the best talent would be chosen, an opinion unquestionably embittered by the exclusion of his own family which contained four lawyers (including himself) and a Virginia legislator of thirteen years' experience (his father-in-law).[26]

In its paucity of lawyers, educated men, and politicians of established reputation, Kentucky's constitutional convention resembled the 1776 Pennsylvania meeting. There, Benjamin Franklin and the few others who had some knowledge of government were so distracted by national events that they did not influence the deliberations. The constitution produced by "well meaning Country men" was the most democratic of the revolutionary era, with a broad taxpayer franchise, unicameral legislature (not new in Pennsylvania), and veto power by the electorate. Replaced in 1790 at a lawyer-dominated convention, the Pennsylvania constitution of 1776 seemed clear demonstration that well-educated convention delegates were needed. In the national convention in 1787, 60 percent were lawyers and almost half had a college degree. Kentucky's convention of 1849 contained 42 percent lawyers. Even in more comparable gatherings, frontier conventions in Tennessee in 1796 and in Ohio in 1803, experience and education were far more prevalent.[27]

Among Kentucky's inexperienced delegates in 1792, George Nicholas's talents stood out, and he hoped to avoid a duplication of the first Pennsylvania constitution. He could be optimistic about his preeminence among the gentry, particularly since the most respected of his fellow delegates were indisposed to challenge him. Isaac Shelby, Revolutionary hero soon to be the state's first governor, was close to him. Judge Caleb Wallace, by nature a willing and capable debater, was ill and did not participate extensively in the convention, but he shared Nicholas's perspectives in any case. So did Judge Samuel McDowell, a veteran legislator and the only delegate who had participated extensively in the Political Club debates during the 1780s when constitutional issues were discussed. One who was not sympathetic to the more elitist of Nicholas's notions was pioneer Benjamin Logan, but he was inept and inarticulate in parliamentary sessions. With most of the gentry agreed upon the main thrust of Nicholas's proposals, he was able to carry them along upon points where they differed.[28]

One potential rival was Alexander Scott Bullitt of Jefferson County, whose background was similar to Nicholas's. Son of a Virginia Supreme Court judge and master of a showplace plantation near Louisville where over fifty slaves tilled the soil, Bullitt was nearly as self-assured as his fellow aristocrat. He had begun to formulate constitutional programs prior to the convention, volunteering to consult with Nicholas and bringing a plan for the judiciary to the meeting. However, at thirty, he was among the youngest of the delegates, and his past did not inspire the confidence of his fellows. He had led a dissolute life before 1790 and was "very changeable." Further, he was thought to mistreat his wife and to have handled her inheritance dishonestly. Thus his political ambitions were foiled in the convention, and he acknowledged with considerable chagrin that Nicholas possessed a "Decided Superiority over every Member of that Convention."[29]

Several members were at least eager to challenge Nicholas upon the issue of slavery. Planter and gentleman James Garrard, who would follow Shelby as governor, had served in several legislative sessions and conventions, but he lacked the "gift of ready speech" and had recently lost influence because he had become "a zealot," a Baptist lay preacher, and a devoted emancipator.[30] The Reverend David Rice, best known of the ministerial contingent, was a tobacco-chewing pioneer, yet also Princeton-educated and chairman of the Transylvania Seminary for four years. He had just published a pamphlet urging that the constitution include a program of gradual emancipation.[31] Rice was replaced midway in the convention by Federal Judge Harry Innes, an antislave sympathizer seemingly even better equipped to offer respectable opposition to Nicholas. But Innes's skills as a well-educated, well-read lawyer, a founder and active participant of the Political Club, could hardly have been tested, since he came into the convention only after the constitution had been drafted.[32]

The democratic committee position had several capable spokesmen. Best known was Samuel Taylor, an active anti-statehood leader in the 1780s under the pseudonym "A Real Friend to the People." So popular in his own county that he was practically unbeatable at the polls, he served in convention and assembly almost continuously from 1788 to 1800. Taylor was blunt and outspoken and had already debated Nicholas in the Mercer County meeting before the election. Opponents criticized his "noisy, pert impertinence" but admitted he was "a shrewd, [although] a crude, politician."[33] Another leader of the popular position was Bourbon County committeeman James Smith, a western Pennsylvanian, known for his exploits as an Indian captive who escaped after four years, explorer, frontier fighter turned Revolutionary, and participant in Pennsylvania wartime politics.[34]

These were the delegates Nicholas needed to dominate, persuade, or conciliate. Debating such formidable opponents as he had faced in Virginia had sharpened his political skills. A man with strong ideas about government, he possessed "uncommon firmness and inflexible perseverance" and was "utterly fearless." Yet he was a shrewd and calculating politician, flexible in his tactics, respected for his "knowledge of mankind" and his "great tact in the management of public bodies." Thus he expressed his disdain for the electorate only privately, while publicly cultivating his popularity in the years after he arrived in Kentucky and in the constitutional convention campaign itself. And his most controversial proposals were couched in popular terms and promised beneficial results.[35]

Advantages Nicholas possessed because of his personal character were enhanced in two ways by the state of Kentucky society in 1792. In the first place, the society was so new that men "see none about them to whom or to whose families they [have] been accustomed to think themselves inferior." Nicholas's complaint that this situation made Kentucky particularly difficult to govern contained an unintentional and unrecognized irony, since it was just such a community without recognized leaders where, briefly at least, a single famous and talented individual could shape events. His prior aloofness from Kentucky politics also augmented his role. The bitterness of the statehood fight had involved nearly every potential leader in the convention. Nicholas alone had not been affected and thus could appeal to all.[36]

The dependence of Kentucky gentry upon him was apparent in their fears about his possible defeat and the elation and relief with which they reported his election. Nicholas himself had not been completely confident of victory but was certain of his role if chosen: "I shall try to form such a government as I think will suit the country." He apparently spent much of the time between the December election and the April convention preparing to fulfill that promise. Reading, taking notes, organizing his arguments, he also penned a final defense of the republican forms of government for the *Kentucky Gazette*. Yet he took such activity in stride and ended a routine business letter to his brother with, "News none."[37]

The convention met on April 2. The delegates disposed of formalities on the first day – elected Samuel McDowell president, named a committee of privileges and elections, predictably headed by Nicholas, accepted petitions from Bourbon County – and adjourned until the next morning when the real work began. Thereafter, in a remarkably brief period, the convention produced a constitution. A committee of the whole met nine days and hammered out a series of resolutions; a committee, again headed by Nicholas, drafted a constitution based on those resolutions. The convention then made a few amendments to the draft, accepted it after only one roll-call vote, and adjourned on April 19 without submitting the document to the people for ratification. The spare words of the *Journal* barely hint at the proceedings but do suggest Nicholas's unique contribution. Midway in the convention, he resigned to run for reelection, whereupon he was formally thanked "for his particular attention to and zealous and useful assistance in conducting the business while a member of this House."[38]

The thanks were for hard work well done. Nicholas had not written the constitution for the convention to ratify, but he knew fairly precisely the kind of government he wanted. In a lengthy opening speech well calculated to impress the delegates, he stressed the importance of the convention's task, the nature of republican government, and the principles crucial to that government. Then, as the convention discussed particular aspects, it was Nicholas who offered a series of resolutions outlining the constitution and defended critical elements with a series of speeches he had already prepared. Thus his proposals formed the basis of discussion and decision within the committee of the whole, to be adopted, amended, or rejected. In the event, he largely prevailed, although some convention amendments significantly altered his intent.[39]

The constitutional package embodied in the Nicholas resolutions is startling when compared to contemporary constitutions. Although almost all individual features had eastern precedents, the elements of the state government – governor, assembly, and Court of Appeals – were drawn from the most conservative models, making Nicholas's plan in toto more conservative than any other eighteenth-century American constitution. Yet this state government is combined with several democratic local institutions and the broadest suffrage in the United States.[40] Such an amalgamation of disparate elements apparently was a consequence of Nicholas's beliefs tempered by pragmatism.

Before moving to Kentucky, Nicholas had shared the appraisal of eastern republicans that lower houses of assembly needed to be checked. Even in Virginia, where gentry control was strong, the House of Delegates was untrustworthy. Men with local or particularistic interests were elected, bad laws were passed. Residence in Kentucky not only confirmed these preconceptions for Nicholas but sharpened them. A new state like Kentucky required a government even more stable and well run than in the east to direct development and encourage proper growth. Particularly was the protection of property needed to insure the immigration of the better sort of citizen.[41]

But such good government would be especially hard to establish. Nicholas now shared the perception of other Kentucky leaders that there were few men skilled in the art of government. The sort of people who would fill governmental slots, "even taking the best we can furnish, . . . cannot be admired." Further, politics in Kentucky were more democratic and unruly than in Virginia, with fewer legal or customary checks upon popular participation. In a new and unstable frontier, lines of authority and deference were not yet established. The statehood conventions and the constitutional convention election itself had mobilized the public and invited electioneering. Finally, at a time when Kentucky republicans hoped to check popular politics, the most widely accepted curb had been yielded. Every eastern state had some kind of suffrage qualification, and several had an even higher property requirement for officeholding. But Kentucky counties had already abandoned Virginia's fifty-acre voter qualification and effectively granted universal free manhood suffrage. Turbulent legislative politics, with infringement of minority and property rights, seemed almost inevitable.[42]

The program forwarded by Nicholas focused upon a cluster of interrelated goals which together were intended to handle these intractable realities. First, he wanted to contain and control the democratic impulse released by an unstable society and the broad suffrage provision. This might be done initially by regulating elections and further by building powerful countervailing institutions to curtail the anticipated excesses of the House of Representatives. These strong state institutions would retain most power at the state level rather than turn it over to local county courts which Nicholas also distrusted. As a final barrier against legislative error, Nicholas proposed constitutional guarantees of several features potentially vulnerable to tampering.[43]

Such a government represented, to Nicholas, the best hope for the future of the state, but he knew that some of these elitist ideas were highly unpopular and were unlikely to prevail unless he accommodated and reassured delegates fearful of aristocratic government. The constitution he unfolded before the convention skillfully intermingled his own ideas with popular and democratic features. And he presented the whole package in terms intended to appeal to most Kentuckians.[44]

In his speeches, Nicholas drew upon extensive notes on the writings of dozens of English, continental, and American philosophers. However, he used these sources not to provide a theoretical framework but to buttress his predetermined position and to overwhelm his listeners with his erudition. He set out to demonstrate that his proposals were based upon long usage, classical and European, drawn from the best of the American constitutional tradition, state and federal, and especially fitted to the requirements of the newly settling area of Kentucky. His most persistent theme, reiterated in a dozen different contexts, emphasized the need to encourage population growth. The government must be framed "in such a way as will satisfy all those who may wish to emigrate to your country."[45] Most delegates responded favorably to such an appeal, since growth provided additional security and companionship as well as enhancing land values. A final attractive feature of this emphasis, for those who concurred in Nicholas's pessimistic appraisal of Kentucky talents, was the incentive his proposals would offer to settlers of the better sort, men who could make a positive contribution to society and government.

The first barrier Nicholas planned against an immoderate House of Representatives was a Senate, made effective by its size, mode of selection, and absolute independence. A small group would deliberate more decorously and wisely, Nicholas thought, proposing that the upper house be no larger than one-fourth to one-third the size of the lower house. The convention concurred. He urged that the senators be chosen as in Maryland, where electors selected in each county met to choose senators, "men of the most wisdom, experience, and virtue." This indirectly elected Senate had gained widespread admiration among republicans for its independence, and Nicholas incorporated the exact language of the Maryland constitution. He thought that such a Senate, even without the property qualification by which the Maryland electors were elected, would provide an "impenetrable barrier" for the security of property, since it would be "composed altogether of men of that sort. I will give up my opinion as soon as I see a man in rags chosen to that body."[46]

Nicholas also intended the Senate to counter the dangerous tendencies of the House by avoiding its localism. Indirect election for the relatively long period of four years would partially accomplish that; further, and to guarantee that the Senate would include the best talent wherever located, he proposed that the electoral college make its choices without regard to residence. In this way, the Senate would consider itself representative of the whole state and would legislate for the general good. Against such a body, a demagogue in the House "might declaim, menace, and foam, with as little impression as the roaring billows produce on the solid beach." The convention inserted a requirement that one senator be chosen from each county before two could be chosen from any, an amendment reflecting "local prejudices" and connoting an entirely different conception of the Senate. The required distribution tied representation to the county. In Kentucky, at least, it negated the ideal of a Senate of the "most wisdom, experience, and virtue," since such men had settled close to one another and were concentrated in a few choice locations.[47]

A far more important check to the House of Representatives was to be the governor, more powerful and independent than in any other state. He should be elected directly by the people, Nicholas argued, not by the legislature. Although Nicholas had doubted that the voters could identify the ten or twenty men in the state best qualified to be senators, he asserted that they could recognize the one man preeminent in the community. More important, direct election would guarantee strong popular support for the governor in any clash between the executive and the legislature. Should the legislature possess the power, desire for reelection would encourage executive subservience. The convention avoided this last evil but gave the choice to the electoral college rather than to the electorate. Nicholas regretted the amendment, believing the governor consequently lacked the public confidence "necessary to support him against the attacks of the wicked and the discontented."[48]

Nicholas was clearly using the provisions of the United States Constitution as a model for the executive. The four-year term of office he proposed was longer than that of any other governor. Furthermore, he had reversed his earlier opinion that the governor ought to serve only one term, a shift perhaps explained by his judgment that there were few Kentuckians qualified for the office. The alteration was significant, since many republicans believed that the executive should only have substantial power if he held office for a specific and limited period; Nicholas discounted such opinion and suggested that reeligibility would provide an important incentive to good administration. Certainly he proposed ample powers for the governor, the key figure in the concentration of powers he planned. The executive would possess a veto, which could be overridden only by a two-thirds vote of both houses, and wide powers of appointment. Unlike other states with a strong executive, he would exercise these responsibilities alone, with no executive council to advise or inhibit him.[49]

Nicholas's stress upon the importance of the executive was in itself somewhat unusual, but even more singular was his proposal on the appointive function. Most republicans agreed that this was a difficult constitutional problem and that no mode of naming either local officials or state officers was completely satisfactory. There were several possible alternatives. All officials might be elected, either directly by the people or by a single house of assembly, as the county committees had urged earlier. Or all might be named by the governor, with or without a council or Senate. A final option operated in Virginia, where local officials were chosen by the county courts and state officials by the legislature. The last choice clearly conceded authority to the gentry, who controlled both assembly and local courts.[50]

While still resident in Virginia, George Nicholas had recognized the dilemma. He thought county court domination of appointments was rotten, but, on the other hand, "popular assemblies make very bad choices." At that time, he had concluded that the governor alone ought to appoint all officials, an idea of which Madison approved although no state practiced it.[51] In light of this early opinion and Nicholas's defense of a strong executive, his arrangement for the appointive powers in 1792 appears puzzling. Seemingly he had shifted to a more democratic frame of mind.

Nicholas introduced his proposal by discoursing upon the power of the people: they were sovereign and government existed for their benefit. Therefore, they ought to make appointments themselves (i.e., elect) "in all cases in which they can make the appointments, without too much inconvenience to themselves, and with as great or greater advantage to the public interest as those appointments could be made by any other mode." However, he continued, popular election contained serious inherent difficulties. Time and distance rendered frequent elections inconvenient for a widely scattered populace. Further, voters might err and suffer greater evils than if they had delegated their appointive function. He suggested, as a solution to the dilemma he described, that the convention decide which cases the populace could best determine and in which ones it would be unable to act wisely and well. For all appointments beyond the popular capability, Nicholas insisted that the governor would make the choice best for the citizens of Kentucky. After all, he thought, "the inclination and int[eres]t of the people and executive coincide in the making [of] proper app[ointment]s."[52]

He devoted most of his speech to the evils he perceived in a legislative selection of officials. The assembly would be tempted to create high-salaried offices to which assemblymen might then be named. Each legislator would have friends and connections he would nominate for positions, while the governor – only one man – would have fewer favorites and connections. As the weakest branch, the executive required the power of appointment to balance the powerful assembly. One man of perception could better assess the abilities of applicants than a body of men, even if that body possessed equal discernment (a possibility Nicholas clearly discounted).[53]

Nicholas's plan to vest the selection power in the people directly and the governor bypassed the gentry – serving either in the county court or in the legislature – just as he had suggested earlier. However, whether deliberately or not, he now incorporated elements of the county committee program by suggesting popular election of some officials. Nicholas was a skilled political tactician who believed that "one of the greatest arts in government is to accommodate itself to [the people's] wishes in all matters which will not distract its energy." Probably he made these democratic concessions to disarm those who feared the powerful executive in his governmental model and gain support from those desiring wider electoral powers. Although no proof of this hypothetical Nicholas-committee alliance exists, in one respect such a link on the elective issue was logical: the elitist Nicholas shared with committee spokesmen a distrust of the local county court oligarchies.[54]

Nicholas originally suggested that the convention decide which officials might best be elected and which best chosen by the governor, but he himself subsequently recommended the division. His resolutions proposed the election of the sheriff and coroner (a minor officer whose most important function was to serve as substitute sheriff) in each county and of low-ranking militia officers. The governor was to name every other official, civil and military, local and state, only excepting the state treasurer who would be chosen by the legislature. The convention accepted his plan and the division he suggested, but with an amendment requiring Senate confirmation of all gubernatorial nominations. Nicholas regretted the alteration, since it allowed the Senate a share of the appointive power.[55]

A conscious linkage of Nicholas's program to popular and democratic ideas espoused by some committeemen may also explain his support of two other constitutional provisions. One was ballot voting, considered experimental in eastern states although potentially useful in curbing undue influence at the polls. The other was universal male suffrage. While in Virginia in 1788, Nicholas had favored a voter qualification requiring the payment of taxes or enrollment in the militia, but by 1792 he accepted a universal vote. Nicholas probably shifted in a realistic accommodation to existing political practice in Kentucky, but he went further than mere acceptance in a strong speech to the convention. The motive in making this address is unclear, since in every other speech he defended a principle under sharp attack, and there was no threat to the existing liberal suffrage. Apparently he thought it politic to place himself on record as its most powerful advocate.[56]

Nicholas employed conservative justifications for the democratic principle. Instead of considering the abstract rights of each man, he weighed the benefits of such a grant to the community. Society would be stable, since men with votes could work through the electoral process to effect changes in government. Immigration would be encouraged because prospective settlers would be assured that their political rights were guaranteed. The poor needed this right to protect their liberties, since "the rich will from their wealth always have at least suff[icien]t degree of influence." Privately he was sure that property would always dominate. "Notwithstanding *all* have a right to vote and to be elected, the wealthy will nineteen times out of twenty be chosen. The house of representatives will therefore always have a majority at least of its members men of property."[57]

Nicholas could support universal suffrage and the ballot, while remaining optimistic about the government, because he hoped that his constitution would reestablish a purified political system in which the natural relationship between the citizens and their leaders would be renewed. The relationship was undermined, Nicholas and other republicans believed, by corrupters obtaining votes through treats or bribes and by demagogues arousing passions in canvassing for support. He argued that universal suffrage, far from debasing the political system, might be instrumental in improving it. With a wider electorate, corruption would be more difficult, since more extensive bribery would be required. Furthermore, by giving poor men "equality as citizens," their fears that the wealthy intended to deprive them of their rights would be proved groundless, and they would not "always oppose the better kind of people, those who are best qualified to serve the public."[58]

The most important cornerstone upon which a pristine republican system would be built was the constitutional provision Nicholas had devised regarding elections. Several other states had attempted to curb bribery and treating by excluding from office those convicted of the practices. Georgia, in 1789, required an oath denying such practices for all entering office. Nicholas endorsed the oath but expanded its provisions: "Resolved that every Senator and representative ought before permitted to act to take oath or make affirmation that he has not directly or indirectly given or promised any bribe or treat to procure his election for the said office; or declared or procured himself to be declared, a candidate for the same." Although the convention watered down the last provision, Nicholas's effort to eradicate active democratic politics was incorporated into the constitution.[59]

The convention's acceptance of a government which cut so deeply into the powers of county court and legislature is distinctive evidence that those political institutions had not developed strength and support in Kentucky. Twenty-five, or slightly more than half, of the delegates had received commissions as justices of the peace before 1792, but several had declined to serve. The rest had no ties with local government – ministers, men new to politics with no record of officeholding, and judges such as Caleb Wallace and Samuel McDowell, whose interests were linked to the central authority enhanced by the 1792 constitution.[60] Since there had been no district assembly, there were few interested advocates of a stronger legislature. The result was acquiescence in the persuasive arguments of Nicholas; nonetheless, the convention altered some of his proposals to shift a share of power to the legislature.

The proposed judicial system was intended to provide yet another check upon the legislative branch and a constraint upon the power of other courts. This section of the constitution was entirely Nicholas's creation. He was so widely regarded as the foremost lawyer in the district that the convention deferred to him after a little opposition.[61] Resistance was hardly surprising, for ordinary citizens found the complexity of the law irksome and regarded courts suspiciously. Also, Nicholas's scheme contained a controversial element which invited comment.

While still resident in Virginia, Nicholas suggested a court system adhering closely to the conservative school of legal philosophy. In order to function effectively as an equal branch of government, the judiciary must be absolutely independent. Hence, judges should be named by the governor, hold office during good behavior, and have their salaries fixed, out of the reach of the legislature. Good men must be attracted, and therefore, "these are the only salaries in the government that ought not to be very low." Predictably Nicholas had included a Court of Appeals, since only the possibility of appeal guaranteed true justice. After three years in Kentucky, he continued to stress the necessity of an independent judiciary appointed by the governor. However, he had concluded that justice moved too slowly in land-title cases – the most important and numerous kind of adjudication in Kentucky – and contended that there should be "some plan adopted by which the land disputes may be specially decided." He asked the convention to vest original and final jurisdiction over land cases in the Court of Appeals.[62]

Nicholas's speech defending this unique proposal began by conceding that a process of appeals was absolutely essential to rectify mistakes of lower courts. Only the most extraordinary circumstance could warrant any exception. However, such an exception was required for Kentucky land cases because there were "an infinite number of disputes" which could not be settled in a reasonable time or at moderate expense. His plan would provide an expeditious mode of settling land questions, an attractive prospect to Kentuckians, of whom it had been reported that fewer than one in ten had secure title to land. However appealing, the proposal violated orthodox legal principles and caused a stir among his fellow delegates. Because of the controversy, Nicholas resigned his seat, ran for reelection, and was returned to the convention. Alternatives were then considered, including one that would have extended the original jurisdiction of the Court of Appeals to all cases, but the convention fixed upon Nicholas's plan. It added an amendment, however, which permitted the legislature to eliminate the original jurisdiction of the high court at any time.[63]

Some contemporaries thought Nicholas's proposal derived from self-interest, since he would stand to gain as the leading lawyer in the state. Humphrey Marshall claimed that Nicholas "required every real, and adventitious circumstance of patronage, which he could combine, to ensure it success."[64] However, if there were considerations of personal advantage, they were intertwined with his conception of the public good. His concern over the lack of qualified leaders had led him to a carefully contrived consolidation in government. Here, too, in the complicated field of land law, he was attempting to delegate authority to those few men he thought best qualified to use it.

By and large, Nicholas had been successful in setting the guidelines of the government. He had ambitious plans both for this government and for the state of Kentucky, for which revenues would be needed. But he – and other members of Kentucky's elite – recognized the popular prejudice against any taxes beyond those required by a simple government and low salaries; they feared that parsimony would bring a well-constructed government to failure. Nicholas proposed to avoid that danger by writing a system of taxation into the constitution: three shillings or fifty cents annually on each one hundred acres and fifty cents for each slave owned. If this were done, he told the convention, the government would be assured of a large and augmenting income with which the legislature could not tamper. It was a tax structure that "will not take from the poor what is necessary for his support & will only take from the rich a small sum or a part of the surplus." Furthermore, the land tax would break up the holdings of speculators, opening opportunities for Kentuckians to obtain land or increase their holdings.[65]

The constitutional tax provision would impose a second constraint upon the legislature, although Nicholas was understandably more reticent about discussing it. Property would be protected against confiscatory legislation, since the rate was a maximum as well as a minimum figure. Men owning poor or inaccessible land believed that there should be a higher levy upon the best land, a discrimination Nicholas dismissed as impossible to administer. His proposal would avoid that and would protect slaveholders from high punitive taxes upon slaves.[66]

Nicholas estimated that the tax structure would bring into the state treasury $81,000 annually. Ample funds would be available for adequate salaries so that the best men would be willing to serve the state. Even after that, Nicholas expected a surplus of $50,000, which he hoped would be used to encourage the development of Kentucky through the agency of a loan office. The office would loan money to small farmers for improvements which would benefit both the farmers and the community; repayment of loans with interest would increase the funds available for lending. No aid was provided for tenants or poor people to purchase land, although Nicholas acknowledged that the majority of the population was landless. The only encouragement he offered was that the fifty-cent tax would break up large landholdings, enabling tenants as well as newcomers to obtain land.[67]

There were two other objectives to which Nicholas hoped the surplus might be applied. Believing that Kentucky's economy should be diversified, he urged governmental support of domestic manufactures. Faced with an agrarian majority in the convention as in the state, he maintained that manufactures were "essential to a flourishing state of agriculture," that farm goods would command an improved price and manufactured goods would be obtainable less expensively. Nicholas also hoped that the state would one day support education and had prepared his case in advance. In the convention, however, resistance to expensive governmental projects was so strong that he refrained from advocating educational support.[68]

As it turned out, Nicholas's careful argumentation and caution went for naught. The convention rejected his entire plan of mandatory taxation with its untouchable surplus. Finances and future governmental activity were left completely to the discretion of future assemblies, precisely the situation Nicholas had tried to avoid.[69]

Slavery clearly became one of the most important issues in the 1792 convention, with the only roll-call vote taken upon its constitutional guarantee. The dominance of the question in the convention seems surprising, considering the muted debate over slavery in the election campaign, but is less so if the national context is considered. Slavery was undergoing the same kind of challenge as other eighteenth-century institutions. Just as egalitarian sentiments based in part upon Revolutionary ideology and rhetoric undercut traditional politics, natural rights philosophy was turned against the enslavement of blacks, and an antislavery movement began to emerge. Northern states began the slow and painful task of proceeding toward emancipation; southern states were challenged by some individuals and groups who wanted to take the same path.[70]

The new western state of Kentucky was a logical place for antislavery proponents to attempt positive action. Elsewhere, southerners believed the preexistence of slavery sharply limited options. The large number of slaves already present would become a dangerous element should emancipation occur. Resistance to any move endan-

Table 1

KENTUCKY SLAVEHOLDINGS IN 1792

County	Householders	Slaves	Slaveholders	% Householders Owning Slaves	Average Size Slaveholding
Woodford	979	1,749	346	35.3	5.05
Fayette	2,735	4,015	863	31.6	4.65
Lincoln	1,164	1,295	320	27.5	4.05
Madison	1,189	798	241	20.3	3.31
Bourbon	1,953	1,143	339	17.4	3.37
Nelson	2,045	1,387	340	16.6	4.08
Jefferson	817	824	123	15.1	6.70
Mason	921	397	116	12.6	3.42
TOTAL	11,803	11,608	2,688	22.8	4.32

NOTE: Slaveholding figures have been computed from the Kentucky County Tax Lists, Kentucky Historical Society. See Appendix for note on method.
Mercer County is not included because there are no extant tax records for 1792.

gering property rights was well entrenched.[71] However, Kentucky was new, still malleable. In 1792 some 23 percent of its householders owned slaves, the holdings unevenly distributed as Table 1 indicates. This was not an inconsequential percentage, but Kentucky had its greatest growth yet before it. Slavery proponent and opponent alike recognized that the 1792 constitution would determine the nature of that population growth. If slavery and the importation of slaves were protected by the constitution, men of position and wealth from the South would be encouraged to make Kentucky their home. Northerners and those opposed to slavery would go elsewhere. Furthermore, the growth of a plantation agriculture would be encouraged by the increase of slaves. Commercial farming was not yet widespread, but the Mississippi promised an outlet for crops and meanwhile slave labor was important in clearing the land. On the other hand, if the importation of slaves were stopped or the possibility of future emancipation introduced into the constitution, southern slaveholders would be discouraged from coming to Kentucky, and the state would develop instead as a region of small farmers. It was evident that the debate involved far more than the rectitude of slavery.

Before 1790 there was a good deal of support for the idea of antislavery, although it was unpoliticized and largely unmobilized, deriving from three distinct though sometimes overlapping sources. One was the group of settlers from the North – Pennsylvania, New Jersey, and New England – where slavery was less approved and less important. Many northern migrants were so poor they could afford neither land nor slaves, so poor they could not even move away from their port of debarkation on the Ohio River. Other northerners were merchants and tradesmen who developed a handful of towns, Danville, Washington, and, most importantly, Lexington, the metropolis of trans-Appalachian society. Both northern townsmen, not dependent on slaves, and northern farmers who owned none were significantly less attached to the institution of slavery than other Kentuckians.[72]

Quite different were some gentlemen who had brought to Kentucky a share of the antislavery liberalism current in Virginia. There, such sentiment had been frustrated, but in Kentucky, perhaps, positive steps could be taken. Politician John Brown, who had formed antislavery views at least as early as a Phi Beta Kappa debate in 1779, thought slave imports ought to be barred. Kentucky's Political Club, with Brown and his antislavery friend Harry Innes participating, resolved that the tobacco culture would not benefit Kentucky. Such expressions were encouraged by the theoretical nature of Kentucky's constitutional inquiry before 1790. These were educated men, engaged in discussing the first principles of government without yet being confronted by the practical dilemmas of political implementation.[73]

Support for antislavery may have been present or latent among some northerners and Virginia gentlemen, but the original core of antislavery activism in Kentucky was in the churches. Religious organizations were of especial importance in Kentucky where there were few other community organizations. Some churches had agitated internally about slavery in the 1780s, but in 1791, religious enthusiasm had turned toward politics.[74] The first positive action was taken at the annual meeting of the Elkhorn Association of Baptists, a denomination which usually adhered to an absolute separation of church and state. Probably with advance coordination, the attendance at the August meeting was unusually high and included two preachers, themselves unassociated with Elkhorn and traveling in the cause of emancipation. The meeting named a committee of three, including emancipator James Garrard, to draft a memorial to the constitutional convention upon the subjects of slavery and religious liberty.[75]

Such action ran sharply counter to Baptist practice, and it aroused strong feelings both on the propriety of memorializing and on the antislavery appeal. The Baptists were the most sharply divided denomination on the issue of slavery, and individual churches were wracked by dissension between strong proslavery and antislavery factions. Within Elkhorn, a subsequent special meeting, ostensibly called to settle an unrelated controversy within a member church, reconsidered the original action. With the two emancipating ministers and delegations from a number of smaller churches absent, the association rescinded the memorial.[76]

Elkhorn might have retreated from its official antislavery stance, but the election results attested to widespread church activity. Seven ministers were elected, including James Garrard and another Elkhorn delegate. Ostensibly they formed a sort of "antislavery party," led by Presbyterian David Rice, author of a pamphlet advocating emancipation. Now a delegate, Rice rose to request convention action and to reiterate the arguments he had already laid out.[77]

Slavery, his pamphlet title declared, was "Inconsistent with Justice and Good Policy." It was unjust and immoral because it made some men the property of others. All men were equal by natural law (which was God's law), and slavery negated this equality. A slave, who was accountable to God for his actions, was obligated to obey orders of another man. Slavery was bad policy because it encouraged idleness and sapped political virtue. He asked the convention to "resolve UNCONDITIONALLY to put an end to slavery in this state" and to work such "fixed principles" into the constitution. A future legislature could then devise the best mode of achieving emancipation. He concluded passionately:

Slavery is the national vice of Virginia; and while a part of that State, we were partakers of the guilt. As a separate State, we are just now come to the birth, and it depends upon our free choice, whether we shall be born in this sin, or innocent of it. We now have it in our power to adopt it as our national crime; or to bear a national testimony against it. I hope the latter will be our choice; that we shall wash our hands of this guilt; and not leave it in the power of a future legislature, ever more to stain our reputation or our conscience with it.[78]

Rice proposed to fix a course for future legislative implementation, but antislavery sympathizers in the convention were entirely divided upon the mode and extent of the effort. A few wanted emancipation to take place immediately; others were content to protect
slave property but wanted to include in the constitution an immediate prohibition of slaves imported for sale (the slave trade) and a
prohibition at some specified date in the future of any slave importation. Such limitation upon the expansion of slavery drew support
from those who considered it a first step to eventual emancipation –
either through future legislative action or through voluntary manumission – and from those who hoped to lessen the potential for black
insurrection.[79]

Rice's cause was weakened by these divisions, but he also hurt it
himself. Even though he cloaked his arguments in the most moderate tones, assuring "men of fortune" he did not reproach them and
stressing the need for gradual emancipation, he must have shocked
the sensibilities of his listeners. He was so obsessed with the immorality and injustice of slavery that he virtually disregarded his own claim
that slavery was inconsistent with good policy as well. He obviously
believed any institution so wrong must be bad policy, but that assumption led him to ignore or gloss over widely shared attitudes
which must be accommodated if antislavery forces were to succeed.
One was the universal wish of Kentuckians to foster economic and
population growth. Rice conceded that emancipation would deter
slaveholders from moving to Kentucky but suggested it would attract
"useful citizens." Delegates who wanted the state to encourage talented, educated, and propertied settlers were not reassured by Rice's
somewhat cavalier exclusion of southern property holders.[80]

Rice dismissed the claim of property rights, suggesting that laws
which made people property were contrary to the laws of God. But
his greatest miscalculation was to underestimate prejudice and thereby shrug off the possibility of miscegenation and racial rebellion, two
obsessive concerns of Americans. He thought that slaves were an "in-
jured, inveterate foe" and that only emancipation would preclude a
rebellion such as the bloody uprising which had just begun in Saint
Domingue. But Rice did not couple emancipation with some plan
for removal, as Jefferson and other Virginians did in their public abolition proposals. White fear of freed slaves was a major barrier to
emancipation, a problem so intransigent that one Kentucky del-

egate, in frustration, proposed to "just get all the Negroes asleep, knock them in the head, and kill every one of them." Rice agreed that miscegenation would occur with emancipation but thought it of small concern, the last an opinion with which few emancipators anywhere in the United States would concur. [81]

For all Rice's somewhat tactless presentation, it was the proslavery delegates who were on the defensive with George Nicholas their forceful spokesman. Built partly upon logic and constitutional reasoning, Nicholas's appeal touched self-interest and emotion as well – the whole core of values which most Kentuckians shared. Constitutionally, emancipation was doubly wrong, first because it would violate the right to property which government was required to protect, second because slaves were not members of the compact forming the government and thus had no rights under it. [82]

Nicholas dwelt longest upon the argument that protection of property was especially important as a lure to immigrants. The Southeast was the most likely source of prospective settlers, he thought, since northerners would generally be drawn to the Northwest Territory. Southerners could choose Kentucky or Tennessee, the latter particularly attractive because the North Carolina cession to Congress bound it perpetually to slavery. Kentucky must write a positive guarantee into the constitution in order to compete for emigrants, as well as to hold Kentucky slaveholders who might otherwise move south into Tennessee. Not only the quantity but the quality of the population would suffer by an exclusion of slavery, since all but the poorest southerners would be excluded. [83]

Nicholas was so eager to persuade that he employed all possible arguments, even contradictory ones. His statement that only poor southerners would come if emancipation were adopted did not jibe with his plea in another speech that all should be given a vote, since only poor and middling people would come under any circumstance. Even within the same speech, he argued that it was pointless to shape the constitution to please the northerners in Kentucky, since most were planning to move away, yet he later asserted that slavery was so beneficent and useful in Kentucky that northerners had adopted it. [84]

He baited the emancipators, although fairly gently. If they were slaveholders, they could prove their principles by emancipating their own slaves; if not, they were only willing to be generous at the expense of others. He declined to investigate the origin and propriety of slavery, declaring it had always existed. But his main thrust was the detrimental effects of emancipation, and upon that topic he could appeal to the fears and prejudices of whites. Emancipation would debase white society, as the blacks acquired economic and political rights. He told a story of black male sexual appetites and assured his listeners that intermarriage would result. "None can say where it will stop," he concluded.[85]

Apparently the pressures of the radical emancipators, demanding an emancipation without paying "anything at all an equivalent to the slave holders," enabled Nicholas to prevail. He was able to convince the delegates that the convention must move "either to give up that property or to secure it." During the debate, David Rice resigned his seat, perhaps hoping to muster public support for his position. In the reelection, he was replaced by the likeminded Harry Innes, but the convention meanwhile had acceded to Nicholas's demand for positive guarantees. For the first time, a state constitution would include a bulwark around slavery.[86]

Nicholas's proslavery constitutional package began with the Bill of Rights. Nicholas defended it as a buttress of individual rights which must be attached to the constitution, but he had every reason to know it might be a two-edged sword. The Virginia Declaration of Rights of 1776 opened with the statement that "all men are by nature equally free and independent," a phrase which some might construe to include slaves. In the 1776 convention, that very point had been raised by Robert Carter Nicholas, George Nicholas's father, but dismissed by his fellow delegates upon the grounds that slaves were not constituent members of society. The intervening years had shown, however, that it could not be so easily waved aside. Virginia's formulation was copied by several northern states and provided a basis for ending slavery in Massachusetts and New Hampshire. Vermont in 1777 explicitly tied emancipation to that declaration of equality, and South Carolina's Charles Pinckney had suggested that support for such a statement in the United States Constitution would come "with a very bad grace" from a slaveholding state.[87]

Antislavery Kentuckians had developed the argument before the convention, insisting that the natural rights of slaves were included in the Bill of Rights, and Rice pressed the issue upon the delegates. Nicholas's speech pointedly denied the contention, but he resolved the intellectual problem the Bill of Rights presented by recasting the terms of the social contract to exclude slaves. Instead of declaring, as Virginia's did, that "all men . . . equally free and independent . . . enter into a state of society," Kentucky's constitution specified that "all men, when they form a social compact, are equal."[88]

Nicholas also incorporated an article forbidding legislative interference with slavery except under severe constraints. Slaves could not be emancipated without the consent of their owners or without paying a "full equivalent in money." The legislature could never prohibit immigrants from bringing in slaves for their own use, though it could close the slave trade. Antislavery delegates who had initially hoped to move Kentucky toward slave limitation or emancipation were confronted, instead, by constitutional guarantees of slavery. In the last days of the convention, they attempted to erase this section on slavery, an amendment which would simply leave the matter to future legislative discretion. The roll-call vote upon this rather limited objective failed to expunge, 16 to 26.[89]

The twenty-six who supported the constitutional provision were undoubtedly swayed by self-interest. They were, as a group, wealthier than their sixteen opponents, with larger landholdings.[90] Not surprisingly, they also owned more slaves, as Table 2 demonstrates. As

Table 2

SLAVEHOLDINGS IN 1792 CONVENTION

Size of Slave-holding	Antislavery Delegates		Proslavery Delegates	
	Number	%	Number	%
0	4	25	0	0
1-4	7	44	5	19
5-10	2	13	7	27
over 10	3	19	14	54

NOTE: Kentucky County Tax Lists, KHS. The 1792 lists have been used when available. However, if records for that year are incomplete, tax lists from other years have been searched.

The slaveholdings of David Rice, who had been replaced, and three men who did not vote are not included. Harry Innes has been included in the group of antislavery delegates holding over ten slaves, despite the lack of a tax figure before 1796. He owned fifteen then and had probably owned slaves continuously since 1787, when he had advertised the leasing of slaves: *Kentucky Gazette*, 15 December 1787, 20 December 1788.

men of property, they found Nicholas's arguments regarding Kentucky expansion persuasive and compelling. Mostly southerners themselves, they had no wish to exclude other southern property holders. Alarmed and offended by some of the emancipation ideas expressed in convention, they agreed that the constitution must protect slave property. There was some reason for their alarm, in fact, since sixteen men had voted to leave the door open for future emancipation and other delegates agreed to support Nicholas's proposal only reluctantly.[91] Antislavery had a somewhat surprising amount of support, which the vote showed to be diffused throughout Kentucky, economically as well as geographically.

Property and slaveholdings (as described in Table 2) may satisfactorily explain the motives of the twenty-six delegates who supported slavery, but they are less satisfactory in explaining the motives of the sixteen dissenters. Among men with large slaveholdings, a handful voted to end an institution from which they benefited. James Garrard was a planter with twenty-three slaves; Harry Innes was another wealthy slaveholder, although as a lawyer-judge, slave labor was less critical to him. More important, the size of slaveholdings is a particularly inaccurate measure of class and wealth under circumstances where slavery was at issue, since it misrepresents men who owned few slaves out of choice rather than economic necessity. Andrew Hynes of Nelson County held but two slaves in 1792, but he was a prosperous man and recognized county leader. During the 1790s, he demonstrated his abhorrence of slavery by emancipating two of his slaves, one immediately after the 1792 convention; at his death in 1800, he freed the five he then owned. Clearly economic measures are not sufficient to explain the entire vote.[92]

Although the sixteen votes came from seven of the nine counties, there were apparently pockets of antislavery deriving from the origins of their settlers. Three votes came from Mason County, a recently developing area in northern Kentucky and home of poor northern migrants. Three votes came from Bluegrass Fayette County, where the town of Lexington was considered to be a northern settlement. Three came from Mercer County, where the district court was located. Finally, three came from Bourbon County, also rich Bluegrass country first settled by small North Carolina farmers who had learned of the area from Daniel Boone. Bourbon was the center of political and religious turmoil during the decade, culminating in the revival at Cane

Ridge during the Second Great Awakening in the early 1800s. Anti-slavery activists there worked through both the Baptist and Presbyterian churches.[93]

Throughout Kentucky, the churches were probably the most significant sources of antislavery energy. Six of the sixteen antislavery votes came from the ministers in the convention; the seventh minister, David Rice, was not a delegate at the time of the vote but had been their most articulate spokesman. Five of the other ten votes came from active laymen in the Baptist and Presbyterian churches. But such religious connections did not mean that the churches were united internally upon the issue. As the Elkhorn Association actions demonstrated, such unity of purpose was entirely lacking among the Baptists.[94] Furthermore, sentiment in the churches did not channel easily into political effort. Nearly all the sixteen antislavery delegates in the convention were nonpolitical, inexperienced, and unpersuasive. Divided among themselves upon their goals, they failed to lay out a political program to implement the widespread antislavery sentiment they represented. Such a political failure doomed any chance they might have had to implant a program of slave limitation or at least reserve future options to do so. The persuasive Nicholas obtained, instead, positive protection for slavery. Slaveholders were freed from any immediate threat of emancipation and might move into the state with assurance. The pattern of settlement from the South was thereby established.

Confronted by an ironclad guarantee of slavery in the constitution, emancipation efforts might well have ceased in 1792. They did not do so, partly because the constitution itself was not permanent. Nicholas himself, for his own independent reasons, had left the constitutional door open just a crack.

Nicholas believed his proposed article on amendment formed the keystone of the constitution. He assumed that Kentucky would soon gain more men of capability, so that the government might be remodeled to incorporate the new talent. Moreover, he wanted the amendment provision to lure people to Kentucky. For these reasons he urged that the constitution insure another constitutional convention at a specified time in the future. The idea was not original to him. James Madison had suggested that a second convention might be appropriate in a new country such as Kentucky. Nicholas had at first believed the second constitution might be written three or four years after the first, but by 1792 he had shifted to a seven-year interval.[95]

He minced no words when he outlined the virtues of such a provision. It would attract settlers, because everyone would expect the future government to follow his own preference. Those satisfied with the first constitution would assume it would remain in force, while those who were dissatisfied would believe they would later be able to alter the government to their own specifications. Besides, he noted, it was impossible to know what the best government would be, since the future of Kentucky could not be predicted.[96]

An important advantage was the opening it left to improve the government. Better qualified men would move in, and a constitutional restructuring would provide an opportunity to fill offices more satisfactorily. "Public good requires [a temporary government], as, by this means, the door will be left open to the ambitious which a perpetual government will shut in most offices &c. This may have great effect on emigration and on such emigrants as will have it most in their power to improve the country. It will also put it in power of the community to select the best of characters there will be in the country at the end of seven years instead of then having their offices filled only with the best as we now have here."[97]

Nicholas was quite emphatic that this should not be an opening for perpetual revision. He was generally quite conservative with regard to change, believing that "more evil is to be feared, than good expected" in most cases. Here in Kentucky, one opportunity for reappraisal during the period of settlement was proper. Any government allowing more frequent alterations would "ever be unstable and subject to convulsions at the return of those stated periods appointed for its revision."[98]

The convention accepted Nicholas's provision for another meeting seven years in the future but specified that a majority of the voters must approve the convention at two consecutive elections before the legislature could call it. If the option for a convention were not exercised at that time, the calling of any future meeting would be left exclusively to the assembly.[99]

Nicholas's speech contained an unintended prophecy. His belief that government would be "subject to convulsions" at the times appointed for revision was true for the onetime revision he called for. In fact the provision for a second constitution invited debate and turmoil for the next seven years. No question could be regarded as irrevocably settled; any objection to policy or procedure could quickly turn into a constitutional controversy.

When the convention adjourned, the gentry expressed general satisfaction and relief that it was much better than expected. Nicholas himself regretted some of the alterations made by the convention to his proposals but thought by and large the document was praiseworthy. Others only criticized the parts where Nicholas had made concessions to the popular position: the election of militia officers and sheriffs, the lack of a property qualification for the Senate. [100] Both in what they approved and what they criticized, the gentlemen observers were testing the constitution against an abstract model derived from the decades-old inquiry into constitutionalism. They did not consider and only time would tell how it fit the realities of Kentucky politics.

3

THE POLITICS OF
EXPANSION, 1792-1800

IN PLANNING the Kentucky constitution of 1792, George Nicholas had assumed that the state would grow rapidly and that it would fill with settlers of the most desirable sort. Whether because he had been correct in his argument to the convention that the constitution itself would attract settlers or because Kentucky was alluring regardless of the government, the population did indeed increase rapidly. The 1790 census had recorded 73,677 settlers, and there were approximately 100,000 in 1792. By 1800 the census total was 220,955.[1] The growth was geographical as well: as land in the central areas was taken up and outlying regions became safer and more accessible, settlement flowed eastward toward the mountains, southward to and beyond the Green River, and along the Ohio River banks to the north.

But Nicholas was disillusioned about the quality of the new settlers. Furthermore, his hopes and expectations about the government's directing and channeling state activity were shattered. Expansion created its own dynamic. The government was placed under pressure to support, but not to direct, the growth. Kentuckians petitioned, and finally demanded, policies tied to their own future advancement: land easily available for those who desired it; an enlarged supply of slave labor to work the land; and an increased number of county units, both to provide convenient government and to satisfy individual ambitions for office. Expansion was not an impulse which could be controlled by cautious politicians but a force which could overwhelm its opponents.

One man who moved into Kentucky soon after statehood was just such a citizen as Nicholas believed the state required. At thirty-three years, John Breckinridge was a veteran of three years in the Virginia assembly. Trained to the law under George Wythe, Breckinridge had long been urged to come to Kentucky, where he had close ties. Yielding to such importunities, he decided to move in 1788, but he proceeded slowly, purchasing a 1,600-acre parcel only six miles from Lexington and setting tenants to clear the land. Only in 1793 did he wrap up his affairs in Virginia and move with his family. Possessed of a large and well-situated estate and twenty-five slaves, he was well set for his life in Kentucky. He developed his home property carefully during the next years, concentrating in stockbreeding. By the end of the decade his slaveholdings had increased to sixty-five, among the largest in the state. [2]

Breckinridge had settled himself conveniently for his law practice as well. He advertised his intention to practice before the two state courts – the Court of Appeals and a Criminal Court of Oyer and Terminer – and the Fayette County Court, all located in Lexington. Clearly he felt no compulsion to scramble for cases in the backcountry. He brought a number of legal commissions west with him and soon obtained more business. As he rose to a prominent place at the Kentucky bar, he and George Nicholas often faced each other in court. The one short, balding, and ungainly, the other tall, slender, with red-brown hair, these two men were natural rivals, deemed by others nearly equal in ability. Nicholas, some six years Breckinridge's senior, did not agree and thought Breckinridge would be hard put to maintain his reputation. [3]

Unlike Nicholas, Breckinridge remained politically ambitious. When he moved west, he resigned a seat in the United States House of Representatives to which he had just been elected. A Virginia friend had advised him to stay out of the faction-ridden Kentucky politics but rather to consider future service in the national government, and Breckinridge's career suggests his intention to follow that advice. Almost as soon as he arrived in Kentucky in 1793, he was elected chairman of the Democratic Society of Kentucky, one of many such groups springing up across the country in support of Jeffersonian principles. He was a candidate for the United States Senate in 1794 but was defeated by Humphrey Marshall. Thereafter, he served as state attorney general from 1795 to 1797, resigning that post to go into the state House of Representatives. He may have intended his service there to aid him in obtaining a congressional seat. He participated actively in the debate on the Alien and Sedition Acts in 1798 and 1799, enhancing his reputation by leading the attack upon these unpopular measures. In 1799 he was elected Speaker of the House; from this post he launched a successful campaign for the senatorial seat of Humphrey Marshall in 1800.[4]

Like many other wealthy Kentuckians, Breckinridge engaged in a variety of projects to enhance his financial position. He invested in an iron works and speculated in land across the Ohio. But most of all his attention focused upon speculation in Kentucky lands, an activity he had pursued in partnership with his half-brothers before he moved to Kentucky. Although he sometimes possessed more, Breckinridge usually held around twenty thousand acres upon which he paid taxes and from which he expected to reap profits by future sale.[5]

Nearly all Kentuckians felt the attraction of the unsettled lands of the state. The disposal of land would determine the wealth of individuals and shape the nature of Kentucky's growth as well. In the separation compact, Virginia had guarded the interests of its citizens by requiring that laws regarding land titles be based upon laws of Virginia in force at the time of separation. Nonresidents could be taxed only at the same rate as residents of Kentucky, thus preventing confiscatory legislation. However, a large amount of land was as yet unappropriated, and over this Kentucky had full control. It could either continue or change Virginia policies.[6]

Unappropriated lands were scattered around the periphery of Kentucky, but the major question was the disposition of the lands in the Green River Military District, set aside by Virginia in 1779 to satisfy claims based upon Virginia military warrants. Kentucky had the right to end the soldiers' exclusive claim to this area, and there was debate beginning in 1792, both in the newspaper and the assembly, upon the propriety of doing so. Opinion fluctuated, but in 1795 the House resolved to terminate the monopoly by a margin of 28 to 11. By then, as "A Citizen" pointed out, there could be no basis for the plea that soldiers deserved special consideration, since the warrants had passed into the possession of other men.[7]

This final determination was probably related to the expansion of population which made the Green River lands of greater importance by the middle of the decade than they had been earlier. The treeless "barrens" of southern Kentucky were appropriate for certain crops and for cattle grazing. The Mississippi navigation rights, finally obtained in 1795, enhanced the value of all western lands.[8] Thus, the question of the disposal of these military lands and other unclaimed acreage became critical. Starting during the assembly of 1794, various methods of disposition were considered, but no decision was reached until February 1797.

Some men believed the lands ought to be used as a source of revenue for the state; if handled correctly, they might be the principal financial support for the state government for years to come. One suggestion was to rent unsold lands on long leases at $1.33 per hundred acres a year. By this means, the state treasury would gain an estimated income of fifteen thousand dollars, and land would be available for those who had no purchase money. But the most frequently recurring proposal which promised to guarantee the state a revenue was to sell the lands to speculating groups.[9]

During the mid-1790s, the Kentucky legislature received at least five offers to purchase part or all of the unclaimed lands. Most were from residents of Kentucky, one from a state representative, but the most ambitious and controversial of the enterprises was a speculative company organized in Philadelphia. Among the five eastern partners were prominent politicians and several who had earlier been active in the Yazoo speculations in Georgia. They sent an agent, Elisha I. Hall, west in 1795 and again in 1796-1797 to negotiate with the legislature for the purchase of all the unappropriated land. He attempted to interest Kentucky leaders by distributing shares in the venture. Secretary of State James Brown, Federal Judge Harry Innes, and lawyers George Nicholas and John Breckinridge were involved in the first effort, with instructions that they use their "*personal influence and information to bring forward and finally to perfect this business.*" Hall's efforts led to a final determination of land policy.[10]

Hall's original offer was $260,000, part to be paid immediately and the rest in six annual installments. The unappropriated land was estimated to be somewhere between four and six million acres, making his offer anywhere between 4.3 and 6.5 cents an acre. Obviously the Kentucky partners had a personal stake in the effort, but they also believed the venture would benefit Kentucky. The legislature was not enthusiastic about taxation to support the energetic government these men wanted. As Breckinridge explained, "No appropriation of these lands will produce the state so much money *certain* in the treasury."[11]

The assembly did not even know what it had for sale and attempted to find out the quantity and quality of land available. Despite a pessimistic assessment, however, the House voted to reject Hall's offer by a margin of 13 to 19, although the Senate approved it, 6 to 4. A year later, Hall made a second effort, with more liberal terms, but this time both houses rejected the offer, and Hall left Kentucky for good. The venture was not popular among Kentuckians, and the westerners with shares in the company kept "entirely out of view." There were rumors that Hall had attempted to interest legislators in the project by promising them portions of the land. However, much of this may have been unknown, because most blame was directed at the Senate for its original approval of Hall's offer.[12]

The criticism of the plan to sell the lands to Hall was tied to the emergence of alternative goals. As population pressure built up in 1793 and 1794, men prepared to move onto the unappropriated lands, simply assuming that the assembly would allow actual settlers the right to preempt the land. Starting in 1793, the legislature began receiving petitions asking that settlers be given their land at a moderate price. In 1795, when the assembly rejected Hall's first offer, it added a resolution that it was impolitic to sell those lands to any one individual. It then passed a bill for the relief of those settlers who had already moved in, allowing each family a preemption of 200 acres at thirty dollars per 100 acres.[13]

The law specifically stated that others ought not to expect the same relief in the future, but this advice was ignored. Families poured into the area thereafter and again petitioned the assembly for preemption rights. Furthermore, those who had settled under the terms of the previous act, but had not yet paid the requisite price, petitioned for further time to discharge the debt. The new governor, James Garrard, was sympathetic and added his plea for relief. The assembly meeting in the fall of 1796 postponed the decision until a second session to be held the following February but suspended the sale of land pending a final determination of priorities.[14] The choice the assembly faced at that time was between sale to a speculative group and sale to actual settlers.

In February 1797, after rejecting Hall's second offer, the assembly voted to sell to settlers. The 1797 law was in some respects more generous than the 1795 measure and in some respects less so. Anyone who moved into the Green River area before July 1798 might preempt 100 to 200 acres of land at a price of sixty dollars per 100 acres for first-rate land and forty dollars per 100 for second-rate. In the course of events, the forty-dollar figure prevailed as all land was presumed to be second-rate. The settlers were given a year before payment was required, thus providing a tremendous incentive to prospective buyers even though the price was higher than before. Men began to move whether they had the cash or not. The same law also provided an extension of time for those who had not yet paid for land obtained under the 1795 act, with 5 percent interest charged upon the unpaid balance.[15]

This enactment opened the door to the most significant sectional split in Kentucky politics. Strong pressure built up to ease the operation of the law, pressure resisted by politicians from the settled Bluegrass region. Many still hoped to use the southern lands as a financial resource for the state government, best accomplished by high prices and no credit. Easy terms also hurt established planters by luring tenant farmers away from the task of clearing Bluegrass lands. And ultimately the shift of population would be reflected by a new political balance in the legislature.[16]

Petitions requested two revisions in the law. First, the price charged for land should be lowered or eliminated. The legislature resisted for a time but finally passed a bill in 1800, setting a price of twenty dollars per 100 acres for those occupying up to 400 acres. A second demand was that the families who moved in should be given several years to pay. In 1798 the legislature yielded, allowing the settlers to discharge their debts in four equal annual installments, with interest upon the amount outstanding. Some politicians predicted the debt would be nearly impossible to collect, a prediction proved true in the coming decades. The legislature was unable to resist the demands of the south country inhabitants, demands which grew stronger as the increased population of the area gave it a larger representation. South Kentucky politicians with a constituency whose land ownership rested upon legislative indulgence were willing to logroll for votes on this crucial question of "relief." In addition to the long-range problem of enforcement, the state had lost its one important source of revenue: by 1799 the auditor estimated that $352,612 was due from the settlers.[17]

The auditor's figure is ample testimony to the speed with which settlers took advantage of the 1795 and 1797 laws. At the very minimum, the figure indicates a debt from 4,400 settling families. While word of the laws may have attracted people from outside the state, apparently it also lured many landless families from the central regions of Kentucky. One gentleman reported from Fayette County "a prodigious spirit for removing to Green River."[18] Thus the land policy of the state after 1795 went far toward making Kentucky a state with a landholding majority. As Table 3 shows, almost exactly one-half of the householders owned land in 1800. The Green River counties of Logan, Christian, Barren, and Green were among the counties with the highest percentage of landholders. Furthermore, since tenants were drawn from thickly settled counties such as Fayette, the proportion of the population owning land must have been raised there as well.

Rarely did families of any high social station move to these developing sections. Gentlemen settled in the central area where life was more comfortable and company was better and were not disposed to move. Lexington, in Fayette County, was the center of genteel society, and one gentleman who built a grand estate nine miles away was told even that was too distant for proper company. The wealthy men who moved into the periphery of the state during the 1790s numbered only a handful, and they did so against the strongest advice. As John Breckinridge told one, "You are in a genteel, agreeable neighborhood. . . . And what are you about to exchange all this for? A country you have never seen: a country when you do see, – you will see filled with nothing but hunters, horse-thieves & savages. And a country where wretchedness, poverty & sickness will always reign." With few established families moving, an opening was left for new men and new families to enter into the political arena. Lifestyles and politics both developed very differently outside the Bluegrass.[19]

One important political result of the population expansion was the growth of county government. The number of counties increased at a rate even more rapid than the population, county formation often preceding population growth. The nine counties existing at the time of separation in June 1792 were increased to sixteen within one year and to forty-two by 1800. A good deal of pressure had built up before 1792, with Virginia moving only very slowly to accommodate the desire for new counties. The immediate increase in the number of counties during the first year was a result of these past frustrations as well as the pressure of population growth.[20]

The numerous petitions for separate county governments re-

Table 3

KENTUCKY LANDHOLDINGS IN 1800

County	House-holders	Land-holders	% Householders Owning Land	% Landholders Owning 1-200 Acres
Logan[a]	769	515	67.0	75.5
Christian[a]	416	262	63.0	75.6
Bracken	405	248	61.2	83.1
Barren[a]	707	418	59.1	73.2
Green[a]	1,035	607	58.6	72.3
Fleming	804	464	57.7	81.7
Livingston[a]	481	274	57.0	76.6
Henry	511	291	56.9	79.4
Scott	945	535	56.6	72.9
Jessamine	718	404	56.3	63.4
Mercer	1,265	704	55.7	60.7
Washington	1,434	794	55.4	69.7
Hardin	498	275	55.2	50.2
Muhlenberg[a]	245	135	55.1	68.1
Garrard	890	489	54.9	72.8
Warren[a]	691	376	54.4	83.0
Cumberland[a]	352	191	54.3	88.0
Woodford	890	466	52.4	62.2
Madison	1,549	798	51.5	76.2
Bullitt	483	244	50.5	65.2
Lincoln[a]	1,323	654	49.4	63.2
Franklin	743	360	48.5	60.7
Gallatin	171	82	48.0	51.2
Henderson[a]	238	113	47.5	67.3
Clarke[b]	1,126	535	47.5	70.7
Nelson	1,485	703	47.3	62.2
Boone	184	87	47.3	55.2
Pendleton	242	114	47.1	62.3
Campbell	290	135	46.6	65.9
Pulaski[a]	642	298	46.4	90.3
Bourbon	1,870	863	46.1	70.8
Harrison	769	351	45.6	76.8
Fayette	1,748	743	42.5	56.5
Shelby	1,271	530	41.7	64.0
Ohio	202	84	41.6	54.8
Nicholas	504	209	41.5	81.3
Breckinridge	147	59	40.1	44.1
Mason	1,928	757	39.3	71.3
Jefferson	1,153	419	36.3	55.6
Knox	178	56	31.5	76.8
Montgomery	1,201	361	30.1	69.5
TOTAL	32,503	16,003	49.2	69.4

[a] Counties located part or all in the Green River Military District

[b] Now spelled Clark

NOTE: These landholding figures have been computed from the Kentucky County Tax Lists, KHS, see Appendix for note on method. Floyd County is not included because there are no extant tax records. Wayne County is excluded because the 1800 law creating the county did not take effect until March 1801.

ceived by the assembly did not claim sufficient population but pleaded the inconvenience of the existing arrangement. The county seat was sometimes so far removed that men had to travel 80, 100, even 120 miles to obtain justice at the county court, to vote, or to conduct other business. Men were thus deprived of equal political rights, since many did not bother to vote and the area close to the county seat dominated elections. Even if men chose to make the trip, they must spend the night, an expense many people could not bear. The argument that men who could not afford a night's lodging could manage even less the expense of new public buildings was not so persuasive as the promise of convenience. In some cases, the expectations of local politicians were self-fulfilling. A petition was sent forward from Campbell County in 1796, asserting that the county seat had been placed in the far north of the county because a division had been expected; consequently, justice was too far removed from the southern portion and the expected division should take place immediately.[21]

Since the arguments of Kentuckians for separation from Virginia had most often dwelt upon the inconveniences and difficulties of a government far removed from the people, such pleas were particularly effective in the first year after statehood. There was little legislative resistance to the creation of new counties in 1792, but thereafter the question of county formation became closely enmeshed with legislative representation, so that it was not so casually handled.

Before statehood, Kentucky politicians had all rejected representation by county as practiced by Virginia, and the 1792 convention – although itself constituted on the basis of five representatives per county – adhered to the principle of representation by number. The constitution apportioned representation among the counties upon the basis of the free male inhabitants over twenty-one (i.e., the voters). In a reapportionment every four years, the assembly should establish a ratio, and counties without that number of electors would continue to vote and be represented with the parent county.[22] Under this provision counties formed for reasons of convenience rather than population were chronically unrepresented. Furthermore, the wording left unanswered the question of how to treat counties formed between the periodic enumerations, whether they should be given representation before the next enumeration if they had the requisite voting population at the time of formation.

Problems related to representation were not slow to arise. Three of the counties created in 1792 had not been given representation because they lacked what seemed an appropriate population. In the following year, after the official census confirmed their small population, the assembly conducted a tedious debate on apportionment. Some delegates believed that these small counties ought to continue voting with their parent counties, since the ratio to be established would be higher than any of the units possessed. But others resisted, and a resolution was offered to give every county separate representation regardless of population. Patently unconstitutional, the proposal received only five votes. Next offered was a measure which specified 336 voters as the ratio required for representation, then allotted each of the three troublesome counties a seat even though none had that number; this also failed, probably because it too clashed with the requirement of the constitution. In the closing minutes of the session, when many delegates had either gone home or else abstained because of weariness, a law passed which specified no ratio and gave the three counties separate representation.[23] Although rejected in principle, representation for every county was achieved in practice.

The next apportionment law in 1795 passed expeditiously and with no roll calls. This time a ratio of 330 voters was specified in the law, but Campbell County – formed in 1794 but left without representation – was given a seat despite lacking the required number. Franklin County, where the state capital was located, was given two representatives with only 417 voters. Such complaisance was beginning to fade, however, and the law specified that the House of Representatives should consist of fifty-six members until the next apportionment; thus any seats given to new counties would come from the representation of the parent counties. Furthermore, any county without the required 330 voters at the time of formation would vote with the parent county until the next enumeration.[24]

Six counties were formed during the next meeting of the legislature. The timing may have been coincidental, or the spurt to county growth may have been an outgrowth of the reapportionment itself, since the representation was broader with fifty-six instead of forty-two delegates in the House. Perhaps the creation of the six counties just after reapportionment was the result of deliberate delay; the legislature may have postponed forming the counties to avoid including them in the provisions of the act. Several of the districts had petitioned for county status before that session, the area that became Montgomery County for the preceding three years.[25]

In writing the laws creating the six counties, the assembly ignored the ratio required by the law but resisted giving representation unless the parent county lost proportionately. The results gave one county a representation to which it was not entitled, while others were unrepresented or underrepresented, as Table 4 demonstrates:

Table 4

REPRESENTATION OF NEW COUNTIES IN 1797

Counties	Voters	Representation
Bracken	284	1
Bullitt	388	1
Christian	293	0
Garrard	827	0
Montgomery	1,238	1
Warren	547	0

NOTE: Figures for voters in 1797 came from county tax lists, KHS. Actually, as in note 23, the figures are for white males over twenty-one. Representation figures came from acts establishing the counties, *Session Laws*, 1796 session.

There was an immediate flurry of activity, as several of the counties attempted to rectify what they considered the inequities. Garrard County petitioned the House of Representatives for separate representation; the request was rejected because of the reluctance of Madison County to lose a seat. On the same day that the House dismissed the petition, the county spokesman turned to the Senate. He finally succeeded, and Garrard County gained a representative while Madison lost one. Warren County also attempted to change the original legislative decision by electing a representative and sending him to Frankfort, only to have the House of Representatives refuse to seat him.[26]

Warren and Christian counties, both in the Green River area, were the two left without representation. Both had been formed from Logan County, which had but two seats itself; thus their claims were necessarily denied so long as the assembly adhered to the principle that the parent county must lose an equal number. The legislature was not only unwilling to yield the principle but became increasingly reluctant to create new counties. A flood of petitions poured into the assembly in January 1798. Many were tabled or rejected, but the House of Representatives acted favorably on five of the applications. Only one passed the Senate, with the new Fleming County receiving and Mason County losing one representative. In the other cases the Senate rejected the bills, twice after a roll-call vote upon representation.[27]

During the fall session in 1798, the logjam was broken. Twelve counties were formed, in eleven cases with a proviso that there would be no separate representation until the number of voters exceeded the ratio to be "hereafter established." The counties, some of which possessed the 330 voters the 1795 law required, would have to await the apportionment scheduled for the following year.[28] Most important, none of these eleven counties would be represented in the constitutional convention called for July 1799.

Even without representation of these eleven counties, the political balance had shifted to some degree. As Table 5 shows, geographically outlying regions were gaining power and the dominance of large counties was lessened. In fact, many Kentuckians resented large counties, preferring smaller units where voters were convenient to the election place and where they would have at least one representative responsive to their interests. Those living in counties with one or two representatives thought it unfair that voters in some counties might elect six or seven men.[29] Within the assembly, a large county delegation voting as a bloc could prove decisive. Thus the whittling down of the power of one county was appealing. In the fall of 1798, the only new county given representation was Jessamine County, split off from Fayette, which lost a seat as a result. John Breckinridge and the Fayette delegation opposed the bill, but it passed by a 24 to 15 majority.[30]

The formation of counties in 1798, some with very small populations – two had less than two hundred voters – led some to suspect that a radical redistribution of power would be attempted in the constitutional convention of 1799. George Nicholas predicted that there would be an attempt to write representation by county into the new constitution. In fact, these tiny counties turned previous opinions about representation upside down. To those who had long considered county representation a means of maintaining power for established areas, it was hard to comprehend that the same rule would

Table 5

COUNTY REPRESENTATION IN LEGISLATURE, 1792-1800

County	1792[a]	1793	1794[a]	1795	1796[a]	1797	1798	1799	1800[a]
Bourbon	5	4	5	5	6	6	6	6	4
Fayette	9	8	6	6	7	7	7	6	4
Jefferson	3	2	2	2	2	2	2	2	2
Lincoln	4	4	3	3	3	3	3	3	2
Madison	3	3	3	3	4	4	3	3	3
Mason	2	2	3	3	5	5	3	3	4
Mercer	4	4	3	3	4	4	4	4	3
Nelson	6	4	3	3	4	3	3	3	3
Woodford	4	2	3	3	2	2	2	2	2
Clarke	b	2	2	2	4	3	3	3	2
Green	b		1	1	1	1	1	1	2
Hardin	b		1	1	1	1	1	1	1
Logan	b		1	1	2	2	2	2	2
Scott	b	2	2	2	2	2	2	2	2
Shelby	b	1	1	1	2	2	2	2	2
Washington	b	2	2	2	2	2	2	2	2
Harrison		b	1	1	2	2	2	2	2
Campbell			b		1	1	1	1	1
Franklin			b		2	2	2	2	1
Bracken					b		1	1	1
Bullitt					b	1	1	1	1
Christian					b			1	1
Garrard					b		1	1	2
Montgomery					b	1	1	1	2
Warren					b			1	1
Fleming						b	1	1	2
Jessamine							b	1	1
Barren							b		1
Cumberland							b		1
Pulaski							b		1
Boone							b		
Pendleton							b		}1[c]
Gallatin							b		
Henry							b		}1[c]
Muhlenberg							b		
Ohio							b		}1[c]
Henderson							b		
Livingston							b		}1[c]
Breckinridge								b	
Floyd								b	
Knox								b	
Nicholas								b	
Wayne									b
TOTAL	40	40	42	42	56	56	56	58	62

[a] The year a new apportionment took effect
[b] The year the assembly passed law creating county
[c] Counties joined together to elect one representative

have a very different result in Kentucky. Nicholas attempted to set the record straight in 1799 for ex-governor Isaac Shelby, who had clearly been confused by the new situation: "You will be satisfied as to the propriety of representation by numbers, if you will attend to the situation of the green river country. They will soon have a majority of counties in that quarter, and if representation by counties should prevail, they will then have our property in their hands. This is one reason why so many new counties have been made lately."[31]

Another set of problems which resulted from the growth of counties came from the need to set up local governments for each of the units formed, to name justices of the peace and other local officials. It was the dawn of an age where men actively sought after local preferment, and some cynics thought that this desire for place was yet another reason for county growth. But forming counties before people had arrived meant that counties were created before there were qualified men to serve in the offices. This dilemma sometimes occurred in developing regions near the center of Kentucky; but it arose more often and with greater difficulty on the fringes. One possible solution was to delay naming officials for months or even years. One gentleman wrote from Clarke County in 1794, urging that petitions which sought commissions be rejected: "It may be a means to get men into the magistracy that may keep better ones out of commition. . . . I expect some men of character to move into this county in the course of another year that perhaps will better soot to fill the place and therefore think it better to suffer some inconveniency in neighbourhoods than justice should be trampled underfoot and men be fixed to execute Laws that never gives themselves the trouble to study either Law or justice." Delay was attempted in the county of Logan, formed on the southern border in 1792, when only three justices were named. But this solution was intolerable to inhabitants who had, after all, insisted upon a new county because they believed that justice had been inaccessible. County after county brought pressure to bear upon the legislature and governor to increase the number of justices or to distribute the men more evenly through the county.[32]

The pleas for more justices rarely included praise for suggested appointees, but were based upon the urgent necessities of particular communities. The fringe areas felt the need most desperately since they seemed to be populated by the most lawless part of the population: Logan County, for example, was nicknamed "Rogue's Harbor." However, even the town of Paris in the heart of the Bluegrass needed more justices because "riots is frequent." Under such circumstances, it seemed enough if a man lived in a community needing a justice of the peace, was "consentable," and had done nothing "a sofitient cause of exception." One note recommended a man "in Every Respect Qualify'd & Worthy, but not of age. . . . But believing the said Brunts will immerse the County less than any other Man, Maturely considering the Scarcity of fair Characters in our County: Tell you his Age (to wit) 18 years, and leave the Decision wholly to yourself." It was a time when men were rarely modest about their abilities, yet a surprising number of letters resigning the post of justice cited what one man termed "a conscinecousness of my inability." Kentucky counties, then, did not possess – particularly in newly developing areas – government by the best men, but by the best available or even by the only men available. By old-fashioned standards, it could not be commended. Perhaps the clearest commentary upon the deteriorating quality of government as a result of expansion was an advertisement that appeared in a Kentucky newspaper in 1797: "Take Notice, a reasonable price in Cash will be given for a good second rate *Lawyer*, to practice in the county of Bracken."[33]

The constitution of 1792, by guaranteeing that immigrants could bring their slaves into Kentucky and that slave property would be protected, set the stage for the development of a slaveholding society. Slave population increased 225 percent before 1800, even more rapidly than total population.[34] Despite the entrenchment of slavery, opponents attempted to dislodge it. However, demographic trends and agricultural patterns combined to make their efforts increasingly difficult.

The pattern of slaveholding suggests that slavery had become more broadly based. The percentage of householders who owned slaves remained approximately the same as it had been in 1792, as Table 6 shows. In 1792, 23 percent had owned slaves, while there were 25 percent in 1800. But the geographical distribution had changed: although still centered in the Bluegrass, slavery had extended into outlying areas as well, only excepting the newest and smallest counties. In 1792, half of the counties profiled (four of eight) had slaveholdings of 17 percent or less; at the end of the decade, only eleven (four with representation) of forty-one profiled had

Table 6

KENTUCKY SLAVEHOLDINGS IN 1800

County	House-holders	Slaves	Slave-holders	% Householders Owning Slaves	Average Slaveholding
Jessamine	718	1,569	292	40.7	5.37
Woodford	890	2,014	358	40.2	5.63
Franklin	743	1,307	298	40.1	4.39
Scott	945	1,681	375	39.7	4.48
Boone	184	282	71	38.6	3.97
Gallatin	171	304	64	37.4	4.75
Fayette	1,748	3,658	594	34.0	6.16
Clarke	1,126	1,479	352	31.3	4.20
Lincoln	1,323	1,713	389	29.4	4.40
Garrard	890	1,168	261	29.3	4.48
Mercer	1,265	2,100	363	28.7	5.79
Bourbon	1,870	2,038	507	27.1	4.02
Nelson	1,485	1,706	397	26.7	4.30
Madison	1,549	1,585	405	26.1	3.91
Shelby	1,271	1,325	331	26.0	4.00
Bullitt	483	581	123	25.5	4.72
Jefferson	1,153	1,890	293	25.4	6.45
Washington	1,434	1,298	349	24.3	3.72
Henderson	238	294	55	23.1	5.35
Mason	1,928	1,658	419	21.7	3.96
Green	1,035	805	220	21.3	3.66
Livingston	481	344	102	21.2	3.37
Christian	416	257	86	20.7	2.99
Pendleton	242	217	50	20.7	4.34
Logan	769	525	157	20.4	3.34
Barren	707	460	144	20.4	3.19
Montgomery	1,201	755	233	19.4	3.24
Campbell	290	243	54	18.6	4.50
Ohio	202	137	36	17.8	3.81
Warren	691	321	122	17.7	2.63
Harrison	769	417	132	17.2	3.16
Henry	511	263	86	16.8	3.06
Pulaski	642	270	94	14.6	2.87
Hardin	498	276	69	13.9	4.00
Nicholas	504	248	63	12.5	3.94
Fleming	804	259	94	11.7	2.76
Muhlenberg	245	98	28	11.4	3.50
Bracken	405	160	45	11.1	3.56
Breckinridge	147	44	15	10.2	2.93
Cumberland	352	87	34	9.7	2.56
Knox	178	54	16	9.0	3.38
TOTAL	32,503	35,890	8,176	25.2	4.39

NOTE: These slaveholding figures have been computed from the Kentucky County Tax Lists, KHS, see Appendix for note on method.

The slave population in each county, when compared with the United States Census figures (cited in Clift, "*Second Census,*" pp. iv-vi), is underenumerated in the tax lists, unquestionably as a tax dodge. The United States Census lists 40,343 slaves, compared with this total of 35,890.

17 percent or less. In counties where slavery had been weak in 1792, it had expanded significantly. Bourbon County's slaveholdings increased from 17 to 27 percent, Mason's from 13 to 22 percent. Even where a plantation system had not developed, slavery had proved useful in clearing new land.[35]

The size of the slaveholdings, however, did differ sharply from area to area. In the central region, where the plantation system was well established, the average size of the slaveholdings was substantially higher than elsewhere. In the Bluegrass counties of Fayette, Jessamine, Woodford, and Mercer, 14 to 17 percent of the slaveholdings were plantation-sized (more than ten slaves), while in the Green River counties of Warren, Barren, and Christian, only 1 to 4 percent were of that size. Changes were under way in southern Kentucky which would alter that, however. Starting in the mid-1790s, the area emerged as a region of commercial farming, particularly of tobacco. After 1796, tobacco inspection stations were established there, beginning the trend which would make Christian County the center of the state's tobacco industry by 1830 and a large slaveholding area as a result.[36]

Slavery was also bolstered during the 1790s as nonslaveholders moved into the ranks of slaveholders and slaveholdings were increased. Some people who had opposed slavery at the time of the first convention obtained slaves during the 1790s. In one sample of men in Madison and Mercer counties, over two-thirds of the slaveholdings increased, as Table 7 shows:

Table 7

CHANGES IN SLAVEHOLDINGS DURING
THE 1790S IN TWO COUNTIES

	Madison	Mercer
Decrease	4	8
Remain the same	9	10
Increase	26	33
Increase from zero	6	5

NOTE: Sources, Madison and Mercer County Tax Lists, KHS.

Nonslaveholders may have acquired slaves because they had accepted a previously distasteful institution or because they could finally afford the investment. Motives were probably mixed for many, as they were for a colony of Jerseymen settled in Mason County. Originally without slaves, partly from principle and partly from poverty, all but one of them finally became slaveholders. "Even good old Uncle Cornelius purchased a man by the name of Clem, and argued from the Bible that it was right."[37]

Geographical and population expansion, the spread of commercial farming, acceptance of slave labor – all these factors combined to augment the demand for slaves. Since natural increase could not meet the need, attention focused upon importation of slaves from other states. After statehood, Kentucky had two sets of constraints upon such importation. The 1792 constitution permitted any immigrant to bring in slaves for his own use but allowed the legislature to cut off importation of slaves as merchandise. The second constraint – in this matter as in all others – was Virginia law, which remained in effect until amended or repealed by the Kentucky legislature. Virginia's code regulated slave importation with great strictness. Migrants were required to sign an oath that they brought in slaves only for their own use; Virginians could only import slaves that they owned at the time of the law's passage (1782) or obtained thereafter by dower or inheritance. Any violation of the ordinance required that the slaves be freed. This law, which apparently was enforced in Kentucky, even after statehood, represented a real barrier to expanded slaveholdings for resident Kentuckians.[38]

Pressures for amendment to the law came from two antagonistic sources. Planters looking for additional labor sources chafed under restrictions limiting the slave supply. And those who were interested in ending slavery altogether recognized that the limitation of slave importation was a critical first step. The legislature first considered Virginia's slave importation law in 1793 but failed to agree upon amendments then. In 1794 it received a memorial from an abolition society (probably the convention of abolition societies which had met earlier in the year in Philadelphia), asking an end to any slave imports.[39] This time the assembly acted, although not as the society wanted.

Upon the issue of slave importation, antislavery forces were on the defensive. In fact, the goal of ending slave imports was not even entertained, and the best that they could attempt was to continue the Virginia law which required an oath that slaves were not imported as merchandise and freed slaves brought in contrary to the law. The House of Representatives discarded the latter provision, 14 to 18, imposing penalties ($3Q0 per slave) rather than freeing the slaves. Both houses rejected the oath, weakening if not eliminating the enforcement mechanism. And Kentucky added a final proviso which completed the shift from a policy of limitation to a policy of expansion. "A citizen of this state or persons emigrating to this state may bring or cause to be brought" slaves for their own use.[40] Although the slave trade as such was forbidden, citizens could buy elsewhere or direct the purchase elsewhere of slaves to be brought into Kentucky.

Antislavery legislators could not resist demands for more labor, but they still could command much sympathy and support. Apparently as a quid pro quo for the new importation regulations, the same law liberalized Virginia's requirements for the manumission of slaves. On the one hand, the liberator was released from rigid requirements to support the freedmen, and, on the other hand, the freedmen were rescued from the strict rules Virginia had imposed on them. Such manumission provisions salved the consciences of legislators unwilling to limit economic growth. Slave labor would be available to Kentuckians who wanted it and could afford it, but those who disapproved of slavery were enabled to free their own bondsmen. Similarly, antislave sentiment was strong enough throughout the decade to keep slaveholders on the defensive on two issues which marginally affected the profitability of slavery but did not threaten its viability. Opponents repeatedly attempted to eliminate compensation to owners for slaves executed for a crime. Property rights of slaveholders were protected in this matter, although usually by a close vote, but slaveholders were denied the tax exemption for young slaves which Virginia allowed.[41]

In the churches, antislavery sentiment was strong in the 1790s. David Rice thought that the Methodists were "generally friends to freedom; the Presbyterian Ministers, and I believe a large majority of the People" were sympathetic, as well. The Baptists were much more divided. Individual churches testified to the immorality of slavery, but "Baptists have a number among them who possess many slaves, and they are too great politicians to see with moral eyes." But antislave churches and church members continued to suffer difficulty in translating religious commitment into public policy. The denominations found it hard to cooperate, even for a common goal. Still more difficult was the approach to the civil authority. An emancipating Baptist church asked its association if the church ought not memorialize the legislature to free the slaves. The ruling body responded that each person might do so but the church could not. Even the Transylvania Presbytery, home of several emancipationist ministers including David Rice, resolved in the midst of a long period of self-searching that "the final remedy [alone belongs] to the civil power," and that meanwhile Presbyterians could do no more than educate their slaves to enjoy the freedom which "they hope will be accomplished as soon as the nature of things will admit."[42]

Rice, however, remained active. He attracted the attention of antislavery groups nationally by his convention speech, which the Pennsylvania Abolition Society reprinted and circulated in the east. The Society sent Rice a packet of antislavery material to be used in any future Kentucky antislavery efforts. As Rice worked out his strategy after 1792, he demonstrated an enhanced appreciation of political reality not evident in the convention. He thought people understood the "moral evil of slavery" but excused themselves because of "Interest, all powerful Interest." To awaken those of sluggish conscience, he inserted a purported dialogue between God and a slaveholder in the *Kentucky Gazette*.[43]

At the end of 1794, Rice attempted to organize an abolition society. In order to remove one obstacle to emancipation which he had dismissed in the convention, he suggested that the Pennsylvania Abolition Society petition Congress to set up a western state to which blacks would remove. The effort to form a society in Kentucky proved abortive, however, because "Some influential Charaters, on whom was considerable dependence, did not chuse, for some political reasons, to enter into such an association." Indeed, by 1797, Rice himself was tiptoeing delicately in political terrain. He and his antislavery friends had decided a low profile would be safer and more productive. There might soon be a second constitutional convention at which "the detestable 9th Article [on slavery] might then be annulled, or altered into a greater consistency with the principles of humanity; if not some political provision made for the Abolition of slavery." An abolition society might alarm the slaveholders so that "the friends of equal Liberty by making a premature exertion, might loose their influence in the election . . . or in the Convention itself." Several dozen brash young Lexingtonians declined such circumspection, openly organizing abolitionist debating societies in 1797.[44]

While these factions worked upon strategies to obtain a favorable vote for emancipation in the convention, should it occur, many of their potential supporters were "voting with their feet": both in-migration and out-migration during the 1790s weakened antislavery in Kentucky. After the Battle of Fallen Timbers in 1794 reduced the Indian danger, Ohio was open to settlement and thereafter provided an attractive nonslave alternative to Kentucky. Furthermore, land titles in Ohio were clear, while many titles in Kentucky remained clouded. With such a choice, easterners supporting slavery moved to Kentucky – at least until the convention prospects renewed a sense of caution – while those with an aversion to it went north. And Kentucky residents, some of whom had only been waiting for secure conditions, began to move north as well, in church congregations and as individuals. The stream of Kentuckians moving into southern Ohio – and later Indiana – drained off some of the people who had been active in antislavery, serving as a safety valve for slavery in Kentucky while providing support for future abolitionist activity in Ohio.[45]

4

COURTHOUSE AND STATEHOUSE POLITICS

THE GEOGRAPHICAL and population expansion seriously affected the government of Kentucky during the 1790s. After a brief pause during which no noticeable change occurred, the centrifugal forces inherent in expansion became apparent, and the locus of power moved to the county court and its natural ally, the House of Representatives. The agencies which George Nicholas had intended to hold power – the governor, the Senate, and the Court of Appeals – could not stop the erosion of their authority, partly because they had made themselves unpopular by certain actions they had taken, partly because there was no practical possibility of a continued domination of the state by these institutions. Centralized control was physically impossible in the face of vastly increased numbers of county jurisdictions and furthermore was intolerable to a widely scattered population.

The emergence of strong county courts was unquestionably related to the necessity of governing localities far from the state capital and, in some cases, occurred quickly. For the General Assembly, strength came with actual experience and with the esprit de corps which developed within a few years after statehood. In both cases, however, the institutions were strong and self-assured before 1799.

The legislators of the new government convened in temporary quarters in Lexington in June of 1792, elected two wealthy Jefferson County planters – Alexander S. Bullitt and Robert Breckinridge – Speakers of the two houses, and turned to business. The customary modes of legislative procedure were adopted by the assembly, and the *Journals* describe what would seem to be routine activity. Yet differences were apparent, and onlookers were dismayed. Only five days after the session began, the House made it a standing order that "no personal nor indecent language shall be used in debate." Before the end of the second session of 1792 and despite such an order, a feud between two members of the House, involving charges of malicious lying, was exposed to the public in the *Gazette* and resulted in an investigation by a House committee. During this second session, a joint resolution was passed declaring that no assemblyman should carry firearms while acting in his legislative capacity. A desirable degree of order and decorum was distinctively missing. [1]

Lack of decorum was not the most serious problem of the assembly. That was but one manifestation of a general lack of experience. Old fears regarding the quality of Kentucky leadership came to the surface. Writing even before the General Assembly met, one observer conceded that the legislators were mostly "very Honoust men" but thought they lacked "some old Experienced hands who would know the Proper rules." He might properly lament, for there was but a single lawyer in the House, and only two members had more than two years of legislative experience. Another gentleman reported that in "our political Body . . . there is the greatest Dearth of Abilities here I ever saw for the number of people, when put to the Test." [2]

The neophyte legislators made certain changes in parliamentary practice. The Kentucky House of Representatives continued the Virginia system of standing committees but enlarged the membership. The committee of propositions and grievances, which was entrusted with most private and local legislative matters, had been the largest committee in the Virginia assembly with up to 60 percent of the House appointed to it. Thirty-eight of the forty members elected to Kentucky's first legislative session were named to this committee, excluding only the House Speaker and one man whose seat was vacated early in the session. Kentucky's committee of privileges and elections was also larger proportionately than Virginia's, with 40 percent of the House appointed. The other three standing committees established to handle religion, claims, and courts of justice were similarly enlarged. [3]

The lack of experience quickly led the legislature to look for help. Only four days after it had convened, the House passed a resolution requiring the state attorney general to attend the session so that he could give his opinion when asked by either branch of the legislature. Thereafter, two of the most controversial and complex measures before the assembly – those dealing with the court system and with revenue and taxation – were drawn up by committees explicitly instructed to have the attorney general draft the bills. One observer described "this particular Crisis when . . . a Set of Novices at the Helm that have got entangled with politics and knows not how to extricate themselves without the Assistance of our Att[orne]y General and if he should refuse or die we would undoubtedly fall to the Ground under the pressure of Government." This appeal to the attorney general for help aroused controversy, and the bill describing his duties was only passed in the November session. The controversy may have been caused by the identity of the man holding the office. The nomination of George Nicholas had been sent to the Senate by Governor Isaac Shelby on June 7 and had been approved.[4]

Why Nicholas took the post is obscure, since he had sworn to remain outside government. He explained he wanted to protect the governor against unwarranted attacks, but another motive surely was involved.[5] He was aware that the legislature could impair the careful centralism he had built into the constitution, either by carelessness or by hostility. He also hoped to institute through legislation the tax program he had not been able to insert into the constitution. It is likely, then, that his term as attorney general – just as his participation in the constitutional convention – was intended to organize government properly. With Nicholas assisting, the legislature did at first elaborate his own ideas, hedging localism as he desired. From the beginning, however, his proposals met stronger resistance than they had in the convention.

One of the most time-consuming issues the legislature faced was the organization of the judiciary. The constitution provided for a Court of Appeals and a system of county courts, but the legislature had to divide the jurisdiction and might erect other courts. It was empowered to eliminate the original jurisdiction of the Court of Appeals in land suits. And the level of pay established would affect the judiciary and the kind of men who would serve.

The House of Representatives first inclined to support a judicial system composed only of county courts and the Court of Appeals, but the Senate insisted upon intermediate district courts. It seems likely that the senators were more concerned about the lack of men with legal training in the counties and had concluded that a district court system would insure more qualified men on the bench. Eventually the House made two amendments to its own proposal, attempting to win senators away from their plan. First the House resolved that a state court of criminal jurisdiction, the Court of Oyer and Terminer, should be established. Two days later, the House resolved that the county court business should be divided. The Virginia county court held all local power; it met two times in three as the administrative and legislative body of the county, the third time as a court of quarter sessions, handling cases under common law and chancery. Now the Kentucky House of Representatives proposed that four of the justices in each county be specifically constituted as a court of quarter sessions, thus presumably guaranteeing that those best qualified would handle legal matters. This compromise was adopted and the final law included no district courts but created instead a three-man Court of Oyer and Terminer and a three-man quarter sessions court in each county, in addition to the regular county court.[6]

The debates on the structure of the judiciary were intricately interwoven with the question of original jurisdiction. Upon this matter the sparsity of the record makes it impossible to understand the divisions precisely. Both Senate and House of Representatives exhibited at some time during the session a willingness to divest the Court of Appeals of its special jurisdiction, but the two houses found it difficult to agree upon a bill. The disagreement was based partly upon different ideas of where the jurisdiction ought to be placed. The House resolved early in the session to give original jurisdiction in all matters to the county court; it seems likely that the Senate desired to lodge the jurisdiction in the district courts it supported. Midway in the session, after the House had resolved to divide the business of the county court, the Senate attempted to vest the original jurisdiction in the quarter sessions court, but the House rejected the proposal. Even though the Senate preferred to take the power from the Court of Appeals, it held to its determination to keep the jurisdiction in courts composed of reasonably well-qualified men.[7]

With a deadlock between the two houses, a series of conferences resulted; in one, the Senate sent eight of its eleven members, apparently hoping to overwhelm the House conferees. When the conferences failed to resolve the differences, George Nicholas became the key figure in the negotiations. Senate Speaker Bullitt went to consult with him. Nicholas was apparently able to convince the House of Representatives that the original jurisdiction ought at least to be tried before it was abandoned. In the end, then, the law left the original jurisdiction exactly where the constitution had placed it, in the Court of Appeals.[8]

Nicholas's efforts in the drafting of the legislation during 1792 were intended both to protect the consolidation of jurisdiction and to guarantee that the appointive power remain exclusively with the governor. The constitutional provision explicitly granted the executive the authority to "appoint all officers whose offices are established by this constitution, or shall be established by law, and whose appointments are not herein otherwise provided for." Only the Senate had any voice, through its right to confirm nominations. But legislation might allow another agency – perhaps the county court – authority to nominate or to reject. This Nicholas clearly disapproved, as his arguments in the convention had demonstrated. He had prevailed at that time, and he was also able to write an executive carte blanche into the first legislation in 1792. The governor was given the power to name county surveyors, without even the previous requirement of a test of competence. He was to appoint sheriffs for new counties or for counties where the post was vacant. So clear did the constitution seem that one law required only that appointments be made "as the Constitution directs," and even the lowest-ranking local peace officers, the constables, were presumed to be included in the executive prerogative. In the June session, the county court was authorized to appoint only one officer – the commissioner named to take in lists of property – and a specific enactment was thought necessary to delegate that power.[9]

Legislative decisions regarding the compensation to the judiciary represented a departure. Logic seemed to demand a change in the case of justices of the peace. Virginia justices had served without pay, but they had been rewarded with the post of sheriff for two years on a rotating basis. In 1792, since Kentucky justices were deprived of that office, the legislature authorized pay for them. For the quarter sessions justices, a salary of two dollars a day was specified; for the justices of the peace, there was a scale of fees for particular services.[10]

Whatever Nicholas may have thought of that innovation, he must surely have been frustrated at his inability to persuade the assembly to follow his advice regarding salaries for the judges of the Court of Appeals and the Court of Oyer and Terminer. He had insisted in convention that judicial salaries ought to be the only ones that were not low, yet the assembly from the beginning demonstrated no willingness to pay an adequate amount. The pay to judges under Virginia law had been $1,000 a year, but the House rejected figures of $500 and $333 before finally inserting $250. When this measure was amended by the Senate, presumably raising the salary, the House refused to pass any bill during the first session. Predictions that "men of ability will not serve" proved accurate, and the nominees refused to accept appointments. After prodding by the governor, the General Assembly in the second session settled upon a salary of $667 for the judges of the Court of Appeals and $100 for the judges of the Court of Oyer and Terminer.[11]

From the beginning, the Kentucky assembly became recalcitrant when urged to undertake schemes for revenue producing and spending. George Nicholas attempted to generate support for the fiscal plan he had presented in the convention but faced tough opposition. He began his efforts by appealing to the public, publishing in the *Kentucky Gazette* "A plan for supporting the Civil List, and raising a Revenue for the State of Kentucky." Although the column was unsigned, the program of raising and disbursing funds was Nicholas's.[12] Undoubtedly he hoped that such propaganda and the position of attorney general might enable him to gain through legislative enactment what he had failed to obtain through constitutional provision.

The assembly entrusted the writing of the tax bill to Nicholas, and presumably the first version of the bill included his tax structure. Both houses then amended it, but the final law reflected his scheme: land and slaves were the most important bases of taxation, with all land taxed at an equal rate. The law, however, set a lower taxation rate than he had recommended, thirty-three cents per 100 acres and per slave.[13] Furthermore, his partial success in setting the structure of taxation was not matched by any success in controlling disbursements. The loan office he had recommended was not started; ample salaries for the judiciary were denied. From the beginning, it was the farmer-legislators who defined the governmental functions, not George Nicholas.

In fact Nicholas's political activity attracted jealousy. His ideas ran counter to the interests of an agrarian society; his wealth, pride, and his position as a newcomer also worked to his disadvantage. The jealousy was heightened by a feud between Nicholas and Senate

Speaker Alexander Bullitt, which became so bitter that a duel would probably have resulted if Nicholas had been willing. Although Bullitt had not opposed the confirmation of Nicholas as attorney general in the Senate, shortly thereafter he denounced him as a "rascal." Resentful of the House of Representatives' dependence upon the attorney general, he became "very clamourous against any person who was not a member of the Legislature being called on to draw bills." In fact the law which required this duty was stalled for the entire June session, then was reintroduced and passed in the fall session just as Nicholas himself resigned the office.[14]

The motive for his resignation after only six months' service is no more apparent than his motive for taking the job in the first place. He may not have intended to remain on the job long, and criticism of the governor, which he had cited earlier, had tapered off by November. The hopes he had entertained of shaping legislation had partially been realized, but, with the increasing jealousy of the assemblymen and his feud with Bullitt, his influence was at an end. Whatever the reasons, the resignation led to his final withdrawal from public affairs. The law requiring the attorney general to draft legislation was repealed in 1793, thereafter leaving the General Assembly to its own devices.[15]

George Nicholas had intended to limit the power of the county court severely, particularly through the executive's appointive power and the centralized judiciary. Further, he had hoped that the elimination of influence and electioneering at the polls would improve the electoral process. All these hopes proved illusory, as the local magistrates gained back much of what had been lost in 1792 within a half-dozen years. Within the county, the magistracy established its ascendency; acting through the House of Representatives, it proceeded to dismantle the centralized government. De facto or de jure, the magistracy became the locus of power.

The election process was supposedly governed by Nicholas's constitutional scheme. He had proposed an oath by each elected official, denying bribing, treating, or seeking office. The convention instead required an oath eschewing bribery and treating; only those convicted of canvassing would be disqualified. But even in the first election in 1792, there were active candidates for office "as numerous as Stud Horses at a Court House of an Election Day." There is no evidence of any effort to prosecute office seekers.[16]

The election of sheriff – new under the 1792 constitution – suggests the disintegration of Nicholas's plan. In 1792 five of the nine elected were the senior justices who would have been commissioned sheriff under Virginia's system or who were acting sheriffs at election time, precisely the sort of men who might be elected in a depoliticized atmosphere. But in the next general election in 1795 only two of the thirteen were justices; in 1798 there were three justices among the twenty-one elected. There were contested elections, men illegally seeking a second term, and overt collusion by sheriff and deputy in trading jobs – first one and then the other seeking election.[17]

Just as active politics emerged, so also did an assertion of the influence of the local oligarchy. Although the practice of viva voce voting had been constitutionally eliminated, efforts were made to circumvent the ballot. Amendments offered to the election law reflected both an interest in swaying the vote and increasing disillusionment with the operation of the electoral process.

Initially the election law required the voter to turn in his ballot unfolded to the sheriff, but an amendment enacted within the year required folding. That official was supposed to ascertain that there was but one ballot but without reading it; clearly he had been exceeding his authority. The original law also specified that the ballot box should not be opened before all votes were cast, a period of several days. Such a provision seemed to promise the most unbiased election results, but it also gave substantial latitude for vote tampering overnight. An announcement of the ballot at the end of each day insured against such dishonesty but provided candidates an opportunity to seek out additional support. Motives were undoubtedly mixed, then, in the legislative move to require a daily tally. In 1796 such a requirement was rejected, but it passed in 1798 by an overwhelming vote.[18]

The same assembly of 1798 debated far more drastic measures regarding election procedure. John Breckinridge first entered the House of Representatives at this time and rose to leadership immediately. He spearheaded the efforts to limit the secrecy of the ballot, first proposing to require that the voter write his name on the ticket, an amendment which was never put to a vote. Another proposed alteration of the same character would have inserted into the law a statement that, "Whereas grossest deceptions are practiced upon unsuspecting and ignorant electors, . . . and whereas secrecy in any public regulation is repugnant to the principles of true republicanism, . . . Be it therefore enacted, That the sheriff shall receive the ballot from the voter, and shall distinctly . . . read the names written . . . But if the person voting shall at the time he delivers his ballot, . . . declare . . . that he does not wish it read as aforesaid, being unwilling that it should be publicly known for whom he did vote; in such case the sheriff shall not read . . . the said ballot." This amendment failed only by the narrow margin of 24 to 27.[19]

Even with ballot voting, local magnates dominated elections for the House of Representatives. The House was usually complacent and rarely unseated members but was compelled to vacate the seat of the Montgomery County delegate in 1797 because of "undue influence and fraudulent practices." The representative, a member of the locally powerful Clarke family, was thereupon reelected by a large majority. The constitution permitted justices themselves to serve, and during the 1790s generally one-half of the legislators were acting justices. Additional assemblymen had previously sat on the county bench but had resigned. Still others were related by blood or marriage to county officials. The description of one man, if divested of the rancor directed at a political opponent, could as well be applied to others: his "Interest is all made by his insinuations and Connections as he has a Long Tail[d] Family here." Table 8 demonstrates the extent of all these connections.[20]

The eligibility of quarter sessions justices was controversial. When the first assembly divided the county jurisdiction in 1792, Governor Isaac Shelby returned the bill, noting in his veto message that quarter sessions *judges* were constitutionally disqualified from sitting in the legislature. The hint was taken, and the word *judges* was changed to *justices* so that quarter sessions officials could serve as assemblymen. Some people doubted the constitutionality of a law permitting salaried judicial officers under any name to sit in the legislature, but Shelby thought it was necessitated by the scarcity of men well qualified for law or government. The assembly in the fall of 1792 rejected a resolution to exclude quarter sessions justices from the legislature, but in 1795, in conjunction with an expansion of their jurisdiction which made such a breach of separation of powers more egregious, reversed itself. The House of Representatives declared the seats of twelve of its members vacated because the quarter sessions justices were not eligible; three senators suffered the same fate. New elections were called in mid-session; seven of the twelve

Table 8

RELATIONSHIP BETWEEN LEGISLATURE AND COUNTY COURT

House of Representatives

Year	House Members	Acting Justices	Ex-Justices	Kin of Justices	Named to Court during Session	Total Justice-Tied	% of House
1792[a]	40	22	2	2	28	30	75
1793	40	19	3	1	6	29	73
1794	42	21	4	0	4	29	69
1795	42	28	4	1	1	34	81
1795[b]	42	18	11	1	6	32[c]	76
1796	56	27	12	2	2	42[c]	75
1797	56	29	12	3	1	45	80
1798	56	21	13	4	2	40	71
1799	58	32	6	3	1	42	72

Senate

Year	Senate Members	Acting Justices	Ex-Justices	Kin of Justices	Named to Court during Session	Total Justice-Tied	% of Senate
1792[a]	11	7	1	1	5	6	55
1793	11	6	1	0	1	7[c]	64
1794	11	7	0	0	1	8	73
1795	11	7	1	0	0	8	73
1795[b]	11	4	4	0	1	8[c]	73
1796	15	4	4	2	1	11	73
1797	15	4	4	3	0	11	73
1798	15	4	4	4	0	12	80
1799	15	5	4	2	2	13	87

NOTE: Table based upon List of county officials in Kentucky counties before statehood, 1780-1792, List of county officials in Kentucky counties, 1792-1799, List of members of the Kentucky House of Representatives, 1792-1799, and List of members of the Kentucky Senate, 1792-1799, see Appendix for sources. Figures for justices include those who served on the county court and on the quarter sessions court. Except where noted, the profile is of the assemblymen seated at the beginning of the legislative session.

[a] The 1792 figures for acting justices and ex-justices refer to commissions from Virginia before statehood. The other 1792 figures refer to commissions issued by the new Kentucky government.

[b] The second set of figures for 1795 profiles the assembly as reconstituted after the election to fill vacancies caused by declaring quarter sessions justices ineligible.

[c] Because ex-justices were among those appointed to the court, the figure for "Total Justice-Tied" does not equal the sum of the previous categories.

representatives and all three senators resigned their posts as justices and were reelected to the assembly, while the rest were replaced.[21]

This particular decision upon eligibility introduced a new feature of the link between local and state government. With concurrent service forbidden, men resigned from the quarter sessions court with their election to assembly; then, presumably when they had decided to end their legislative service, they often regained the local posts in the closing days of the session. Such alternating accounts for the large number of ex-justices who served in assembly. It also partially explains another aspect of the tie. As the table indicates, the relationship had become a reciprocal one: for those assemblymen who were not acting justices, the tenure in Frankfort could be used to gain such an appointment or to regain a position previously held on the county court or the quarter sessions.

Without assuming that every assemblyman with close ties to the local court was directly and personally interested in the aggrandizement of the county court, Table 8 does make the actions of the General Assembly during the 1790s explicable. Individual justices were protected, and the county court was given wider jurisdiction in matters of administration and justice. Furthermore, the conception of the state government which prevailed was that held by the county squires, emphasizing cheap and local institutions.

The first legislation benefiting the justices of the peace was the schedule of fees set in June 1792. From the beginning, the justices thought it insufficient and petitioned for an increase. The new scale set in the fall of 1792 was so high that Governor Shelby protested the fees were beyond the financial resources of the poor; under this pressure, the legislature reduced the fees in 1793 but not to the first level. The institution of fees encouraged men to seek the post. Friends thought one nominee deserving because he had served as a justice under the Virginia government when there were no fees and ought to have the same opportunity when he could gain by it. A candidate seeking a commission in 1794 commented that "altho it is not profitable it may be more so in future than at present." His optimism was justified when the assembly increased the rates again in 1798. Occasional efforts to eliminate fees were quickly rejected in the House of Representatives.[22]

The desire of individuals for place and pressure from communities in need of a peace officer contributed to a proliferation of justices. The first law which had stipulated the number of justices for each county – from three to sixteen – was amended to increase the size of the commission in most counties by as many as four. The executive was granted discretion to add still more. A 1796 law merely specified that "a competent number" of justices should be appointed. With such an indeterminate limit, court sizes were dramatically increased, with Bourbon County gaining nine justices at that session and other counties a half dozen or more. Within a year, a law requiring the concurrence of a majority of county justices in levying the county tax was unworkable.[23]

The friendly protection of the legislature was most apparent in the way it treated complaints against particular justices. When citizens petitioned the assembly regarding an errant justice, a majority of both houses might send an address to the governor to remove him. During the 1790s fifteen cases involving individual magistrates were handled by the House of Representatives, usually with great solicitude. The petition was generally referred to a select committee which called witnesses – in one case, twenty-two of them. Based upon this, a recommendation was reported to the whole house, considered and frequently reconsidered, sometimes referred back to a reconstituted committee, and finally rejected or accepted. For all such agonizing, only three times did the House of Representatives approve a removal address. Two of those were routine, with no select committees, one involving a justice who was insane.[24]

In the other twelve cases, the House declined to address the governor for removal, no matter what the recommendation of the select committee. Upon several occasions the charges were judged unproven or declared insufficient grounds for removal; in another instance the House concluded that the "crimes" had been committed while the justice was not acting in his official capacity. The culpable actions of another justice were not taken "from impure motives." In one case, torn between conscience and inclination, the House first agreed with the select committee that the accused magistrate ought to be removed, then rejected the address to the governor. The inescapable conclusion is that the legislature protected the magistracy from public complaint. In 1794, "A Farmer" protested that the assembly, largely composed of "Squires," ought not sit in judgment on the squirearchy. He urged the voters to elect farmers and mechanics instead of justices, but his advice was not heeded.[25]

Even while engaged in such direct assistance to the magistracy, the assembly was shifting the balance of power from state to local government, vesting authority in the county court which it had never held or which it had temporarily lost in 1792. Some administrative functions such as the establishment of towns were decentralized. Virginia and Kentucky procedure had required a special enactment for each town, specifying location, trustees, and their authority, with supplementary acts often necessary to change outdated regulations or to add trustees. Faced with an increasing number of petitions for town formation, the legislature surrendered the power in 1796. At first, the assembly considered authorizing any individual to set up a town, but the final law gave the county court authority to locate the town and name the trustees. At the same time, the court was given jurisdiction over ferry service.[26]

The constitution was so explicit in giving the appointive power to the governor that there was no serious attempt to transfer the authority to the county courts, but signs of erosion appeared. One minor official – the overseer of the poor – who had been popularly elected under Virginia law was after 1792 appointed by the court. The authority to appoint constables had been presumed to belong to the governor in 1792, but in 1798 a statute transferred that power to the court. Furthermore, the assembly was increasingly willing to delegate responsibility for the inspection of commercial crops. A 1794 law merely specified twelve counties where new stations should be located, leaving the choice of location and inspectors to the county courts. When local courts proved inadequate a year later, they lost those powers but retained supervisory authority. They could not appoint the inspectors but could request the removal of any inspector.[27]

The centralized judicial system established in June 1792 was unpopular from the moment of its inception. Both the Senate and the House of Representatives tinkered with alternatives, the Senate preferring a district court system, with the House finally registering a preference for circuit courts in each county. The two houses deadlocked during 1792 and 1793, but in 1794 matters were brought to a head by a Court of Appeals decision which almost completely depleted its stock of public confidence.[28]

Kenton v. *McConnell* was one of the many land cases that arose because of overlapping or conflicting claims. Both adversaries based their case upon the settlement and preemption rights of the 1770s and the determination of those rights by a court of land commissioners in 1779-1780. In a split decision in 1794, the Court of Appeals ruled the Kenton claim invalid because the land commission had exceeded its original instructions. The judgment cast doubt upon the validity of all titles based upon the land commission rulings, long considered the most secure in Kentucky. Anger and alarm were intensified because McConnell's lawyer was George Nicholas, already suspected of initiating the Court of Appeals' original jurisdiction for his personal gain.[29]

In the wake of this decision, petitions were sent to the 1794 legislature urging a reversal. The court was already unpopular for other decisions, and now there was an effort to gain the two-thirds vote needed to remove the two offending judges, Benjamin Sebastian and George Muter. When that failed, the assembly censured them, declaring that the ruling was "contrary to the plain meaning and intent of the law" and that it derived "from a want of a proper knowledge of the law, or some impure motives, that appear to discover a want of integrity."[30]

A sense of legislative prerogative had emerged in the House of Representatives, and it resolved unanimously to call the two judges before the House where they might answer the charges against them and show cause why they should not be removed. The judges declined, denying the authority of the House to question them or their decision. This lofty insistence upon the separation of powers was soon undercut by their publication of a pamphlet defending their position, attacking the entire assembly, and probing the motives of several legislators. Those who had refrained from joining in the attack on the court feared with good reason the effects of the judges' diatribe. The original ruling of the court and the later actions of the two judges brought down upon the Court of Appeals what the third judge, Caleb Wallace, described as "a very extraordinary degree of malevolence." The original cause for the attack upon the court disappeared when Judge Muter reversed his decision on land titles during the following judicial term, but the rancor remained.[31]

The overhaul of the judiciary was undertaken in this acrimonious atmosphere. Both houses were prepared to discard the existing court system and divest the Court of Appeals of its original jurisdiction. They still differed on two points. The Senate proposed concurrent jurisdiction in land cases to county quarter sessions courts and district courts. The House continued to reject district courts, and it insisted that the quarter sessions justices, to whom it wanted to give sole land jurisdiction, were ineligible to sit in assembly. This the senators refused to accept. Final action was postponed until the 1795 General Assembly, by which time both sides demonstrated a willingness to compromise. The Senate then concurred in declaring the quarter sessions justices ineligible; in return the House finally accepted the district court plan long sought by the Senate. The Court of Oyer and Terminer was abolished; its entire jurisdiction and the original jurisdiction of the Court of Appeals was vested in six district courts. The quarter sessions court was given concurrent jurisdiction with the district courts in all but criminal cases.[32]

The district court system was an uneasy compromise and was attacked by both those who thought it had gone too far and those who thought it was still too centralized. John Breckinridge led an effort to return to the Court of Oyer and Terminer in 1797-1798, but without success. Before the decade was over, the legal establishment clung to these same district courts as preferable to other likely alternatives. There were renewed demands for circuit courts rather than district courts. In an effort to avoid such further fragmentation of the judiciary, the assembly added a district court in southern Kentucky in 1798. But the men who desired a decentralized court system remained unsatisfied.[33]

During this same decade, any support for an active state government was given up. Taxes were slashed and expenditures minimized in a program compatible with the desires of the agrarian population. The tax reductions began almost immediately after Nicholas had resigned in 1792. A majority was prepared to change the revenue law during the fall term but failed to agree upon an alternative. Starting in 1793, the initial tax of 33 cents upon each 100 acres of land and upon each slave was progressively lowered; furthermore, the land tax was assessed upon a graded scale. By 1798 the tax rates were 17 cents per 100 acres first-rate land, 10 cents for second rate, and 6.25 cents for third. Slaves were taxed at 6.25 cents. Most other levies had also been lowered or eliminated. The reductions were accomplished in a remarkably haphazard fashion, often through one-year reductions of one-fourth, one-third, or one-half of the established tax rate. Since the land policy of the state was not calculated to yield revenue, the state treasury was seriously affected. It was empty in 1797, and by 1800 retrenchment measures were required.[34]

The activities of the government were the reverse side of the same coin, as the assembly avoided any excess expenditure. Salary increases were always a matter of legislative contention. A variety of petitions for loans or money grants to start cotton or hemp manufactories were all rejected. The only two successful petitioners, both asking assistance in starting iron works in the backcountry, received no money but obtained legislative authorization to purchase land at a reduced price.[35]

Kentucky statesmen considered the improvement of land transportation to the east essential to the public good. If the Wilderness Road were made a wagon route, goods could be imported more cheaply and western produce more profitably exported. Private efforts organized immediately after statehood were not enough, and Governor Shelby proposed in 1795 that the state build the road with an anticipated budget surplus. John Breckinridge and others attempted to convince the farming population that the road would redound to their financial benefit. The General Assembly passed a bill authorizing the project but cut the appropriation from a recommended $50,000 to $6,667. Another $2,167 was authorized in the following year for repair to the main road and the building of a branch, but at the same time the assembly provided for turnpiking and farming out the contract to the highest bidder. Henceforth, it was declared, money for repairs would come only from the turnpike receipts. One farsighted provision exempted those moving to Kentucky from payment of the tolls, but it was soon repealed. Economy prevailed as the assembly stated explicitly that it wanted to pay no more for the road.[36]

The same tug-of-war between idealism and economy was evident in the reform of the penal code. In the tradition of the Enlightenment, there had been a sustained effort to eliminate the long list of capital offenses. The attempt was finally successful in 1798; under the revised penal code, only first-degree murder was punishable by death. Yet to fulfill the promise of the reform, supplementary legislation was required, authorizing the building of a penitentiary. The new code would result in more prisoners, and they must be well housed and rehabilitated. The assembly was reluctant to authorize the expenditure, and the penal act passed only after an unsuccessful attempt to institute private subscriptions for the penitentiary. For three subsequent legislative sessions, the General Assembly wrangled over the amount to appropriate for the building and the jailer's salary, eventually trimming the allotments.[37]

George Nicholas had hoped that the state government would eventually expend part of the anticipated budget surplus for the encouragement of education. Senate Speaker Alexander Bullitt also desired government support for schools to help eradicate distinctions among Kentuckians from different sections of the country. Kentucky education did in fact need help. The largest and best-known school was Transylvania Seminary, founded by the Presbyterians in 1783. Torn by religious factionalism during the 1790s, it had been rechartered as Transylvania University in 1798. Except for Transylvania, however, there were only a handful of academies. For these schools the General Assembly had done no more than to pass acts of incorporation and to authorize private money-raising through lottery or subscription.[38]

In February of 1798, past practice was reversed. The education law was prefaced with Enlightenment idealism, declaring that government could only be good if administered by wise men and that it was the duty of government to promote the education of those men. The Kentucky assembly did not fulfill this self-proclaimed duty by providing money but instead gave land: 6,000 acres of Green River lands were donated to each of the four academies already existing and to each of two new academies incorporated in the act. All six were located in the well-settled areas of central Kentucky, but other sections could anticipate a similar endowment, since the law set aside part of the vacant lands south of the Green River for such academies as future assemblies might establish throughout the whole state. In December, twenty more institutions were incorporated and given 6,000 acres each.[39]

It was a policy clearly tied to the county system. Each of the academies was located in a county where no other school existed; altogether, the existing schools and those incorporated in 1798 would bring education to virtually every county. One amendment which would have added a school in an area overlapping two counties, both of which possessed academies, was rejected 2 to 35. As a final means of tailoring the schools to local needs, any county still without an academy was authorized to establish one and appropriate 6,000 acres to its use. The program exemplified the widespread desire for accessible institutions, but it was characterized by Humphrey Marshall as suffering from "the country disease – multiplicity, and bad government."[40]

The boards of trustees named by the assembly – including from nine to eighteen men – were given great power. Self-perpetuating in nature, the boards could locate the academies, hire and fire the faculty, dispose of the land, conduct lotteries, and take subscriptions to raise money. Inclusion on the list was important enough so that most senators and representatives from counties where academies were incorporated were careful to assure their own nomination. Two judges from the state bench gained the places that their rank and education demanded. Several young but yet unestablished lawyers also were appointed, in deference to ability and promise. For the most part, however, the lists represented the triumph of the local oligarchy. Almost precisely one-half of the 235 trustees included in the list were acting justices of the county courts. Another twenty were past justices. County clerks and county surveyors were included, as were relatives of court members. Substantially the boards were extensions of the county court.[41]

The law was designed to fit the desires of the local magnates rather than the population at large, and subsequently complaints were registered against the actions of the boards of trustees. In Jefferson County, some contended that the board had chosen the site of the academy because of the interests of certain board members rather than community needs. The 1799 General Assembly received numerous petitions urging that the law be repealed. The grants to academies were unconstitutional, it was claimed, since the land was the property of the people. Unappropriated lands ought to be sold to settlers at a modest price or given to them by headrights. Despite the large number of petitions, a bill to repeal the academy law was not even passed to a second reading.[42]

During the 1790s the General Assembly, particularly the House of Representatives, learned the political ropes, developing a group of experienced and capable legislators. Men now attended year after year instead of an occasional term in Richmond. Including both houses of assembly, twenty-four men sat in at least five of the seven assembly sessions before 1799. Within the House alone, thirteen had served that frequently. Such continuity contributed to a regularization of procedures, as the large unwieldy committees were pared down. The committee of propositions and grievances, which had included thirty-eight of forty men in 1792, contained nineteen of fifty-six in 1798. In the same interval, the committee of privileges and elections was cut from fifteen to six members. As committee size was decreased and the legislators became acquainted with the capabilities of their fellows, certain members emerged as an unofficial but important leadership through committee assignments and chairmanships. A minority of the House controlled a majority of the committee assignments: some six or seven held one-third of the committee seats, while another four or five possessed about one-fourth more. As the decade progressed, leadership ranks became tighter as the proportion of the House members included among the leaders decreased. House membership was expanded from forty to fifty-six by 1798, but the number of leaders remained constant.[43]

Using number of committee assignments as a key, some thirty-five men ranked as legislative leaders during the period from 1792 to 1798, and among them lawyers were prominent. There was a continuing popular antipathy to men of that profession, so that few were elected to the House. But once chosen, ability and training were recognized, and eleven lawyers – virtually every one elected – were among the thirty-five. In addition to well-established men like John Breckinridge, two young lawyers not yet of the requisite age of twenty-four were included – John Rowan and Ninian Edwards, destined to be governors, respectively, of Kentucky and Illinois. Capable lawyers were included even when their politics were unpopular. In 1798, ex-Attorney General William Murray entered the House. A man of Federalist views, he had spoken publicly in support of the Alien and Sedition Acts; in the House of Representatives, he voted consistently against the Kentucky Resolutions, in several cases casting the only negative vote. Although this opposition occurred at the beginning of the legislative session, it did not affect his role in the House. He was in the top echelon of the leadership, ranking above Breckinridge himself.[44]

As the inclusion of Murray demonstrates, the eleven lawyers hardly constituted a united group, a "legal party" with shared principles. Even upon the lineaments of the state judiciary, they were divided. When John Breckinridge attempted to reestablish the Court of Oyer and Terminer, William Garrard, lawyer son of the governor, was among his opponents. The lawyers and the rest of the leaders were, in fact, spokesmen for various interests. Samuel Taylor was consistently in the top echelon, but few others of his democratic persuasion were included. Many of the leaders were planter-magnates, men long dominant economically and politically in their own counties and now potent in the assembly. Green Clay of Madison County was one such figure, another was Robert Johnson, reputed to own one-third of Scott County.[45]

The Senate participated in the training of political leaders to some extent, but it took its responsibilities rather lightly during the first assemblies. With only eleven members until 1796, it must have seemed more like a club than a deliberative body. There was a leisurely quality to the proceedings. The Senate often convened later than the House and held shorter sessions. It took extended weekends, not obtaining a quorum on Saturday and setting a late meeting time on Monday. Such a measured pace was possible because the Senate normally acted as a council of revision. There were exceptions, but usually the upper house awaited bills drafted by the House of Representatives and reshaped them. Even in this relaxed atmosphere, at least one man arrived at political maturity: Alexander Bullitt, Speaker of the Senate for eight years and increasingly influential.[46]

The Senate was elected by an intermediate body deliberately fashioned to remove it from popular control and was composed of some of the wealthiest men in their respective counties. It would have been one of the most controversial institutions of Kentucky's government in any case, but its actions invited censure. During the June 1792 session, several senators resigned to fill higher posts – more lucrative ones, one critic later charged. By the constitution, the Senate filled these vacancies itself. Upon the first occasion, it elected a man then serving as state representative, Henry Pawling. Pawling resigned from the House and was sworn in as a senator, but one day later the Senate resolved that it had erred in voting without taking an oath as an electoral body. The senators then took the oath and chose another man; Pawling, after having been chosen first representative and then senator, was left with no post. While Pawling's fate was not widely decried, critics in the *Gazette* denounced the action as "stupendous for its eccentricity." Furthermore, the constitutional provision allowing the Senate to become a "self-created Kentucky nobility" quickly drew attack. In 1794 it was pointed out that the Senate had elected a majority of their own members, "a thing unequalled before in America."[47]

Public criticism grew stronger because of Senate behavior regarding land legislation. The Senate's approval in 1795 of the sale of all the Green River lands to Elisha Hall was reprinted in the *Kentucky Gazette*. The public found even more reprehensible the senatorial rejection of a measure dealing with what were termed "occupying claimants," another legislative item necessitated by the confusion over Kentucky land titles. When one man had claimed land under what he had believed was a valid title, then was ejected (perhaps years later) by a man with a better claim, questions of reciprocal obligations arose. Should the first be required to pay rent for the years he had lived on the land? Should he be repaid for any valuable improvements he had made? Popular opinion in Kentucky supported the loser, and many petitions for relief came before the assembly. He should be paid for his improvements but without owing rent. In 1794 and 1795 such bills had passed the House only to be blocked in the upper house. Not until after the 1796 election, when the Senate membership was changed and enlarged to fifteen, did the bill become law. Public demands for constitutional reform of the Senate, aroused by such actions, were intensified by stubborn Senate opposition to legislation calling for a convention.[48]

The united attack of the Senate and House of Representatives upon the Court of Appeals in 1794 demonstrated that the legislature was willing to challenge the separation of powers on that occasion, but there was no concerted legislative attempt to encroach upon the other branches of the government. Perhaps the only encroachment that could be noted was upon the all-inclusive appointive power of the governor. From the beginning the General Assembly made certain appointments by naming them in the statutes creating the offices. In doing so, it was following the precedent of Virginia assemblies, but going against the letter of the Kentucky constitution. For the most part, there does not appear to have been any particular pattern; sometimes the assembly preempted the appointment power, sometimes delegated it to the governor. Only in one case was the transfer of power made explicit and permanent. In 1794, the assembly claimed for itself the annual appointment of the public printer, a rich political plum.[49]

Relations between the executive and the assembly were relatively harmonious, particularly during the term of the first governor, Isaac Shelby, who seems to have been as popular when he left office in 1796 as when he entered it. Although granted large powers by the constitution, Shelby was cautious in their use, tactful and reticent in relations with the assembly. The formal relationship between governor and assembly was determined by an annual address to the two houses. Shelby and his successor, James Garrard, dwelt longest upon those matters on which Kentuckians were comparatively united, such as Kentucky's relationship with the national government. The executive elicited substantial support upon such subjects as the opening of the Mississippi River, the injustice of Jay's Treaty, the right of Kentucky to collect certain debts from the national government, and the unconstitutionality of the Alien and Sedition Acts.[50]

Shelby moved carefully in domestic matters, cautiously mentioning laws which he believed were required by the constitution or which needed revision. Only occasionally did he make definite suggestions, as when he insisted in 1793 that county court fees be lowered, when he urged three successive assemblies to authorize higher salaries for the judges of the Court of Appeals and the Court of Oyer and Terminer, and when he suggested that the state build a road to the east in 1795. Despite the unpopularity of these particular proposals, Shelby's ideas generally coincided with those of the legislators. In 1793 and 1794, he noted surplus revenues and suggested tax reduction.[51]

Shelby's caution was reflected in his handling of the road project. He supported the general principle in his 1795 address but without details. Then, in response to a private inquiry from one legislator, Shelby outlined a specific plan of building and maintaining the road. That representative introduced a bill conforming to Shelby's specifications.[52] On other matters, there is no evidence of such guidance. Opportunity no doubt existed in Frankfort, the small town designated the capital by a 1792 law, to exchange ideas. But if such contacts were made they were informal, and the governor refrained from obvious executive "interference."

Shelby was also delicate in his exercise of the veto. Only in 1792 did he suggest any displeasure with the assembly. He made personal notes upon what he designated the "omissions" in the revenue and court acts, but he did not veto or publicly comment upon the revenue law. He did veto the bill erecting county and quarter sessions courts, but refrained from including in his message his private opinion that the salary of the quarter sessions justices was too high. Instead, his veto was confined to two points, one a badly written and contradictory phrase, the other the use of the word *judges* in describing the quarter sessions, by which description these men were constitutionally ineligible to serve in assembly. If anything, then, this veto was a favor rather than a disservice, since the legislators proceeded to change the word to *justices,* thus rendering the men eligible. Even so, he was criticized for his tyrannical use of authority, but he vetoed no more legislation during his four-year term, avoiding an "alarm [to] the democracy."[53]

Shelby was censured for his use of the appointment power during June of 1792. The chaotic first month of government made any routine impossible and criticism inevitable. Shelby was faced with literally hundreds of appointments to be made at every level. He was besieged by recommendations and requests for appointment; every decision disappointed someone. The limitations of time added to the pressure. The assembly had to pass laws specifying what positions were to be filled before the governor could make the nominations. He in turn must submit the list before adjournment so that the Senate could confirm the appointments. Often he had only twenty-four hours to make his choices.[54]

Even this initial session revealed a serious flaw in the logic of Nicholas's constitutional arrangements. He had argued in convention that one man (the governor) would have fewer friends and connections than fifty men (the assembly) and thus could make better choices. He assumed that the governor would know the best men available, but, even in the nine counties then existing, Shelby demonstrated no such self-confidence. To help draw up the slate of justices for Bourbon County, he turned to the United States Senator-elect, John Edwards, for advice, only to be criticized by a Bourbon County politician who believed that the men representing the county in assembly ought to be the ones consulted.[55]

As counties multiplied and people moved further from the center, the necessity of advice was greater and Nicholas's assumption increasingly invalid. After that first hectic session, Shelby came to depend almost completely upon assemblymen and justices. At no time were petitions – a procedure of nomination which could be construed as more democratic, since petition signatures were some evidence of popular support – successful in affecting the governor's choice. In 1792 Shelby received eleven petitions, only four of which were considered. For two of these four, Shelby made a point of seeking corroborative testimony from trusted friends. On the other hand, during the rest of 1792 there were five requests from members of the county court or legislature, all but one of which were honored. The same balance was maintained thereafter. In 1793 there were twelve letters from assemblymen and seven from justices; the comparable figures in 1794 were twelve and six. In nearly every case these nominations prevailed. Petitions and letters from other individuals dropped in number and continued less successful in obtaining a desired nomination.[56]

As the procedure became institutionalized, there was an increase in collaborative nominations. In 1792, of the five requests coming from legislators or county court members, only two represented a joint effort, while ten indicated collaboration in 1793. In most instances, the men writing in 1793 composed the entire county delegation in the assembly, unless one was nominated for a particular position when modesty apparently demanded that he not sign that portion of the letter.[57]

Although this was always a customary rather than legal modus operandi, it was one accepted by both sides. The governor occasionally asked others for suggestions, but far more typically he sought and accepted the advice of the court or the assemblymen. Counties where one faction dominated so that counsel was unchallenged, as with Madison County under the Clays, were particularly successful in obtaining the recommendations desired. So also were exterior counties from which presumably few opinions reached the governor except those of the representatives or of a united county court. The court of remote Green County wrote in 1793, "Being impressed with a sense of the importance of recommending to you proper persons to fill the office of Justices of the peace; as you are unacquainted with the Characters of our County; We have assembled to consult upon the matter." Shelby fell in with the nomination then, and in 1795 wrote, asking the court for its advice. Within certain limits, the governor was willing to name "any Other that may [be] recommended to me from the County." Courts sometimes addressed Shelby diffidently, or with an apology, but they clearly believed it was appropriate to influence the nominations.[58]

The strongest challenge to Shelby's power of appointment came from proud Woodford County court justices. A senior justice of the county court was elected sheriff in 1792, but his seat was subsequently vacated because he lived in a county carved off from Woodford in 1792, and the Kentucky law included a residency provision. Shelby then named a replacement, only to have the county court refuse to commission him. The justices claimed the law giving the governor the power to appoint sheriffs in such circumstances was unconstitutional. They won their point, retaining their original sheriff for the full term.[59]

In contrast to civil appointment procedure, Shelby apparently neither solicited nor received many letters dealing with the militia, despite his responsibility to name all officers above the rank of captain. Only occasionally did anyone, usually a high-ranking officer, offer suggestions and then only apologetically.[60] Shelby and other Kentuckians no doubt considered the governor quite capable of handling such appointments himself, since his reputation was high in military matters. Yet militia appointments were in some respects more difficult than civil ones. The county courts might always be expanded, while only a fixed number of officers was required. Furthermore, seniority on county courts was determined by the date of commission so it could not be juggled, while the governor could ignore seniority within the militia. Conflicting with the custom of promoting men from lower ranks according to seniority was the continuing migration to Kentucky of experienced military men.

The selection of a colonel in Woodford County illustrated Shelby's dilemma. In 1792 the governor was urged to name Marquis Calmes, former county lieutenant and colonel of Hampshire County, Virginia. Men of the "best abilities" ought to be named, it was argued, "however unpopular or obscure." But when Shelby appointed Calmes in 1793, the ranking officer, Bennett Pemberton, protested that he was entitled to the promotion. The merits of his case seemed equally apparent to his supporters: "Pemberton is a man of influence & enterprise & the people have confidence in him, more so than in any man in the County. . . . Calmes is a stranger . . . has not the confidence of the people. . . . The one is entitled to the appointment from Custom – the other can expect it only from favor. . . . It will be prudent to fill the vacancies from the line where the characters are deserving." Thus, with all these pressures and with no institutionalized method of choice, even Shelby's nominations aroused dissension.[61]

Shelby was succeeded in office in 1796 by James Garrard after a contested election. The first ballot of the electors produced no candidate with a majority. A second vote was then taken on the two leading candidates, Benjamin Logan who had been first and James Garrard who had trailed, whereupon Garrard gained a majority and was declared elected. Logan immediately protested and called upon Attorney General John Breckinridge for support. He argued that there was no constitutional requirement for a majority and that he should have been declared governor on the first ballot. Breckinridge refused to issue any official opinions but published his opinion "as a lawyer," supporting Logan. The outcome was in doubt until the assembly met, five months later. Then the issue was presented to the Senate for a decision, as a 1792 law mandated, but the senators declined to consider the case, declaring that the law giving them jurisdiction was unconstitutional. Logan had no further recourse, but the efficacy of the electoral system was placed in doubt.[62]

There are fewer documents extant from Garrard's administration by which to judge, but apparently he used executive authority in a different way than his predecessor. Garrard was more insistent upon state expenditure for development. Twice he advocated reform of the penal code and, after it was revised, he urged adequate appropriations for the implementation of the new law. Shelby had twice noted a surplus to suggest a tax reduction; Garrard urged greater spending. Shelby had largely avoided personal involvement in factional disputes, but his successor pleaded in 1796 for relief for the Green River farmers who had been unable to pay their debt. Garrard refrained from mentioning the heated question of a constitutional convention in his addresses, but his known antislavery position and his candidacy for the 1799 convention as an emancipationist placed him firmly in the political arena. In contrast to Shelby's disinterested stance, Garrard appeared somewhat partisan.[63]

The second governor employed the veto more frequently than did Shelby. Five times before 1799 he sent back a law, specifying the features he considered unconstitutional. In 1798 Garrard rejected three bills creating new counties on grounds which touched the raw nerve of patronage. By the constitution, each county court had the right to choose its own clerk; he pointed out that the assembly had illegally vested the authority in the county court of the parent county.[64]

Under Garrard, the institutionalized procedure for civil nominations apparently deteriorated. There is little evidence of dependency upon county court or assembly for nominations, and only two letters were collaborative efforts. His independence was demonstrated when he refused to appoint prominent legislator John Caldwell surveyor of a new county in 1796 on the grounds that the candidate did not live within the bounds of the county. For his refusal, Garrard earned Caldwell's denunciation for being "squemish stomached" about the nomination.[65]

Garrard asked for and got more advice upon militia appointments – from superior officers, county courts, and assemblymen. Though he frequently followed the nominations, the same dilemma that had confronted Shelby continued, as rank-and-file officers were sometimes displaced. Thomas Sandford, newly come to Campbell County in 1798, was appointed a major because the captains did not seem "adequate to the office," and Sandford was "a Respectable Charracter and a Military Man." By 1798, there was widespread agreement that the militia was in complete disarray, with wholesale resignations. One resignation letter explained: "I think the present mode of Commissioning of Men, that are not in the Line – will always have a tendency to create Divisions, – and keep the Militia in Disorganizations, as there is no Encouragement for any good Man to except of A Captaincy while this is the case That we cannot have good Men to fill those Offices."[66]

Garrard also clashed with the militia over his insistence that officers below the rank of major be elected, as the constitution required. High-ranking officers found this provision constraining and attempted to circumvent it. One planter-politician and militia colonel from Mason County, Philemon Thomas, recommended a slate of officers for a new company, with a relative of his as company commander. When Garrard asked for an election, Colonel Thomas reiterated his previous nomination: "there was five or six small parties making up a Company of all sorts and without any orders or Regular method of proseding. . . . as I think that and Infantrie Company aught to look well and be kep in good order – the offiseres aught to be such men as would fill the place with Credit." Garrard backed down and commissioned Thomas's slate.[67]

Although Garrard was somewhat more forceful in his administration of the government, even he had avoided scathing criticism before 1799. Some aspects of the executive office seemed flawed – the election machinery and nominations for civil and militia appointments – but in the increasing clamor for constitutional reform, it was the office of the governor which escaped most lightly.

5

THE CALL FOR A CHANGE

FROM THE MOMENT the constitution went into operation, there were substantial attacks upon it. Some were the predictable complaints of men disgruntled at the appointments being made and the laws being passed. But those angry at particular actions often proposed to remedy their dissatisfaction by rewriting the constitution, a solution invited by its guaranteed reconsideration. Pressure for another constitutional convention existed through the decade, varying in strength and in the nature of the changes desired.

Dissent over the constitution blended at times with the emerging national divisions between the Federalist and the Democratic Republican interests. Most Kentuckians supported the Jefferson-Madison clique, denouncing Hamilton's fiscal measures and the pro-British bias of foreign policy. Such unity, however, did not obliterate domestic divisions. Instead, national political activity exposed the ambivalent role of the Jeffersonian leadership, while providing an arsenal of weapons to contending domestic factions. Kentucky gentlemen, who considered themselves the natural leaders of Kentucky society and politics, railed against the artificial aristocracy which they believed was created by Hamiltonian policy. But the ideology and rhetoric which they employed against the "Federalist aristocracy" might become a two-edged sword, cutting against the Kentucky aristocracy as well. Potentially, their enemies in intrastate controversies might turn institutions formed for national partisan purpose – the democratic republican societies of 1793-1795 and the public meetings held to oppose the Alien and Sedition Acts in 1798 – to local issues. On the other hand, these Kentucky gentlemen might be able to bolster their local leadership role by popularity achieved in an important national cause.

Criticism during 1792 was sporadic and disorganized. Some writers focused upon the "partiality" of Shelby's appointments. A group of dissidents met in Madison County, complaining of laws passed in the June legislative assembly and petitioning the fall session for relief. At that time, a variety of radical petitions were received, demanding that salaries be kept low, taxes be slashed and made payable in farm produce, and the licensing and practice of lawyers be regulated. While not specifically attacking the constitution, all these proposals reverted to parts of the committee program of 1791-1792. Perhaps in conjunction with this petitioning activity, a resolution was offered in the House calling for a constitutional convention. It was tabled for the consideration of the next assembly.[1]

A good deal more agitation had surfaced before then. A Fayette County lawyer, Reuben Searcy, opened direct attacks upon the constitution in the *Kentucky Gazette*, starting in the spring of 1793 and continuing off-and-on for the next eighteen months. His complaint was a favorite radical one – expensive government – but his solution was unusual. Instead of proposing the elimination of the Senate and the election of all county officials, he wanted a return to the Virginia county system: if the sheriff's office was rotated among the justices, then county court members could take over the duties of quarter sessions and of tax commissioner gratis. Furthermore, if only two representatives and one senator were elected from each county – and chosen directly with no electoral college – more would be saved. He estimated the savings would be $4,400, a figure he later revised upward to $5,200.[2]

Searcy originally suggested that his reforms be accomplished by legislative action, a procedure not sanctioned by the constitution. A "NOTICE" inserted without comment in April went further, claiming that people have "at all times" the right to change the constitution and instructing them to vote for a convention in the May election. Presumably, *Gazette* editor John Bradford was tacitly supporting the convention effort by inserting the notice, but he reported no results so the response must have been inconsequential. During the spring and summer, other columnists began to focus their attention upon the Senate and the justices of the peace. Such criticisms became stronger and more comprehensive when they merged briefly with another stream of dissent. During the summer, democratic republican societies were organized in Kentucky, as elsewhere, in response to national and international events.[3]

The first of these groups was the German Republican Society of Philadelphia, soon outshone by the Democratic Society of Pennsylvania. Drawing upon both the American Revolutionary tradition and the Jacobin Clubs of France, these societies declared that their political principles included the sovereignty of the people, the duty of the citizen to watch government, and the right of citizens to change their government. The societies were tied closely to the Jeffersonian faction by these sentiments and by their membership. Their dual functions were, first, to disseminate political information, to bring "objects of general concern" to the attention of citizens, and, second, to coalesce the exertion of individuals so that it might have an impact. To obtain these ends, it was suggested that every county in the country form a similar society. Kentuckians responded by organizing the Kentucky Democratic Society at Lexington.[4]

The Lexington society was fostered by leading citizens to rally popular support for the national interest. Committees to draw up by-laws and to correspond with other groups contained prominent townsmen. But the society, in an effort to encourage broad popular participation, suspended the membership rules and promised a new election of officers by the enlarged membership. In order to spread participation further, the society invited Kentuckians elsewhere to "form meetings in your several counties" and to correspond with it. Apparently only two counties responded. In Scott County, a corresponding committee became active, and, in Bourbon County, a group specified that it was a "Democratic Society on the principles of that of . . . Fayette." From its inception, the Bourbon County Democratic Society defined itself as an independent unit.[5]

The pro-French bias of the national party was reflected in the activities and aims of the democratic societies. They denounced the British and the negotiations conducted by John Jay. The clubs supported the French Revolution, sometimes insisting that all aid short of war ought to be given to the French. But local interests often dovetailed with this national concern. In western Pennsylvania, three of the democratic societies stubbornly opposed the hated excise tax on whiskey and eventually became involved in the Whiskey Rebellion. In Vermont, a project was conceived to attack Canada. In Kentucky, the attention of the democratic societies immediately focused upon the longtime interest of Kentuckians, the navigation of the Mississippi.[6]

The Mississippi question could be tied to national politics because Kentuckians believed that the Federalist government had made no effort to protect what they considered their rights. John Jay had once proved willing to bargain navigation rights away, and in the spring of 1794 he was named minister plenipotentiary to Great Britain. Furthermore, in any struggle to gain the Mississippi, revolutionary France – at war with both England and Spain – was a natural ally. The French might send aid to attack the mouth of the Mississippi. The French ambassador, Edmond Genêt, encouraged such expectations and aspirations by sending French agents west with army commissions, including a general's commission for the aging George Rogers Clark, for an expedition to force passage. Kentuckians became enthralled with the project and the Lexington society gave some help. Most Kentuckians and all three branches of the democratic society agreed that they had a right "by Nature and by stipulation" to navigation, although there was no consensus upon appropriate tactics to achieve it.[7]

Below the level of agreement and cooperation upon the Mississippi question, the three groups were different – in membership, in procedure, and in political posture. The Lexington meeting was originally composed of "Citizens of the town of Lexington," and it remained distinctly urban, despite the inclusion of some planters in its ranks. Mississippi navigation was so important to this commercial center that townsmen of all persuasions joined, including Federalist William Murray. Under the careful chairmanship of John Breckinridge, the members were rarely distracted from national issues, the Mississippi, the excise tax, Alexander Hamilton's abuses of power, and the British negotiations. Despite the original promise to communicate on all matters of general concern, the only local issue taken up by the society was the reformation of the state penal code, which Breckinridge persuaded the society to endorse.[8]

The Scott County committee was composed of well-connected planters, in sympathy with the goal of the Lexington parent group but much more cautious in tactics. Instead of calling open meetings to orchestrate protest, it proposed to arouse the citizens by passing the remonstrance to those "persons . . . best qualified from inclination and influence to render the most service." Plans to send a vessel down the Mississippi to test the Spanish met with so much disagreement at the Scott County meeting that they were tabled. The meeting would only support a remonstrance to the national government.[9]

The distinctive group was the Bourbon County society, which was apparently captured by radicals. A pioneer settler was chairman of the first meeting, but he was soon replaced. The chairman and clerk thereafter, William Henry and John Boyd, had held the same positions in the Bourbon County committee before statehood. Like several of the other members, they were obscure figures of little property. Wealthy and educated Kentuckians politically allied with Jefferson also joined this society, which acted in conjunction with other groups upon the Mississippi issue. But in other matters, it went its own way.[10]

From the first announcement, the Bourbon County Democratic Society echoed its committee predecessor. It elected its committee of correspondence *"by ballot."* When Lexington suggested the appointment of county committees to cooperate in the Mississippi effort, Bourbon elected two men from each militia company, then called upon all counties to follow its example in "taking the sense of the people by committee." Rather than confine itself to national politics, it broadened its goals and began to apply the principles of the democratic republican societies to governments closer to home. In March 1794, "A Farmer" published a long letter at the request of "a pure *Democratic Society*," sharply critical of the Kentucky constitution.[11]

The description by "A Farmer" of the "pure" democratic society suggested a distinction between his and other branches. Bourbon County was again the runaway, the renegade, among the local societies. One contemporary defined the difference when he assured his readers he was "no enemy to the institution of them, when they are conducted by men of understanding and prudence; but when, on the other hand, ignorance prevails in them, . . . they are a nuisance, and are only calculated to promote dissention, and prejudice the minds of the people against the government and those in office; especially when a few under the name of a democratic society will dare to speak in the name of the people of the county, as the society of Bourbon have done."[12]

The dissident organization developed its constitutional critique over the next eight months. It had been "the rich, the great, the designing" who had urged separation earlier, it was claimed. The ordinary citizens had fallen victim to their arguments, despite the efforts of "the plebeian's real friend," Samuel Taylor. The farmers had received no benefits from the change, since the gentlemen had acquired the best offices for themselves. Now, with separation an accomplished fact, the constitution ought at least to be altered to give the farmers the government they wanted and deserved. The executive and the upper house ought to be abolished as useless and expensive, only serving to limit the power of the people vested in the House of Representatives. The House had been willing to keep the salaries of government officials low as popular will demanded, but the Senate had insisted upon a more expensive government. The Senate was partly self-created, the Bourbonites claimed, neatly turning Washington's pejorative description of the democratic societies against Kentucky's upper house. The electoral college was expensive and also undemocratic; the central court system operated against the interests of the plebeians. But most oppressive of all, the columnists thought, was the operation of county government.[13]

It was a breach of separation of powers to permit the justices to sit in the General Assembly. The point was not a minor one, since justices could use their legislative powers to protect themselves from irate citizens, indeed enact measures legalizing their own past actions. They could establish still more lucrative positions they later expected to obtain. As legislators, these local officials could use their influence with the governor to obtain appointments for their connections. The local government under the magistracy was characterized as "two hundred and twenty-five petty tyrants in a petty state." To eliminate such tyranny, "A Farmer" suggested that "pure Democratic Societies" be formed to elect assemblymen responsive to the demand for constitutional reform. Farmers ought to agree upon a slate of candidates – farmers and mechanics – and vote for no justice of the peace. Lest legislators have lingering doubts about the will of the electorate, voters ought to write the word *Convention* on their ballots and send memorials to the General Assembly. One set of instructions closed upon an ominous note: "if they still persist in refusing to comply [with our wish for a convention], we know the last resource."[14]

The Bourbon County society and its denunciations undoubtedly added fuel to the fire of public discontent. It was after all an era of much popular participation in politics – invited and encouraged by Republican leaders such as John Breckinridge. By couching the arguments for a constitutional convention in terminology then widely in vogue, a certain legitimacy was gained. Most legislators did not accept all the suggested reforms, but they could not resist the demand for a popular referendum. People claimed the right to change their government if they chose, a principle with which Democratic Republicans could hardly argue. Action upon a convention had been stalled in 1792, but bills for a referendum easily passed in the House in 1793 and 1794.[15]

Each time the House of Representatives adopted the bill for a referendum, it lost in the Senate. Senators recognized the widespread popular hostility and feared a convention might eliminate the indirect election of the Senate, limit its powers, perhaps even abolish it entirely. Consequently, they advocated delay, arguing that the constitutional requirement for a vote in 1797 precluded an earlier one. There was no good evidence, they thought, that a majority of the voters really favored constitutional change. But such dilatory tactics only added to their unpopularity.[16]

By 1795 the intensity of criticism was lessening. The democratic republican societies were less active, if indeed they continued in existence. Democratic Republican fury was turned against Jay's Treaty and United States Senator Humphrey Marshall who had voted for it. The issue of Mississippi navigation was quieted by the collapse of the Kentucky expedition and renewed negotiations with Spain which finally opened the Mississippi. The Bourbon County society disappeared, and the number of columns attacking the constitution dropped. Radical denunciation of local and state government faded.[17]

Without strong popular pressure, the House handled 1795 petitions asking for a convention cautiously. Seemingly to avert the previous impasse with the upper house, the House of Representatives proposed that a joint committee examine the need for reform. The committee reported that the constitution was indeed defective, although the only flaw it specified was the Senate's right to fill its own vacancies. Following this report, a resolution was offered that a referendum be taken, but it was rejected by the House, and the issue was dropped.[18] In the 1796 session, there were no petitions to the assembly, and no columns appeared in the paper. Nor did the petitioning resume when the General Assembly met in February 1797.

The mid-1790s was a time "of considerable quiet, though of much expectation," no doubt because the constitution required a poll on the issue of a second convention in 1797. If a majority of those voting in 1797 and in 1798 also voted for a convention, then it would be called. George Nicholas had opposed the referendum, believing the second convention should be automatic, but as the constitution was written it seemed clear enough. The malcontents postponed column and petition, and the assembly took the matter for granted. In the February 1797 session, with no debate or disagreement, it adopted a law providing for the poll to be taken at the May election.[19]

Whether by design or accident, the law lacked any requirement for extensive publication in the newspapers or distribution of the act to the counties, although the election was but two months hence. The sheriff was instructed to post notice of the law on the courthouse door and to read it each day before the opening of the polls. The vote on a convention was to be returned to Frankfort with the election results for representatives. The law was published only once in the *Kentucky Gazette*. With so little publicity, little debate ensued.[20]

When the next regular assembly convened in January 1798 and received the returns of the secretary of state, the convention referendum results were hopelessly unsatisfactory. In several counties the sheriff made no return on the convention. In a half-dozen others, the return was incomplete: the votes for a convention were noted but not the votes against it or the total votes for representatives. The House was so befuddled by such inadequate information that its first report included transparently contradictory totals: 5,001 for a convention, 425 against, 1,194 silent on the question, but a total of only 4,688.[21]

One of the thorniest questions was how to categorize the men who had voted for representatives but had cast no vote on the convention. Delegates opposed to a convention insisted that these "silent voters" ought to be counted with those who had voted "no." After all, they argued, silence meant that the voter was content with the existing constitution, since he had not bothered to register his preference. Other representatives, regardless of their personal opinions about the convention itself, agreed that was the proper interpretation of the constitution and the law, and that a majority of those voting must support a convention. An amendment to count the silent voters with those opposed was rejected only by a narrow margin of 20 to 24. Although some snorted that the phrase "silent voters" was contradictory, "never heard of in the world before," the most telling argument in the debate was that voters who had not known of the law could not fairly be counted as opposed.[22]

The two houses acted independently. The Senate required the secretary of state to send to the sheriffs for additional and more complete information. The House refused to participate, a majority favoring the second vote in May and an adamant minority opposing it. The House majority finally decided to accept only the original official returns which showed a majority in favor of a convention, brushing aside doubts it had about the figures. The representatives passed a bill calling for a second vote, but their actions on the preamble demonstrated their discomfiture. A Senate proposal, which would make the May vote only informational and upon which the next assembly might act if it chose, was rejected. On the other hand, the House rejected a preamble stating that the voters had unequivocally favored a convention in the first vote. The House had decided to require a second ballot but refused to admit it had an obligation to do so. [23]

The Senate meanwhile awaited new returns from the sheriffs. The information received from some counties was definite, but from others it was based upon vague recollections by sheriffs who clearly thought they were being blamed unfairly. The Green County sheriff answered defensively that the act "was not affixed at the court house, neither was it read every day at the opening of the polls; and the reason was, that the acts of 1797 never were transmitted to Green for some months after the election; therefore it was impossible to read the act every day, when we had not received it." The Senate proceeded to supplement its meager information with testimony from assemblymen and other citizens who happened to be in Frankfort. Based upon all this evidence, a progression of tabulations was compiled, indicating that the convention had a doubtful majority at best. [24]

These figures and the prejudices of most senators against a convention influenced their handling of the House bill. They made numerous amendments, including the preamble which proposed to make the May vote only informational. The House was unwilling to accept all the amendments and a deadlock ensued. With the end of the session approaching, the House attempted to gain its objective another way, adopting a resolution that the people "qualified to vote for representative shall" also vote on a convention. The governor should make the resolution known to the sheriffs and generally throughout the state. Again the Senate amended lower house phraseology. The requirement that people *should* vote was altered to *permission* to vote. Furthermore, the Senate did not specify that the sheriffs must be notified but only that the resolution be published three weeks in a row. The House refused to accept the Senate amendments, and again there was a deadlock.[25]

Faced with such an impasse, the House resolved that the bill originally introduced into the House be published in the newspaper. Apparently believing the public would approve their action, the Senate concurred, also printing their proceedings and the oral and written testimony received on the previous balloting. And so the matter rested. The public could read an account of the wild session, including excerpts of the debates.[26]

Apathy disappeared as the public prints reported the story. An unsigned letter appeared, denouncing the upper house and insisting that the people had an absolute right to vote in May despite the lack of enabling legislation. The letter called for committees of correspondence in each county to formulate a plan by which the vote could be taken and regular returns made to the secretary of state. Throughout April, a series of articles supported a poll on the convention. Although signed with a variety of pseudonyms, the articles were so well orchestrated that probably a single group produced them. The writers were profoundly reasonable and moderate, declaring that the main question was the right of voters to make the decision. An aristocratic minority – the Senate – had blocked this legitimate prerogative and by doing so had demonstrated how difficult future amendment would be if the convention were not called now. "Gracchus" insisted it would be "morally impossible." The question was "not whether this or that article . . . is to be altered. . . . [But] whether your power of amending your constitution is to depend, in all future ages, on yourselves, or on the good pleasure of two-thirds of the senate and two-thirds of the house of representatives." The Senate, by its refusal to pass the referendum bill, had provided the best argument for the convention.[27]

"Gracchus" disclaimed interest in particular changes, but some of his fellows suggested reforms, always stressing their moderation. The writers claimed opponents of a convention were attempting to frighten the voters with allegations of plans to enact laws dividing land or confiscating property. That was nonsense. Instead, the intent was to prune bad features carefully. The Senate, a majority of which was at that moment self-appointed, should be reconstituted. The ju-

dicial system might need some change, and the gubernatorial election procedure certainly required amendment. Free men could surely
be trusted to make improvements, to "lop off the aristocratical
part," without destroying the whole fabric of government as their
opponents predicted. As "Gracchus" summarized it, the argument
that a convention would make the constitution worse instead of better, if "reduced to plain English, says you are an ignorant and be-
sotted people."[28]

Emancipation surfaced as a campaign issue, but the convention
supporters discussed it nervously, fearing the impact it might have.
They accused the opposition of raising the possibility of immediate
emancipation as "an over-grown aristocratical bug bear, calculated to
frighten the people from exercising their rights." However, as the
writers were compelled to confront the charges, they shifted ground.
"A Voter" thought no citizen wished for the immediate liberation of
slaves, and that a convention could not endanger slaveholders, since
it would be composed of such men. But, he added, many thought
slavery a crime which must be "*gradually* removed." By the end of
the campaign, "Scaevola" and "Cassius" had admitted that they
wanted the convention to establish some plan of emancipation, although they agreed that it must be gradual.[29]

These active publicists were probably more interested in emancipation than in the other constitutional reforms they espoused, just as
their opponents claimed. A year before, David Rice had, on the one
hand, outlined a campaign to amend Article 9 on slavery and, on the
other hand, cautioned that the effort required extreme circumspection. Members of several groups in Lexington exchanged ideas on the
means of achieving emancipation, including the two brothers of
Senator John Brown, lawyer James and doctor Samuel, and some of
the merchants. Henry Clay, only recently arrived in Kentucky, joined
in and penned the "Scaevola" article against slavery. But the immediate objective was to obtain a favorable vote for a convention, best accomplished by other lines of attack. As Humphrey Marshall observed, "the emancipation of slaves was not an uncommon topic.
. . . But the more adroit politicians . . . talked of 'the aristocratic
Senate.' "[30]

Convention opponents sniped at the emancipators from the end
of the assembly session but did not immediately undertake a sustained campaign. They no doubt hoped that the furor would die

down, but, when it did not, they felt compelled to join the public discussion. Anti-revisionists such as John Breckinridge and Judge Caleb Wallace, writing under pseudonyms, defended the Senate's actions in seeking oral testimony when faced by confused election returns. The upper house had been correct in preventing a second vote, since there was no mandate for it. Rather than meriting the opprobrium of citizens, the Senate deserved their thanks for opposing "a violent and prevailing faction," consequently preserving the law and the constitution. A constitutional convention could be accomplished in an orderly fashion in the future by a two-thirds vote of each house.[31]

The anti-revisionists differed among themselves upon whether the constitution needed any amendment. "Algernon Sidney" acknowledged that there were flaws in the document but feared a convention to remedy them. Reform of the Senate and emancipation were the two goals of convention proponents; emancipation was a goal he "warmly applauded" but thought it ought not be attempted when popular opinion was enflamed against the Senate. The reforms needed in the upper house were slight enough so they required no immediate attention. The citizens should "prefer a certainty for an uncertainty."[32]

Others were more uncompromising defenders of the status quo. John Breckinridge, styling himself "A Friend to Order," maintained that the constitution was an excellent one in which he had "not discovered a single defective operation." He claimed that the real motive of his opponents was to institute radical agrarian laws and achieve the emancipation of slaves. Breckinridge hammered upon the theme of emancipation, insisting that it was the "polar star" guiding the pro-convention forces. "A Voter" had called slavery a crime, but Breckinridge protested that emancipation was equally wrong. "And where is the difference whether I am robbed of my horse by a highwayman, or of my slave by a set of people called a Convention?" Both were "species of Property . . . equally sacred." The issue was a compelling one for him, and he published a heavy-handed parody of the existing abolition societies. In his mythical society, the first qualification for membership was that the candidate own no slave unless he was a minister. He could own no more than 100 acres of land unless he had acquired them by selling his slaves. Breckinridge deliberately developed a distinction between men of substance, who respected personal rights, and men without property, who were willing to tear up the old constitution in hopes of acquiring more under a new document. He clearly believed that emancipation was a potent political weapon he might turn against his opponents and that abolitionists were in the minority.[33]

Another division Breckinridge sought to exploit was countryside against town. He wrote a series of resolutions published under the heading "At a meeting of a large number of the Farmers and Planters of the County of Fayette, at the Big Spring," which stated, "That the publications, squibs, hand-bills, and bellowings, in favor of a convention, did not one of them originate among us the people of the country; (as we do not covet each others property,) but had their birth very near the Printing-Offices."[34] It was a blatant appeal to rural prejudice, as well as a reasonably accurate if exaggerated assessment of the main source of emancipationist sentiment.

By laying such heavy stress upon emancipation, the anti-revisionists were as guilty of trying to camouflage their true concerns as were the emancipators. They were desperately worried that a convention might destroy the balance between government branches by eliminating the Senate or the independent court system. The convention might change the basis of representation or break the compact with Virginia, thus calling old land titles into question. But, however much opponents disapproved such potential revisions, these issues were not stressed.[35] Defense of an independent judiciary and a high-toned Senate was not calculated to gain votes.

And so the campaign ended after a month of "publications, squibs, hand-bills, and bellowings" from both sides. The revisionists had hoped to gain a majority vote for a convention and to elect a legislature receptive to that sentiment. In both goals they were successful. Remarkably, in the absence of a law requiring the vote and of any official notification, eighteen counties returned figures on the convention vote, while only six failed to do so. Furthermore, the results of the balloting were unambiguous, and there could be no juggling of the figures. A majority of those voting for representatives endorsed a convention, in some counties overwhelmingly. Madison County had returned a vote of 907 in favor with but one opponent. There had been 16,388 voters, of whom 9,188 approved a convention.[36]

The effort to elect convention supporters to the House was also successful. In Fayette County the electorate had been informed that four of its representatives had doggedly opposed the convention in the past assembly. In the bitter campaign, Samuel and James Brown worked for a pro-convention slate of candidates and against their kinsman, John Breckinridge. Breckinridge himself was reelected, but the three who had sided with him were turned out. In neighboring Bourbon County, the two incumbents who had opposed a convention were also defeated. One of them wrote a plaintive letter on the eve of the election, asking Breckinridge to certify to the voters that the two had not consistently voted together. He did not "think it a scandal to Agree in Opinion with you" but was being accused by convention advocates of "having no opinion of my Own."[37]

Election results demonstrated majority support for a convention but not for any one amendment to the constitution. Emancipation efforts had heated up the fight, and no doubt all antislavery voters supported the drive. But some citizens resented the apparent attempt of a minority to block the popular will and considered this a last chance to reform the constitution, since a two-thirds vote of the Senate would be required thereafter. Newly developed outlying areas which believed themselves underrepresented disliked the constitution which permitted such inequity. It was a vote "actuated from local, or incidental impulses; and not from any general principle."[38]

After the May elections, citizens ceased their agitation on the convention, as they awaited assembly action in the fall. Instead, during the summer, Kentuckians turned their attention to national events. As in 1793 and 1794, the political causes of the Democratic Republican party dominated local politics. Initial concern over the possibility of war with the French soon was submerged by a wave of outrage at the Alien and Sedition Acts.[39]

In a number of respects the Democratic Republican element in Kentucky operated in the same way in 1798 as it had earlier. Influential Kentuckians allied with the national leadership attempted to mobilize popular support. In 1793 the vehicle had been the democratic republican societies, while in 1798 it was a series of county meetings. John Breckinridge, chairman of the Kentucky Democratic Society earlier, spurred the effort to call mass rallies. He himself wrote the resolutions to be offered at two meetings before illness forced him to travel east to Virginia's Warm Springs in late August.

The rhetoric employed was also the same, urging popular resistance to an aristocratical and tyrannical federal government and stressing the right of the people to oversee the actions of government officials. These county meetings were probably more widespread than the earlier societies. They were held in at least eleven counties during July and August; in fact the traditional Fourth of July celebrations, with their patriotic speeches and toasts, served as a warmup in several places. For this long hot summer, Kentuckians were generally united in condemnation of the laws, although two petitions to President John Adams supporting war measures against France contained 222 signatures.[40]

The unity in Kentucky was demonstrated by the largest of the meetings held, in Lexington on August 12. The audience of perhaps four or five thousand was enthusiastically partisan. George Nicholas, whose brother Wilson Cary Nicholas was one of Jefferson's lieutenants in Virginia, gave the main speech lasting several hours. Then, in a shorter extemporaneous outburst, Henry Clay reiterated the arguments more emotionally. Several, including Federalist lawyer William Murray, attempted a refutation, but the crowd was with the Republicans. Carried away by enthusiasm at the end of the meeting, the people put Clay and Nicholas in a wagon and pulled them through the town.[41]

Although the meeting demonstrated the widespread Kentucky opposition to the Alien and Sedition Acts, it also illustrated an anomalous feature of Kentucky politics. The two Republican orators cheered by the crowd were on opposing sides of the convention question. Clay had worked for the convention and was allied with other emancipationists. Nicholas had come to regret his insistence in 1792 on a second convention, and his natural conservatism regarding changes in government had come to the fore. None of his early optimistic expectations of an influx of capable leaders had been fulfilled. The localism of the legislature was abhorrent to him. Complaints abroad against the Senate, the judiciary, and against slavery caused him to fear the worst from a convention. By the beginning of 1798, Nicholas had joined forces with Breckinridge, with whom he had not previously been close.[42]

Cooperation with Breckinridge was one thing, but active participation in the campaign quite another. Whereas John Breckinridge invited popular disfavor by overtly opposing a convention and by introducing legislation which would limit the ballot, there is no evidence that Nicholas joined in the fight against the convention. Instead he was "*perfectly* silent" on the topic of slavery as he assiduously cultivated his popularity. During the summer he demonstrated his practical political instinct when he wrote a cautionary note to Breckinridge. "A convention I do not wish to see, but opposition to it, will only increase the fever, and render the opposers personally obnoxious." In the same letter, Nicholas suggested to Breckinridge that the assembly ought to fulfill an obligation it had under the 1792 constitution to pass a law protecting slaves from mistreatment. Such an enactment would take some ammunition from emancipation in the convention, particularly since Nicholas reported an especially grievous case in Lexington.[43]

The 1798 activity surrounding the Alien and Sedition Acts does not seem to have had the same direct impact upon domestic politics that it did in 1793. Historian Humphrey Marshall later recalled that criticism of the national government intermingled with discussion of a Senate, of a burgeoning aristocracy, of local representation, and of emancipation, but the published accounts do not verify his recollection. No maverick group applied Democratic Republican rhetoric, defending personal rights against a growing aristocracy, to local issues as the Bourbon County Democratic Society had done in 1793-1794. Most of the chairmen of county meetings were local gentlemen, several with strong ties to the Virginia gentry. Even when such men did not preside (as in Bourbon), there was no hint of local controversy to disturb the unity on national questions. The resolutions passed at the county meetings and the toasts offered at the Fourth of July celebrations without exception were devoted to a recital of Federalist iniquity. The local oligarchy may have been more firmly in control by the latter year.[44]

Perhaps some of the Democratic Republican leaders succeeded, this time, in turning national political activity to their own domestic political gain. John Breckinridge assumed the leadership in Kentucky's assertion of states' rights, introducing the Kentucky Resolutions – originally written by Jefferson and amended by himself – into the Kentucky General Assembly in November 1798. By such activity in such a popular cause, he may have regained popularity he had lost in the previous spring. Nicholas did not think him popular, but Breckinridge was reelected to assembly in 1799 by an increased majority and in fact was elected Speaker of the House. Possibly Nicholas himself, the crowd pleaser at the Lexington meeting in August and an active seeker of popularity in 1798, may have benefited most of all from the national party effort. As in 1792, his noninvolvement in intrastate squabbles in 1798 enabled him to retain his high standing. But despite any personal popularity, the anti-revisionist suggestion that the convention issue be dropped to insure unanimity in a time of national crisis was not accepted.[45]

For the first days of the assembly, the veneer of unity survived. Governor James Garrard devoted his opening address to national events. Not only were the Alien and Sedition Acts unconstitutional, he declared, but Kentucky's reputation and security were endangered. Kentuckians were being accused of disaffection, even of planning to withdraw from the Union. He called upon the legislature to declare their principles and their loyalty, a call the assemblymen were more than ready to answer. A series of resolutions was offered by John Breckinridge and quickly passed, with no more than three representatives voting against any one in the House. The Kentucky Resolutions denounced the repressive legislation and proposed methods of putting pressure for repeal on Congress which followed the lines of the county resolutions of the previous summer; Breckinridge had deleted the resort to nullification included in Thomas Jefferson's original draft.[46]

Thereafter the harmony dissolved as the assembly turned to the thorny question of a convention. The assembly received returns of the May vote from the secretary of state, a vote taken with no legal sanction and incomplete since six counties had sent in no vote; nonetheless the return showed a majority in favor of a convention. The General Assembly had to decide whether to accept that 1798 extralegal ballot and what to do about the confused 1799 return which was still at issue: did the votes require a convention call or, if not, would it be politic to call one regardless?[47]

The division in the House of Representatives was approximately the same as it had been in the previous year, with thirty-odd supporting a convention and about fifteen opposed. Again the Senate was unenthusiastic, but there was one notable change in attitude. Breckinridge did not heed Nicholas's injunction against opposition to a convention, and he fought it bitterly, but others were less adamant. A small group of men in the House who had resisted a convention in

January 1798 supported it in November. A proposed amendment to the bill suggested their motive. They preferred to preface the law with the statement that the General Assembly had deemed it "expedient to call a convention."[48]

The most outspoken senator resisting the convention was John Pope, a lawyer of only twenty-eight who had recently obtained a seat despite having as yet made no mark in Kentucky law or politics. Most probably he was accorded the place as a young Breckinridge protégé, the son of a wealthy Virginia and Kentucky family who was forced to make his way in life by his wits after losing an arm in a childhood accident. Only a month after entering the Senate, Pope offered a resolution that a two-thirds vote was needed in each house to call a convention, since the majority of the voters in the two past elections had not demanded it. The balloting had been illegal in 1798, he insisted, but, more important, it was unwise to call a convention in such troubled times. He concluded by assuring his fellow senators that 10,000 votes were no evidence of discontent with the constitution.[49]

Speaker Alexander Bullitt disagreed. He was convinced that the election showed that the people did indeed want a convention and that the Senate would not be able to prevent it. In such a situation the Senate ought not to "make a stand on the ground of nice Constitutional distinctions. . . . It was a matter of moment that no events might take place which would afford a reason or a pretext in that body, for expunging those parts of the constitution which gave existence to an unpopular, perhaps, though an essential part of a well organized government."[50]

Bullitt acknowledged another motive for preferring the convention at that juncture. There were proposals before the assembly to delay the convention until after the enumeration and reapportionment required in the following year or, alternatively, to reapportion before the convention in 1799. Thus the convention would be properly representative of the population. Such proposals would particularly benefit fringe areas where the population had burgeoned since the 1795 enumeration. Realizing the additional strength such areas would obtain, Bullitt preferred a convention before reapportionment. He argued that the constitutional convention would be less numerous than in the future and more successful as a "*deliberative* assembly." Large bodies were too unwieldy to work well. An enlarged delegation would include men new to politics and unaccustomed to deliberation.[51]

The senators were persuaded by the arguments of their Speaker, not those of the inexperienced John Pope. They rejected Pope's resolution requiring a two-thirds vote, 6 to 7. In a further accommodation to the public temper, they passed the convention bill by a two-thirds majority. Then they attached an amendment which might cool tempers over what Green River malcontents believed a lack of "equal representation" and defuse demands for representation by county. The Senate had previously blocked efforts to give seats to new counties without subtracting them from parent counties, but now it added two seats to the assembly and to the convention, one each from Warren and Christian counties.[52]

After a long and bitter struggle, then, the bill to call a convention passed, providing for an election of delegates in May 1799 and a convention beginning in July. The final step was accompanied by some efforts to limit the bitterness and the consequent ill effects. George Nicholas summed up the coming campaign and its requirements for those who had originally opposed it. "A convention has been called. . . . [Every good man must] turn his serious attention to it. If the people can be kept in good humour," there would be no danger.[53]

The campaign for the May election began shortly after the legislature adjourned at the end of 1798. The conservatives, those who supported the existing constitution, were worried and acted first. George Nicholas and John Breckinridge took charge, collaborating as they had done in the 1798 anti-Federalist activity. Nicholas outlined the basic strategy to ex-Governor Isaac Shelby, whom he hoped would join the effort. With so many "mad and wicked schemes" afoot, he thought, people might be distracted from making "choice of such men as they really have confidence in." These circumstances required "a union of the good men in the different counties to send proper representatives . . . agreeing on and supporting one ticket."[54]

Nicholas had grasped the political realities of 1799. At the time of the 1792 convention, he and his allies had denounced slates and instructions, and Nicholas had included a prohibition of canvassing in the constitution. But that was an anachronism which had not functioned in the intervening six years. Now, without wasting time bemoaning the failure of his original scheme, he adapted committee tactics to his own end. A ticket would concentrate the conservative vote, but, to prevail, it must include "good men, but such of that class as are most popular." Carefully enumerating the prospects in some counties, he asked Shelby's advice about others. Even as Nicholas encouraged certain people to run, John Breckinridge solicited prospective candidates.[55]

Not only were Nicholas and Breckinridge attempting to handpick the delegations which would be elected, Nicholas was thinking ahead to leadership within the convention. Regrettably, he himself could not run, though he thought he could have a nearly unanimous vote: he would be charged with hypocrisy if he broke his pledge never to serve in public office. By remaining on the sidelines and not arousing the jealousy of others, he could be more influential in promoting proper elections. But he thought his absence made Shelby's election imperative. There was no one else who "will possess the confidence of that body, that we ought to have confidence in." He assessed other possible leaders, perhaps exaggerating their weaknesses to exert more pressure on Shelby to serve. Alexander Bullitt, John Breckinridge, Caleb Wallace, James Garrard, Benjamin Logan – all these men were either too uncertain in their principles or too unpopular to have much weight in the convention. Only Shelby himself was trusted by the people and was obnoxious to no party and thus could be of "real service" in the convention.[56]

Leadership and a slate of candidates must be considered in the campaign, but fully as important was a platform. In 1792 it had been the committees which had wanted to establish guidelines, while their opponents preferred free deliberations in the convention itself. But, by 1799, certain key portions of the constitution were under such concerted criticism that candidates must be pledged to support them. Again, Nicholas and Breckinridge had adapted radical tactics to their own purposes.[57]

To implement this strategy, Nicholas arranged for a Fayette County public meeting on January 26, a date early enough to encourage imitation in other counties. The meeting was called at Bryan's Station, outside of Lexington and in the heart of the county's slaveholdings. Every effort was made to bring out the people, and the result was a crowd of probably four hundred. Nicholas keynoted the meeting himself with a two-hour speech, claiming that no convention ought to have been called, since the voting had been inconclusive. The people must now submit, he conceded, but they ought to agree upon the basic principles of the constitution in order to avoid serious blunders within the convention. No one should be elected who did not endorse these tenets.[58]

He then presented what he called the essential principles in the form of five resolutions written by himself and approved by Breckinridge before the meeting. These resolutions, which the meeting adopted, included representation by numbers rather than by county; an independent judiciary; protection of the compact with Virginia; no legislative emancipation, immediate or gradual, without consent of the owners or without paying the owners full value in money prior to emancipation; and a two-house legislature, with the Senate elected "for as short a time and as immediately by the people, as . . . consistent with the proper design of that institution." The last was an obvious attempt to couch the resolution in the most popular phraseology possible. Nicholas privately admitted the resolutions were not "exactly what we could wish," but he thought "they are as good as can now be got, . . . and [will] give us a government, that will be as good as the present temper of the times would allow us to expect." There would never be a constitution as good as the first one, but the resolutions, weak as they were, would secure "a safe government" and the protection of property.[59]

After the platform was adopted, the meeting considered a proper method for choosing the slate. Nicholas, having first taken over committee tactics, now appropriated the device of a committee itself. Each religious society and militia company ought to elect two to meet in a committee, where a slate of candidates pledged to the resolutions would be picked. Nicholas explained that this was the best way to learn the will of the electorate, but the workings were clearly controlled. The committee met in March, its forty-four members representing those groups within Fayette which had chosen to participate. Breckinridge and Nicholas had agreed in advance upon the candidates and ascertained that men would be ready to vouch for them. The poll demonstrated the success of such careful planning. None of the six received less than thirty-six votes, while Breckinridge himself received all forty-four. The slate was a balanced one, with Breckinridge and a Virginia-educated lawyer and judge, Buckner Thruston; three wealthy planters, two of whom had not been active in politics earlier, and John McDowell, legislative leader and Breckinridge ally in the House; John Bell, the sixth candidate, was probably chosen in deference to the militia representatives. Almost unmentioned in

county records, he would turn out to be the maverick of the delegation. For the moment, however, it was assumed that these men were
committed to the Bryan's Station resolutions.[60]

Having nominated a slate of candidates pledged to a set of five
principles, the conservatives centered their election campaign upon
the emotional slavery issue, subordinating defense of the Senate and
judiciary to that. With Breckinridge in the forefront, the publicists
labeled their opponents as emancipators, dangerous to all society.
Slaveholders or men hoping to become slaveholders were natural
allies of Breckinridge. But the writers cautioned other property
holders that emancipation would set a precedent for future property
confiscation. Furthermore, since any compensated emancipation
would be expensive, all property holders would pay higher taxes. The
emancipators were slaveless and propertyless men, ready to overturn
the government in hopes of gaining some wealth. Breckinridge, as
"Don Quixotte," told Kentuckians that one could measure emancipation fever by a "political thermometer." The fewer slaves a man
held, the warmer his sentiment; those hottest for emancipation
owned none at all. Other columns defended slavery in positive
terms, as an institution both necessary and sanctioned by scripture.[61]

The pro-convention campaign demonstrated that the major issue
was indeed slavery, with little comment upon any other constitutional question. Emancipation sentiment ran strong in Lexington,
and the townsmen who had actively sought the convention in the
previous spring set out to incorporate a provision for gradual emancipation in the constitution or at least to eliminate the section which
prohibited future action. As in 1798, the plans of the emancipators
were carefully drawn. The campaign coordinator was apparently
Robert Patterson, a Pennsylvania pioneer, founder and ofttimes
trustee of Lexington, land speculator, and a prominent Presbyterian
layman. Unhappy about slavery in Kentucky, he was considering a
move to Ohio where he owned land, but for the moment he put his
energies into a campaign to eliminate it. A publishing effort was organized and money was collected to pay the costs of printing hand-
bills. Every one of the contributors was a townsman like Patterson.
There were several lawyers – Henry Clay, James Brown, and James
Hughes – publisher John Bradford, a half-dozen merchants. Over
half of the eighteen owned slaves, two owned as many as six. In this
respect the group resembled the town as a whole, for 38 percent of
Lexington's householders owned slaves in 1799.[62]

With the money contributed – some $140 was noted on Patterson's rough memorandum – and the free space the emancipators received in the newspapers during the campaign, the group was able to develop its argument and attempt to convert the citizenry. As in 1798, the authors exercised extreme care in discussing the issue. Slavery was wrong and impolitic, they reiterated, but its eradication should be accomplished cautiously. Gradual emancipation was preferable to immediate freedom for blacks who must be educated for freedom. Their major concern was to assuage the concern of property holders, who were particularly susceptible to the conservatives' arguments. The convention itself should not adopt emancipation, the writers insisted, but simply eliminate the stringent constitutional requirement to require full value in money paid before emancipation, which made the step impossible. If not prohibited from doing so, a future legislature might discover modes of emancipating consistent with fairness to the slaveholder. The state's free land might be employed as compensation or slaves be permitted to work off part of the cost.[63]

In order to maintain the moderate tone of the emancipationist argument, more radical publications were screened out. The editor of the *Washington Mirror* acknowledged receipt of an abolitionist dialogue, but "thinking many of the expressions rather too harsh, and more calculated to *irritate* than *convince* we decline its publication." An article written by Benedict Swope, a minister and delegate to the 1792 convention, was apparently suppressed by Robert Patterson. It contained a plea for emancipation but also included a proposal to eliminate all courts save the county courts, an attack upon the Senate, and a diatribe against lawyers and educated men who ought not be allowed in the convention. Patterson unquestionably believed the selection would hurt his cause and thus did not publish it.[64]

The emancipators attempted to bolster their case by drawing upon Kentucky's opposition to the Alien and Sedition Acts. "Wilberforce" arraigned George Nicholas for employing arguments in his speech at Bryan's Station contradictory to the principles he had espoused in his fiery oratory against the national legislation. If he were as devoted to the cause of liberty as he claimed, how could he condone the institution of slavery? By dismissing emancipators as "Thieves, Robbers and beardless boys," Nicholas had sunk beneath the dignity of a gentleman. Nicholas was sensitive to the charge of inconsistency and published a handbill in reply, as well as sending his answer to the press. His earlier speech had defended personal freedom and a limited government, he explained, while the latter claimed the rights of property. "If there is an inconsistency in these speeches, all the patriots in the southern states, who were slave holders, have been guilty of the same inconsistency, from '76 to this day."[65]

Two other attacks were employed against the Bryan's Station party. Perhaps more a product of the emancipators' imagination than of fact was the charge that the conservatives were planning to include a suffrage requirement in the new constitution. The emancipators admitted that there was nothing in the resolutions passed at Bryan's Station to prove their accusation; however, they believed the omission of any positive statement about the suffrage had been deliberate. The Bryan's Station candidates were all wealthy, since only persons of substance had time to attend committee meetings. For men already accustomed to oppressing blacks, it would be but a short step to the oppression of poor people and the elimination of their voting rights. Such an intent was proved by the private opinions of the candidates, if not the public resolutions. "A Slave Holder," claiming to support the Bryan's Station ticket, seemingly substantiated the charge by proposing a constitutional requirement "that no man should have a vote, unless he has either a tract of land or a slave." But his column appears so obviously calculated to antagonize the public that it may have been an emancipatory ruse. The charge was a potent one, and, in at least one county outside Fayette, a candidate was accused of plotting with Breckinridge to insert a property qualification.[66]

A final target was the conservatives' procedure, the adoption of a platform and the use of a committee to pick a slate of candidates. The resolutions had been written by one man, read aloud, and adopted by a small group, the emancipators claimed. Yet the resolutions were to be the test for any candidate, and he would subsequently be bound by them. In this way, the views of only a few would prevail and free debate in the convention would be cut off. The whole process of committee choice of candidates constricted the independence of the voters.[67]

The emancipators were in a weak position to criticize a coordinated ticket, since they had run a slate in Fayette County in 1798. They became more vulnerable when they did so again. Whether they

had intended to from the beginning, the Bryan's Station organization now doomed them if they did not run a slate. Their announcement carefully specified that a meeting of "a considerable number of
the citizens of Fayette County, principally from the country," had
been held at the end of March. Realizing the critical need to shed the
appearance of a radical and urban group, they nominated six candidates, four of whom were planters and countrymen; the two Lexingtonians were publisher John Bradford and lawyer James Hughes. All
were well-to-do and all but one owned at least five slaves. Five had
served in the assembly, and Edmund Bullock had been Speaker of
the House for the past four years. In an attempt to differentiate their
actions from those they had so recently criticized, the emancipators
specified that the candidates had been given no test, that they shared
only a dislike of some of the Bryan's Station resolutions, and that
they favored gradual emancipation. Thus they were free to profit
from convention debate.[68]

"The Cat Is at last let out of the Bag," the conservatives triumph-
antly proclaimed. The emancipators had planned the step all
along but had hoped to delay until the last moment so that the opposition would not have time to organize. It was the same strategy
they had followed in 1798. Not only were the antislavery forces now
adopting the tactics they had so recently denounced, but the contrast
of the two meetings was strong. The Bryan's Station meeting had attracted four hundred or more, the other had been a small gathering
in a private home. Finally, the conservatives pointed out that the
voters knew where the Bryan's Station slate stood on important issues
of government, but the emancipators remained silent on most questions. Again the advice was not to "give up *a certainty for an uncertainty*."[69]

The Fayette County fight was undoubtedly the best financed and
organized on both sides, with two newspapers to articulate the arguments, but other counties emulated their organization. On the conservative side, a meeting in Bourbon County unanimously adopted
the Bryan's Station resolutions, with a committee later nominating a
slate of candidates. A Jessamine County meeting was called to do the
same. Elsewhere, committees may not have been used, but Nicholas
and Breckinridge encouraged and sponsored individual candi-
dacies.[70]

Emancipators were also active. Samuel Taylor, his own election in

Mercer County taken for granted, conferred with potential candidates elsewhere. David Rice probably participated, but he had moved to remote Green River by 1799, where he could not have much impact. In Bourbon County, an antislavery slate was formed, including Governor James Garrard and his lawyer-legislator son William. Members of a small offshoot Presbyterian church in Scott County named a slate of candidates to the convention and another to the assembly, as well as publishing a strongly worded and wide-ranging platform. Slavery ought to be abolished as soon as equity and safety would admit; all officers of government ought to be elected, the branches of government completely separated, and the government undertake the support of education, since it was vital to the community.[71]

The debate on slavery was apparently statewide. Emancipation was the main issue in Montgomery County in eastern Kentucky; the same was the case in Logan County in the south where an election-day debate was waged on the subject. In Mason County, where the *Washington Mirror* was just as active as the Lexington papers, a lengthy series was published by "Emancipo." One candidate there felt compelled to declare that "he would wade to his knees in blood before it should take place." Another Mason County gentleman was so troubled by the divisions within his county that he declined service in the convention. Miles W. Conway, a delegate to the 1792 convention who had then voted for emancipation, cited bad health and private business, but also "on a reconsideration of the importance of some particular points, which seem to engage the public mind, the great diversity of opinions thereon at present makes it difficult for a public agent to act agreeable to the general wish of his Constituents, which I have always thought it my duty on particular subjects, in preference to my private opinion or interest."[72]

The net effect of this widespread dialogue on emancipation was, however, virtually to ignore other issues. Bourbon County, from which had sprung much of the previous criticism of the constitution, was largely silent. A single column appeared from Bourbon three months before the election, containing the same principles as the earlier radical program: direct election of all officers, instruction of assemblymen, and the elimination of the Senate. But no other columns took up the questions. At the last minute, "Another Reader" published what purported to be a "Fragment of an Ancient Chronicle." The chronicle described a long battle between groups known as Mammonites and Manumites, and citizens could hear nothing but their dispute. A council (convention) had been called because of a number of unsatisfactory elements in the constitution: the method of choosing the Senate and governor, the malfunction of the ballot, the inadequacies of the method of selecting militia officers and sheriffs. In the campaign, however, nothing was known of the candidates except whether they were Mammonites or Manumites.[73]

Upon emancipation then, if on no other issue, the ballot yielded a final determination. To the immense satisfaction of the conservatives, it was overwhelmingly defeated. In Bourbon County, a slate including the popular governor was defeated by a conservative and lesser-known group. The Fayette County tally was two to one for the Bryan's Station slate. Most people had voted for one ticket or the other: the six conservatives received from 718 to 751 votes, the emancipators from 329 to 376. The Mason County gentleman who had promised to wade in blood to prevent emancipation was elected. The emancipators had financed and organized a rousing campaign, but they could not overcome the racial prejudices and economic ambitions of their fellow citizens. By one report, only four delegates "in favor of emancipation on any plan however modified" were elected. They probably included three men who had voted for emancipation in 1792, Samuel Taylor, Harry Innes, and John Bailey. However, despite the rout of the emancipators, Breckinridge and Nicholas could not be completely satisfied. Isaac Shelby had chosen not to serve, and only two of the five men Breckinridge had encouraged were elected.[74]

6

THE 1799 CONVENTION
FIXES THE PATTERN

AFTER ALL the heat surrounding the convention call and the delegate selection, the public apathy thereafter was surprising. Another public affair in Frankfort partially diverted attention. A Woodford County justice of the peace, Henry Field, was accused of the bloody murder of his wife and was tried in the Frankfort District Court during the latter days of the convention. The rich and well-connected Field was first represented by George Nicholas, then Henry Clay. The trial, attended upon occasion by a number of the convention delegates, achieved much notoriety. The issue of guilt or innocence became entwined with the question of whether rich and poor could obtain equal justice. When Field was pronounced guilty and sentenced to die, some wealthy Kentuckians contended that the verdict had resulted from the prejudices of the poor.[1]

Within the convention itself, the ideas of the Bryan's Station party did not prevail – as George Nicholas's ideas had in 1792 – despite the seeming success of the party at the polls. This convention differed in composition and in its deliberations from the first meeting, and the constitution it drafted amalgamated the preferences of the whole membership. Unhampered by ideological preconceptions, the men weighed the 1792 document against their own experiences of the past seven years. They discarded features which seemed outmoded or constraining or which simply did not work satisfactorily. The convention and the population accepted this second constitution which fixed the government of Kentucky for the next fifty years with little fanfare because it incorporated trends already begun by assembly actions.[2] The pattern it set in 1799 in at least some respects moved Kentucky toward nineteenth-century politics.

On the surface, 1799 seemed a replay, with delegates and proceedings not materially different from 1792. Humphrey Marshall thought so, describing the delegates as "very similar to those who formed the first constitution; with the exchange of John Breckinridge, for George Nicholas." The similarities were indeed there, but were more apparent than real. John Breckinridge was not George Nicholas, and the delegates were in no way so pliant.[3]

Some Kentuckians considered Breckinridge the convention coordinator and sent him their recommendations for the constitution, including one suggestion that Kentucky should eliminate the right to keep and bear arms, since the frontier stage had passed. As Breckinridge prepared for the convention, however, there is no indication that he took these unsolicited proposals seriously or asked for advice from easterners. However, unlike Nicholas's unaided effort in 1792, Breckinridge worked in concert with others in planning the deliberations. He drafted a series of resolutions, which he then circulated for suggestions and amendment. Nicholas and probably Caleb Wallace helped refine them.[4]

As before the 1792 convention, there were efforts to influence the deliberations by submitting instructions, although the election results had discouraged many who had agitated for a convention. Some hoped to negate those results. A notice inserted into the *Kentucky Gazette* wishfully asked if federal officers and those in the executive or judicial branches of the state government had any right to act in a legislative capacity within the convention. Since the elected delegates included three state judges, one federal judge, and the state treasurer, the question was a pointed one. The notice concluded by asking, "Would it not be advisable for those counties which have chosen federal officers, and others not eligible, (or supposed not) to be in readiness to choose others, if by the constitution, law, and good policy, the convention should be of opinion that they were not elligible?" Another inquired if those who had treated or canvassed to obtain election ought not to be excluded also. But the fighting spirit had flagged. There was no response to these suggestions, no further agitation, and the convention received no petitions. For better or for worse, the constitution was in the hands of the fifty-eight delegates.[5]

Those delegates in many respects were similar to their 1792 predecessors, as Humphrey Marshall indicated, but some differences may be noted. Marshall himself commented that there was "greater disparity between the extremes" of Kentucky society in 1799 than

there had been in 1792. The delegates were almost without exception men of substantial property, mostly planters with expanding
estates. Only one was a nonslaveholder – Patrick Brown of Hardin
County – and he had earlier rid himself of slaves because he disapproved of the institution.[6] The greater wealth as well as the greater
acceptance of slavery may be seen by comparing the slaveholdings of
the 1792 convention delegates with those of the 1799 delegates in
Table 9.

Table 9

SLAVEHOLDINGS OF CONVENTION DELEGATES, 1792 and 1799

Size of Slave- holding	1792		1799	
	Number	%	Number	%
0	4	9	1	2
1-4	13	29	7	12
5-10	10	22	22	38
over 10	18	40	28	48

NOTE: This table is based upon Kentucky County Tax Lists, KHS. These figures
for the 1792 convention vary slightly from those in Table 2 because the latter was a
profile of the men voting on the slavery question. Here the profile is of the forty-five
men originally elected to the convention.

Even more than the members of the first convention, these men
were respected county figures. Philip Buckner of Bracken County
had organized the migration of his family and friends, sold land to
them, and donated the land for the county town. Robert Clarke, Sr.,
had paid for the Clarke County courthouse. Twenty-seven of the
fifty-eight were acting justices of the peace or quarter sessions justices; nine more had served at some time since statehood. Strengthening the forces of the local magnates were a county attorney and
three county court clerks, including Humphrey Marshall's brother-
in-law, Thomas Marshall, Jr. In all, 75 percent had close connections
with their local courts. Twenty-two were acting militia officers at the
time of the convention, and several others were retired.[7]

Religious representation was noticeably smaller than in the first
convention, and the moralistic tone may have been less pervasive.
Only three ministers attended, all Baptists. John Price, a proslavery
lay minister of distinctly aristocratic views, was known as a man of
zeal, disposed to carry his opinions to extremes. He had aroused a

tempest in his congregation earlier in the year by offering a resolution that those who favored emancipation but continued holding slaves were deists. Sharply different from Price was John Bailey, a 1792 convention emancipator, now representing frontier Logan County. Well known for his pulpit oratory, Bailey was so popular he could not be ejected from the Baptist Association for his heretical Universalist views. Also from the south country was a little-known Baptist preacher, Alexander Davidson. For the rest, religious ties were less important than in 1792, although one new element was identifiable. A large Catholic population in Washington County had gained sufficient political strength to elect one of their laymen, Robert Abell.[8]

If the religious contingent was smaller than in 1792, the bench-and-bar representation was larger. There were nine compared with four in 1792, but the group was sharply divided. Five clearly composed the eastern-educated legal establishment. In addition to John Breckinridge himself, there were Court of Appeals Judge Caleb Wallace, Federal District Judge Harry Innes, as well as State District Court Judges John Allen and Buckner Thruston. All but Wallace were lawyers by training and had studied law in Virginia. Members of the Virginia gentry, they were well set up in life before they moved to Kentucky. Now at least thirty-five years of age, all had consolidated both their financial and professional positions in Kentucky.[9]

Quite distinct from these men were four young lawyers who had literally grown up with the country. One of the first white men born in Kentucky – William Logan – was among the convention delegates. His presence demonstrated that Kentucky had its own native citizens at last and also signaled the emergence of a new political generation, barely of age and educated in the west. Whereas the older judges and lawyers were by and large content with a system of government and a judicial system satisfactory to themselves and designed according to the tenets of classical republicanism they had studied, the young men were restless and ready for change.

William Logan was hardly known in 1799, except as the son of one of Kentucky's most respected pioneers, Benjamin Logan. George Nicholas, with whom he had studied law, placed much faith in his "proper ideas of government" and had urged him to run for election in hopes he would influence the vote of his famous father.[10] Another delegate was John Rowan of Nelson County who had moved to Kentucky as a young man, attended an academy run by Dr. James Priestley, then studied law. He began practicing in 1795, and by 1799 he had obtained both a reputation as a criminal lawyer and some wealth, which he displayed ostentatiously by being driven about in a four-wheel carriage.[11]

William Bledsoe was the oldest of the "young turks," and perhaps not yet a trained lawyer although he became one. At one time a Baptist preacher, he had so strayed from those origins that sectarians described his career as a progression to "a universalist, then a deist, and finally died a reckless horse racer." He had tried surveying, planting, and running a store, before he finally turned to the law. From the time Garrard County was created in 1797, Bledsoe had actively furthered its interests and now served as its representative.[12] Felix Grundy was not yet twenty-two, but already a practicing lawyer of several years' experience and the commonwealth attorney for Washington County. He had been Rowan's classmate at Priestley's academy, then had studied law with George Nicholas. His law teacher was apparently less certain of Grundy's principles than of William Logan's, for he was said to have cautioned Grundy upon his election to the convention to be "honest in all your purposes, and never deceive the people." Stocky and red-faced, with his hair pushed back behind his ears, Grundy had both the appearance and the manner of a frontiersman. The convention was his political debut, and in his first speech he attempted unsuccessfully to lower the age requirement for state representative from twenty-four to twenty-one.[13]

These four young lawyers had very limited experience in the assembly as yet, and the older jurists and lawyers similarly had little: only Breckinridge had served more than an occasional term. But many of the delegates were veteran legislators. Precisely half of the members had served in the assembly since statehood; ten delegates had attended at least five of the seven General Assemblies. Of more importance, a number had become effective legislative leaders. Measured by committee assignments, eleven delegates had been among the leaders of the House of Representatives.[14] Another, Alexander Bullitt, had been Senate Speaker since 1792.[15]

Delegates in the 1799 convention, whether then experienced or not, were eager and anxious for future advancement. By contrast, members of the first convention had exhibited little political ambition. George Nicholas himself declined James Madison's request that he enter Congress. The three judges within the convention remained on the bench after statehood but aimed no higher. Only two of the delegates served in Congress at any time; two were elected governor; one was chosen lieutenant governor; one sought and obtained an appointment as a judge. The rest were farmers who retired to their plantations after the convention and, with few exceptions, disappeared even from state politics within a few years.[16]

In 1799 lawyers young and old aspired to higher office. Three judges, as in 1792, were content with their present posts, but Judge Buckner Thruston went on to the United States Senate before obtaining a federal judgeship in the District of Columbia. John Breckinridge gained the position of United States Senator in 1800, and in 1805 he became United States Attorney General, serving until his death in 1806. Of the young lawyers, William Bledsoe obtained no post higher than state senator, but the other three all served in high state office and in Congress. Four others went to Congress, one acted as governor, and two as lieutenant governor. A dozen more were members of the state legislature.[17] These, then, were politicians vitally interested in the lineaments of the government they were going to create.

The differences between the two conventions meant that the deliberations in 1799 could not be dominated by one man. The triumvirate of John Breckinridge, Caleb Wallace, and George Nicholas had prepared its set of resolutions for the convention, but success in incorporating them in the constitution was not so certain as Nicholas's success had been in 1792. As for Nicholas himself, voluntarily on the sidelines after helping to plan the conservative tactics, he was not available for further consultation. He died on July 25, apparently quite suddenly, three days after the convention began. The *Kentucky Gazette* published an obituary – a notice rarely used in eighteenth-century Kentucky – testifying to his preeminence within the state.[18]

When the convention met on July 22, the delegates immediately proceeded to business and unanimously elected Alexander Bullitt president. Committees were named to draw up the rules of order and to consider the election returns. Both committees routinely carried out their tasks, without the delegate challenges which had been threatened. The convention agreed to reconsider the constitution section by section, which it did, conducting most of the work in committee of the whole. Frankfort summers can be terribly hot in midday, a condition unquestionably responsible for the convention's routine of meeting for one session at nine o'clock in the morning, then adjourning until late afternoon.[19]

Because the debates of the convention were never published, the records of the four-week convention are scanty. The *Journal of the Convention* is a brief notation of official actions which does not include any record of the speeches. Amendments to the first convention are specified, suggesting the pace of the debates. Much more important is the series of votes upon which a roll call was demanded. Unlike the 1792 convention in which only one issue prompted a roll call, the second meeting recorded twenty-six. John Breckinridge took some cryptic notes upon the debates for the first half of the convention, scribblings made apparently for his own use in planning rebuttal. He rarely specified the arguments with which he concurred, since there was no need to address himself to those statements. Instead he jotted down the points of his opponents and his counterarguments, often sarcastic. Small "x's" in the margins probably mark the statements he refuted. Difficult as the worksheets are to understand, they provide important clues to the dynamics of the convention.[20]

Even with such scanty materials as are available, it is obvious that there was no unanimity of opinion within the convention, nor did one group or philosophy dominate. Long after the convention, Felix Grundy asserted that "every man wrote his own constitution," then the differences were debated and ironed out. Since no other source confirms the story, it is probably apocryphal, but certainly the deliberations were freewheeling and open. A dozen men, over half of whom were experienced legislative leaders, led the debates, with the majority of the delegates silent and listening. The main spokesmen for the Bryan's Station party – the group which supported some centralization of power and a careful separation of powers within the state government – were John Breckinridge himself and Judge Caleb Wallace. Samuel Taylor and John Bailey contested nearly every point from what was a fairly consistent democratic position and with considerable animus directed at the Breckinridge clique.[21]

Other individuals represented points of view distinct from those of Breckinridge or Taylor. The young lawyers challenged their elders, often in cooperation with Taylor, upon the lineaments of the judiciary and of the state government. Alexander Bullitt, Robert Johnson, and Philemon Thomas – all wealthy planters and veterans of the assembly – challenged the Bryan's Station party upon the doctrine of separation of powers, fighting instead for legislative supremacy. Often with them was another planter-politician, Green Clay, but he seemed perversely to delight in outraging the convention. He defended the despised Alien and Sedition Acts and asserted that the national government now had all significant powers. State governments existed "only to mind the poor & straighten the roads." The convention ordered him to be silent at one juncture, and Breckinridge later noted beside his summary of a Clay speech, "give no answer to this man."[22]

Two other delegates defied stereotypes. Harry Innes spoke less frequently than might have been expected of a man long interested in constitutionalism, but, when he did, he detached himself from the other members of the legal-judicial establishment. He shared their concern for the separation of powers and an independent judiciary but objected to aspects of their program which would make the government less responsive to popular will than under the 1792 constitution.[23]

Another independent was John Adair, a South Carolinian and Revolutionary War officer who had served in the Carolina assembly and constitutional ratifying convention before moving to Kentucky in the late 1780s. In a number of respects, he supported a strong republican government leaning to a democratic rather than conservative republicanism, but he was inconsistent. He dismissed as inconsequential many axioms of republican government, such as separate qualifications for House and Senate members and a rotation in office. Although Adair voted most often with the young lawyers, the debates exhibited his independence. He shared with other pragmatic Kentucky politicians within the convention an interest in function and not theory.[24]

The membership of the convention committees verified this estimate of convention leadership. The two committees chosen at the beginning of the convention included the senior legal establishment and the most experienced legislators, unquestionably the men then expected to dominate. Ten days later a committee was named to draft a constitution based upon convention resolutions. This important group included spokesmen of every articulate opinion within the meeting. John Breckinridge, Caleb Wallace, and the two other judges closely associated with the Bryan's Station platform were named. Also included were Samuel Taylor, three of the young lawyers – William Bledsoe, Felix Grundy, and John Rowan – Harry Innes, and John Adair. The wealthy planters were least well represented, but the doughty Benjamin Logan was named and Green Clay given the important position of chairman.[25]

Although the spokesmen for various viewpoints can be identified by studying the debates, the divisions within the entire convention are less easy to discern, since many members remained silent. In an effort to uncover formal groupings or parties or to identify coalitions which formed on certain issues, two statistical techniques have been applied to the twenty-six roll-call votes. Only imperfect results could be expected, since many important issues were settled without such a record vote. Incomplete or not, however, these votes on widely scattered questions help to explain the convention proceedings.

The first method was an analysis of the percentage of the time each delegate voted with each other delegate, to discover groups who voted together consistently enough to be considered voting blocs.[26] The tabulations, shown in Chart 1, indicate that blocs did exist but that divisions were blurred. The most clearly defined group predictably contained followers of the Bryan's Station platform, some eighteen fairly closely allied delegates. Since conservatives worried about the breakdown of a government they thought protected their rights, they wanted to maintain that governmental structure but to eliminate some existing democratic features for even stronger safeguards. Even within this well-coordinated group, discipline was not complete. A number of the party members failed to show a strong association with the first three men on the list, the three judges allied with the party. Their loyalties did not extend to the issue with which the judiciary was expressly concerned, judicial independence.

There were three other blocs, smaller and less cohesive than the Bryan's Station party and with substantial overlap. Many of the Bryan's Station followers who separated themselves from the judges were also associated with a small group of planters, themselves totally separated from Bryan's Station, including Green Clay and Robert Johnson. Entrenched in the county leadership and in the assembly, they were willing enough to narrow access to the political system and leave others outside; but, within that system, they took dead aim at constraints on the legislature. A group clustering around John Adair and the young lawyers shared the planter-politicians' preference for legislative supremacy. However, most of this group were still outsiders, resentful of possible limitations upon their ambitions, such as efforts to keep attorneys out of the assembly. More attuned to the voters upon whom they depended for fulfillment of their aspirations, they preferred an open political system. Farthest from the Bryan's Station bloc was a small and ill-defined group clustered around John Bailey, democratic and parochial in their concerns.[27]

Since the lines between these blocs were indefinite, and since people did break away upon certain questions, another statistical method was employed. To discover if it was a convention of shifting coalitions instead of firm parties, a factor analysis measured the intercorrelations among the issues. If a group of issues is highly intercorrelated within one factor, it means that these issues tended to divide people along the same lines.[28]

Social scientists using a factor analysis assume that the variables within each factor are intercorrelated because of the presence of an underlying factor, a concept or dimension which the variables (issues) have in common. For example, a number of issues highly correlated on one factor might all relate to economic status and thus indicate divisions along class lines. In another factor, the underlying concept might be democracy and the division upon such questions different from the economic factor. Once the underlying factor or concept is identified, if it can be, the relationship of each issue to that concept may be measured: if the delegates perceived a specific question as affecting economic status, that issue would be highly correlated in the "economic factor." On the other hand, if the delegates did not perceive the issue as affecting economic status, the degree of correlation would be low.[29]

The results of the factor analysis of the 1799 convention are reproduced in Table 10. Nine factors were separated out. In no single factor were more than four issues correlated to a significant (more than $\pm$ .5) degree. The convention did not divide consistently upon any underlying principle. The same lack of a strong ideological component manifested in the debates is shown by the factor analysis. Decisions upon many questions were made quite independently.

The factor analysis demonstrates that no strong and persistent co-

	Thruston	Allen	Wallace	McDowell	Price	Breckinridge	Coleman	Steele	Sandford	Carr	Harrison	Clarke	Marshall	Henry	Wilmott	J. Logan	Griffith	Duncan	Huston	Allin	Innes	Owens	R. Taylor	Johnson	G. Clay	B. Logan	Payne
Thruston	—																										
Allen	87	—																									
Wallace	83	88	—																								
McDowell	75	88	85	—																							
Price	75	88	84	92	—																						
Breckinridge	79	92	88	96	88	—																					
Coleman	79	84	81	81	88	85	—																				
Steele	86	82	96	83	83	83	83	—																			
Sandford	75	80	77		76		88	78	—																		
Carr	86	95	83	91	91	96	96	80	87	—																	
Harrison	91	91	87	96	86	96	87	90	78	95	—																
Clarke						77	85		81	83	78	—															
Marshall		75					80				76		—														
Henry	80	86	77	86	90	86	100	81	91	100	90	86	81	—													
Wilmott		75				75	83	76	83	81	77	92		85	—												
J. Logan			76	81	80	76	86	84		78	83	76	75	89	80	—											
Griffith				76	76		80			77	77	88		86	87	85	—										
Duncan				81	80	77	85	78	81	83	83	92		91	92	87	96	—									
Huston				80	79	76	76							76		75		76	—								
Allin	78		80					82		77						75				—							
Innes																				88	—						
Owens		77								75												—					
R. Taylor																						81	—				
Johnson							79		83	76				80	82									—			
G. Clay														77	79	81		77						79	—		
B. Logan														77		76	76	81				77			81	—	
Payne														80	82	81	79	79					89		89	79	—
Irvine																											82
Boswell										75						79	79	83							75		
Casey																										85	79
Rogers																							79				
Sudduth																78	78	83								78	76
Prather									77													77				77	
Rowan																		76				81					
Bell																											
Minor																											
Hickman																											79
Adair																											
Y. Ewing																					83						
Abell																											
Grundy																											
W. Logan																					75				80		
Buckner																											
Baker																											
Bledsoe																											
R. Ewing																											
Bailey																											
Stockton																											
Thomas																											
Brunner																											
Davidson																											
T. Clay																											
Brown																											
S. Taylor																											

Chart 1

VOTING CHART OF THE 1799 CONVENTION

Percentage of votes each delegate cast with each other delegate.
Only percentages of 75 or higher are included.

	Irvine	Boswell	Casey	Rogers	Sudduth	Prather	Rowan	Bell	Minor	Hickman	Adair	Y. Ewing	Abell	Grundy	W. Logan	Buckner	Baker	Bledsoe	R. Ewing	Bailey	Stockton	Thomas	Brunner	Davidson	T. Clay	Brown	S. Taylor
Irvine	—																										
Boswell		—																									
Casey		79	—																								
Rogers		95	76	—																							
Sudduth			75	96	—																						
Prather				78	82	—																					
Rowan							—																				
Bell					85	80	78	—																			
Minor									—																		
Hickman										—																	
Adair		77		75	77					82	—																
Y. Ewing												—															
Abell													—														
Grundy				76	79								81	—													
W. Logan		79	77	80	78	77	84						79		—												
Buckner		79		78	77		84						82	88	92	—											
Baker		87	76	82	80	75							81	87	76	84	—										
Bledsoe		79				75							86			80	88	—									
R. Ewing									77				81	80	76			88	—								
Bailey										78						80				—							
Stockton															77	75	96	91			—						
Thomas																	83	79		77		—					
Brunner																75	76	84	79	82			—				
Davidson							77									77			88				84	—			
T. Clay																			76					81	—		
Brown																									88	—	
S. Taylor																									86	91	—

alitions existed within the convention. It also suggests the inaccuracy of the assumption that convention divisions were based upon a fundamental democratic/aristocratic or liberal/conservative cleavage. In fact some issues did divide the convention in just such a way, or perhaps more precisely along democratic/elitist lines. In Factor 9, four issues which are highly intercorrelated do relate demonstrably to "democracy." They were a high property qualification for state senators (Issue 11), a possible return at some unspecified time in the future to ballot voting instead of the viva voce system (Issue 17), the institution of a circuit court system which would be cheaper and more convenient than the centralized courts then operating (Issue 2), and a system of representation which would increase the number of representatives in the lower house and approximate the principle of representation by number (Issue 20). A number of other issues which have traditionally been explained in the same terms are not highly intercorrelated, however: the popular election of the sheriff (Issue 9), the election of militia officers (Issue 8), continuation of suffrage for free blacks (Issue 4), the eligibility of ministers to the General Assembly (Issue 5), and the creation of the office of lieutenant governor (Issue 1). Clearly the motives of the delegates were more complex.[30]

The information acquired from the factor analysis and the charted definition of voting blocs within the convention confirm the impression obtained from the *Journal* and the record of debates. The convention delegates were far more varied than might have been expected. With this variety and with no firm coalitions or parties controlling a majority of the delegates, the constitution represented a series of accommodations based upon pragmatism rather than ideology.

One fundamental question, at least, had been settled by the election and thus caused no controversy in the convention. The Bryan's Station platform was quite explicit upon the issue of slavery if not upon other questions. The campaign had focused upon it, and the "disorganizers" had been defeated. As a consequence, the subject of emancipation itself never arose. The new constitution incorporated the 1792 constitutional provision verbatim, permitting legislative emancipation only with the full consent of the slaveholders or after full payment prior to emancipation.[31]

Slavery was more entrenched in 1799 and the convention closed

Table 10

FACTOR ANALYSIS OF THE 1799 CONVENTION

Issues	Factor 1	Factor 2	Factor 3	Factor 4	Factor 5	Factor 6	Factor 7	Factor 8	Factor 9
1. Lieutenant Governor	.313	-.163	-.147	**-.658**	.088	-.156	.210	.030	-.259
2. Circuit court	.184	.245	.344	.107	.213	.151	.236	-.105	**.589**
3. Implementation of schedule	.496	.165	.132	.100	.166	.165	**.642**	.066	-.033
4. Free black suffrage	-.460	-.478	.015	-.076	.046	-.213	-.093	-.062	-.353
5. Clergy eligible to Assembly	.419	.459	.048	.310	-.214	.074	.113	.310	-.150
6. Lawyers ineligible to Assembly	.094	**.902**	.125	.053	.036	-.111	-.015	.102	.042
7. Lawyers ineligible (var.)	.161	**.931**	.118	.105	.045	-.078	-.005	.068	.008
8. Election, militia officers	.126	.122	.306	-.138	-.060	.033	.199	**.763**	.147
9. Election, sheriff	.224	.057	.142	.258	**-.663**	.201	.163	.249	.203
10. District representation	.113	.307	.179	.124	**.754**	.144	.139	-.094	.048
11. Property qualification, Senators	-.110	.138	-.170	-.122	.056	.121	.083	-.190	**-.785**
12. Prove facts before judges' removal	-.131	-.165	**-.734**	.107	-.128	-.044	.053	-.206	-.215
13. Judges' pay not lowered	-.080	-.498	**-.668**	-.021	-.119	-.036	-.180	-.011	-.186
14. Judge not removed for official act	-.093	-.108	**-.868**	-.269	.023	-.005	-.049	-.210	.035
15. Appoint new justices	.050	.245	.323	-.161	**-.665**	.388	.128	-.209	-.040
16. Amend Virginia Compact	.118	.138	.197	.402	.045	**.661**	.133	.125	.318
17. Future ballot option	.266	.134	-.091	.038	-.055	.443	-.102	.171	**.621**
18. Amendment of constitution	**.787**	.133	.184	.119	-.134	.120	-.093	.060	.105
19. Shorten election	.336	.070	-.019	.238	.144	-.015	**-.698**	-.080	-.048
20. Broaden representation	.370	.103	.044	.236	-.254	-.242	.320	-.143	**.514**
21. Tenure, county attorney	.100	-.293	-.105	-.188	-.142	**.794**	.316	-.029	-.123
22. Halt importation of slaves	.002	.416	**-.641**	.219	.232	.124	-.016	.198	-.020
23. Halt sale, mistreated slaves	-.038	.279	-.009	.440	-.117	.027	-.198	**.512**	.126
24. Amendment of constitution	**.752**	.097	.029	-.038	.013	.041	.108	.063	.341
25. Amendment of constitution	**.879**	.071	.063	-.186	.055	.019	-.103	-.007	.071
26. Accept constitution	-.083	-.047	.065	**-.831**	-.103	.107	-.011	.020	-.051

NOTE: Issues correlated to a significant ($\pm$ .5) degree are boldface. For note on methodology, see Appendix.

up loopholes to tighten the guarantees. The Bill of Rights, already carefully drafted to exclude slaves, was made more precise. The convention added the word "free" to the preface, so that it read, "all free men, when they form a social compact, are equal." The 1792 constitution had given the suffrage to all free men, by intent or accident including free blacks. The convention now specifically excluded free blacks, mulattoes, and Indians and rejected a motion to reinstitute free suffrage, 22 to 30. One proposal to eliminate the clause requiring the sale of mistreated slaves – presumably freeing such slaves instead – received only the two votes of committed emancipators Patrick Brown and Samuel Taylor.[32]

A large majority of the convention delegates favored the protection of slavery, but the issue of slave importation split proslavery ranks. The 1792 constitution protected the right of migrants to bring in slaves for their own use and allowed the legislature to limit the slave trade. A 1794 law contained such permissive language that Kentucky residents clearly possessed mechanisms to expand their holdings through arranging importation. But by 1799 some of the elite had second thoughts about unlimited increase of slaves. No longer concerned about setting the tone of Kentucky immigration, the Breckinridge clique had concluded that slave importation might someday have to be halted. The Breckinridge resolutions prepared before the convention included two possible limitations. One would permit the assembly to halt slave importation after a certain date (left blank in the resolutions); the other would allow a temporary halt during insurrections before that date. The convention finally voted upon a more general provision by which the legislature would have full power to prohibit future importation, which it rejected by a decisive 14 to 37 margin.[33]

The division on this issue was intriguing. Two distinct groups formed the minority, those who supported possible limitation. Six of the fourteen – including Samuel Taylor, John Bailey, and Patrick Brown – owned few or no slaves, disliked the slavery system, and presumably hoped that its limitation might pave the way for future cutbacks. A number of large slaveholders voted with them, including five of the Bryan's Station ticket. These two groups – pertinacious democrats and wealthy conservatives – opposed each other on almost every other convention issue. Quite possibly these wealthy and established men had enough laborers to answer their present and future requirements. All of them came from the inner Bluegrass country which was just turning to livestock raising instead of tobacco planting: John Breckinridge had been interested in stock breeding as early as 1796. Such a shift resulted in a decreased labor need, and Breckinridge had begun to hire his slaves out. With their own labor requirements satisfied, these men could afford a public-spirited concern over the dangers a large slave population posed.[34]

The thirty-seven men in the majority that rejected such considerations were slaveholders, just as anxious to continue the expansion of Kentucky and of their personal estates as they had been throughout the decade. Any slave limitation would inhibit immigration and retard the growth of the state economy. Many of these men had not yet reached what they considered a comfortable economic position but were still increasing and accumulating their holdings.[35] A complete shutoff of the slave supply would limit their ability to expand.

Factor analysis of the voting partially corroborates an interpretation based upon the needs of the delegates, in which the well-settled men who preferred a safe and comfortable status quo were aligned against those men still scrambling for more. Factor 3 showed this vote on slave limitation (Issue 22) intercorrelated with votes defending the independence of the judiciary against legislative encroachment (Issues 12, 13, and 14). The large slaveholders who favored limitation included the legal-judicial establishment; men not solely interested in farming, they were not concerned about expanding their slaveholdings. On the other side, those who rejected a possible constriction of the labor supply included those who wished to subordinate the court system in order to avoid a repetition of the 1794 *Kenton* v. *McConnell* decision which had endangered their landholdings. The young lawyers allied themselves with these planters, since they were equally concerned about future economic opportunities.[36]

Except for the question on importation, there was wide consensus upon the topic of slavery. Similar broad agreement existed upon the powers of local governments. No notes upon these debates exist, but evidence is strong that the convention concurred in the establishment of a strong county court government without major conflict. The convention merely ratified changes already under way through legislative and executive action. Furthermore, although local government had not been an issue in the convention campaign, the nature of the campaign biased the results in favor of the county court. In their efforts to defeat the emancipators, the conservatives had promoted the candidacy of men who were trustworthy but popular. The voters responded by electing men of substance, but men whose power rested in their counties, either as associates of the county court, as sometime representatives to the assembly, or as both.

The vast majority was predisposed to favor the county courts, and no man in the convention opposed. Whereas in 1792 Nicholas had circumvented the local oligarchies, the Breckinridge resolutions prepared before the convention willingly conceded a shift of power to the courts. They only hedged by proposing precautions against abuse of power. Nicholas reversed his previous stance and supported these resolutions, which included an amended means of appointing county officials. His original system of dividing the power between the governor and (through election) the people had not worked as he intended.[37]

With no strong dissent, the convention agreed upon county court control, granting broad appointive powers to the magistrates and protecting the justices from easy removal. Only a few issues required a roll-call vote – Issue 8 and Issue 9, providing respectively for the selection of militia officers and of the sheriff; Issue 17, which concerned viva voce voting; and Issue 15, which dealt with the continuity and seniority of justices of the peace. No firm coalition supporting the local oligarchy emerged upon these issues; factor analysis shows no significant intercorrelation between them. The delegates made their decisions upon the basis of practical considerations and their own preconceptions of what had worked well in the past seven years and what had not. Thus individuals deviated from support of oligarchic control and no solid "county party" emerged. Nonetheless, the preponderance of local-power supporters was great enough so that on each issue a majority favored the transfer of power to the county.[38] In its actions on local government, the convention accepted Breckinridge's proposals only so far as he favored county court authority but ignored his efforts to limit county court abuse of power.

In retrospect, the appointive powers vested in the governor by the 1792 constitution had clearly been too broad. The 1799 convention gave the county court exclusive authority to appoint all inferior officials whose jurisdiction was confined to the county. The local court also obtained the power to nominate more important officials. The Breckinridge resolutions had specified that the courts nominate two men to fill the posts of justice, coroner, or sheriff, one of whom the governor would commission. The convention added the office of surveyor to the list and specified that the courts, when choosing nominees for sheriff from among their own members, must pay "a just regard to seniority in office and a regular rotation."[39]

There were few divisions upon this delegation of power. The mode of selecting the sheriff did require a roll call, in which a motion to continue popular election was defeated, 23 to 32. Although the issue (Issue 9) might seem to be directly related to democracy, it was not highly intercorrelated in the factor analysis with other issues perceived as democratic. Other considerations were more influential, including the disrepute into which the office of sheriff had fallen. Sheriffs were often incompetent or corrupt in their collection of taxes, sometimes buying popularity by their laxity.[40] Justices serving two-year terms might be more honest. Perhaps, too, government expenses might be cut. Breckinridge did not record the main debate upon the election of sheriff, but, in a discussion of the judiciary, he suggested that the plan to name the sheriff from the county court would obviate the necessity of fees for individual justices of the peace and salaries for the quarter sessions justices. If a two-year appointment as sheriff replaced the system of court fees, the populace would save money. A publication several years later claimed such arguments were decisive. The Kentucky constitution seemingly reinstituted the Virginia system of rewarding justices for long, faithful, and unpaid service.[41]

In fact, the actions of both the convention and of succeeding legislatures suggest that this tradition of unpaid service had deteriorated and that the most compelling motive was a desire for the profits of officeholding. The convention eliminated a clause from a first draft of the constitution which would have prohibited quarter sessions justices from becoming sheriff. Furthermore, it added a clause authorizing salaries to the quarter sessions justices but declaring them ineligible to the legislature so long as they were paid. Fees for justices were eliminated by the assembly in 1799 in accordance with the convention intent but were reestablished within three years and raised to new highs by 1805. Similarly, the fees of sheriffs were raised. At the same time, justices appointed to the post of sheriff began farming it out, selling it to another. Without taking on the duties of the post, they were now able to profit by it.[42]

The convention had originally voted to continue the existing commissions of the county court justices instead of issuing new commissions. But after the delegates had agreed to the appointment of sheriffs from the ranks of the county court according to seniority, there was an effort to terminate the existing commissions and to allow the state representatives to draw up new ones for each county. The convention rejected the proposal, 17 to 37 (Issue 15), in a vote correlated with the vote on sheriffs (Factor 5). Most delegates who had supported the county court nomination were satisfied with the existing commissions, while many who had unsuccessfully supported the elective method now desired to revise the commissions, presumably to improve their own position.[43]

The mode of choosing militia officers provoked the only other roll-call vote upon the choice of local officials. The 1792 constitution divided the power between governor and people, as Nicholas had preferred. Breckinridge's resolutions (approved by Nicholas) recommended one change in 1799: company officers – captains, lieutenants, and ensigns – previously elected by men enrolled in the company should be chosen by field officers of the regiment. The convention accepted that alteration but removed authority from the governor. Instead, each superior officer was to name his subordinates: colonels their regimental staffs, brigadiers their brigade majors, etc. An effort to reinstitute election of low-ranking officers was defeated by a close vote, 25 to 30. This vote (Issue 8) was not highly correlated with the vote on sheriff or with any other vote in the convention. Dissatisfaction over lack of proper order in the militia had surfaced well before 1799, but even the militia officers in the convention divided on the issue. Of twenty-two active officers, thirteen favored selection by fellow officers, nine preferred the elective system. Although most of the highest ranking officers – colonels and generals – preferred selection, two did not.[44]

The dominance of the local magnates was assured in matters of appointment, at the expense of the governor on the one hand and the people on the other. Furthermore the second constitution secured the tenure of the local justices. Breckinridge had proposed to expand local powers, while at the same time hedging against abuses. Errant justices were already subject to removal upon address by both houses of assembly, and Breckinridge wanted to give the Court of Appeals the power to try them for misdemeanors. Dislike of the high court combined with reluctance to face a tribunal less friendly than the assembly, the convention rejected Court of Appeals' jurisdiction. Furthermore, assembly removal was made more difficult, a simple majority in both houses being amended to a two-thirds vote.[45]

Closely related to local politics was election procedure, including the method of voting. Breckinridge had challenged the secret ballot in the legislature in 1798 and now did so again. He supported the substitution of Virginia's viva voce, insisting that the ballot system, by its frauds and bad votes, sapped the foundation of representative government. Viva voce provided the only way for the poor man to exert his influence: only by voting aloud and seeing his name recorded could the citizen be sure his vote was correctly counted.[46]

Although few delegates supported this wholehearted endorsement of viva voce, still fewer defended the ballot. John Adair believed that viva voce would destroy republican government in Kentucky, where a few landlords holding most of the land would control the votes of their tenants. But disillusionment with the operation of the ballot was strong, and Adair drew little support. The usually staunch democrat, Samuel Taylor, initially insisted that the ballot was "important to *indigent men*" and that "Gent[leme]n are seeking to change the mode because these have found it wont ans[we]r *them*." But Taylor admitted that the existing ballot system had "a great deal of *Hypocracy*." The convention adopted voice voting without a division but later voted on an amendment which would allow the assembly to reconsider every seven years. This offered a hope of reestablishing the ballot at some time in the future when fraud seemed less likely to occur, but even this was rejected, 24 to 30. The question (Issue 17) was one of the democratic issues, as the factor analysis indicates (Factor 9). Several delegates who had favored the establishment of viva voce voting in the debates demonstrated their theoretical predilection for the influence-free ballot by supporting an option for future change.[47]

The return to viva voce represented a reversion to an old-fashioned style of politics, but, in other aspects of the electoral process, the convention moved away from tradition. Nicholas's 1792 effort to reinstate deferential politics by barring electioneering had manifestly failed, and he had capped the failure by himself participating in an issue-oriented election campaign with candidate slates, platforms, and active proselytizing. Now, in convention, there was no effort to maintain the principle. With only a short debate and without a division, the convention adopted Green Clay's motion to eliminate the oath and, at the same time, dropped the prohibition upon canvassing.[48]

Delegates were much more troubled by the associated question of representation. By 1799 the Nicholas-Breckinridge clique had become absolutely convinced that representation by numbers was an essential safeguard against Green River strength and radicalism.[49] Although most Kentuckians paid at least lip service to the principle of representation based upon population, ample room remained for differences. Politicians from fringe counties believed they had legitimate grievances against the existing system; they resented the time lag between population growth and representation and the requirement that new county voters continue to vote in the county seat of the parent county. Faced with the current inequities, many convention delegates advocated some change in the system, and a few demanded representation by county.

The Bryan's Station platform had unequivocally supported representation by number, but Breckinridge's resolutions included some concessions to the small counties. A county with less population than the established assembly ratio would gain separate representation if an adjoining county had extra population to add to the small county's total. If not, the small county would be represented with its parent county as before, but a separate voting district would make voting more convenient.[50]

Such a concession hardly conciliated the border county delegates, and John Bailey engaged in a spirited debate with Breckinridge. Bailey argued that representation by county would be more equitable. Existing apportionment methods were wrong because a voter in Fayette County chose six representatives, while voters in his own Logan County chose but one. The present mode neglected the exterior counties which were vitally important in the defense of Kentucky. At the moment, he pointed out, seven counties had but four representatives. Breckinridge rejoined sarcastically, "Pretty thing a county without people." Only the buffalo in the exterior counties were presently neglected.[51]

Samuel Taylor joined Bailey in attacking the existing system. He declared that he had always supported the principle of representation by numbers but added that he disliked the power of "large intriguing counties" which could combine and be dangerous. He proposed laying off the counties into election districts so that each voter would choose the same number of representatives whether he resided in Fayette or Logan County. He threatened to support Bailey's proposal for representation by county if the convention rejected the election-district plan, a threat Breckinridge shrugged off as a "scarecrow." Green Clay supported election districts, but at the end of the debate the delegates rejected both Taylor's and Bailey's plans. The group hammered out a statement endorsing representation by numbers, then gave each county existing at that time at least one representative. Such a provision would benefit – temporarily – the unrepresented fringe counties.[52]

So the matter rested, and the draft constitution submitted to the convention on August 10 incorporated this plan. But, during the concluding week, the delegates continued to tinker with the apportionment section. One attempt to eliminate even the mention of counties, to lay off the entire state in election districts, received only five votes. Since Samuel Taylor and Green Clay had supported a similar plan in debate and now voted against it, a compromise had probably been worked out. The convention dropped the provision for representation of all existing counties; instead, two or more adjoining counties each with insufficient population to satisfy the established quota could be joined together for the purpose of electing a representative.[53]

The convention made a final change two days before it adjourned, providing additional opportunity for representation. If two adjoining counties had "residuums" above the ratio set by the assembly which together met the required number, the county having the larger residuum would be entitled to an extra representative. The stipulation would have two results. The number of representatives in the lower house would be increased, since fewer people would be omitted in the apportionment. Also, with this clause, the apportionment system approximated the principle of representation by number as closely as was possible without abandoning the county units for election districts. Whether for one or both of these reasons, the convention approved by a one-sided 33 to 14 vote.[54]

Probably for the foregoing reasons, this vote (Issue 20) intercorrelates in the factor analysis with such democratic issues as the ballot vote (Issue 17) and the refusal to insert a property qualification for officeholding (Issue 11). A majority supported this issue while rejecting the ballot because the method of apportioning representation fitted the preconceptions of the county magnates. Whereas the earlier attempt to provide perfect representation by number through election districts which ignored county lines received only five votes, a pattern of approximate representation by numbers which used the existing county divisions received broad support. Breckinridge and some of his supporters formed the minority. Breckinridge insisted in debate that he desired representation by numbers, but this vote demonstrated that he preferred representation to be limited in extent rather than widened. As in the other issues in the "democratic" factor, he and his group exhibited a desire to narrow popular participation in government.[55]

The convention added one apportionment provision that Breckinridge had drafted and Nicholas heartily approved. The 1799 constitution authorized separate representation for towns which had sufficient population to meet the ratio. When a county seat obtained separate representation, the county voting place must be outside the town. Although most delegates apparently desired to apportion representation fairly precisely, Breckinridge intended to minimize the voting power and influence of townspeople and avoid a repetition of election results during the 1790s when Lexington had dominated the balloting for Fayette County.[56]

Although the fight on representation had been a hard one, much more bitterness surfaced in the discussions on the state government. Nicholas had advocated a careful separation of powers as a check upon the popular branch of the assembly in 1792, and Breckinridge took the same position in 1799. He sought no basic changes but defended the first constitution and employed many of the same arguments. But a majority, intent upon establishing the supremacy of the House of Representatives, overwhelmed him and his supporters.

An intense dislike of the Senate was central to the continuing call for a constitutional convention throughout the decade. The public deplored the method of choosing the senators and the Senate's willingness to ignore popular opinion. Such widespread feeling forced Breckinridge and Nicholas to include in the Bryan's Station platform a statement that the Senate should be elected as directly as "consistent with . . . [its] proper design."[57]

The resolutions they prepared, half of which concerned the election of Senate and governor, clarified what that meant and attempted to eliminate causes of minor criticisms. The resolutions acknowledged the need to fill Senate vacancies differently and proposed that the House of Representatives should be authorized to fulfill that function. No man serving in the electoral college could be chosen as senator or governor; senators should be named from districts rather than at large. Finally the Senate term should be shortened to three years. The governor's term should also be three years, and a majority of the electors must concur in his election. But, changes in details notwithstanding, the basic principle of indirect election was reasserted.[58]

Even the seeming victory of the Breckinridge forces at the polls did not guarantee the continuation of the indirect method, particularly considering the ambivalent statement to which the Bryan's Station delegates were pledged. In fact, the structure and composition of the Senate required one of the longest debates recorded in the convention. When the topic was raised, Breckinridge was immediately put on the defensive: Philemon Thomas, wealthy planter and assembly leader from Mason County, moved that the people elect the Senate directly, claiming that electors "sometimes choose improper men." Conservatives need not fear that a popularly elected Senate would provide no protection for property, since the voters also had their property at stake and would not elect men who would take it away.[59]

Thomas noted that there had been much clamor throughout the state against the Senate. The course of the ensuing debates demonstrated that many of those who supported direct election were responding to the popular antipathy which existed against the old method. Their most active spokesman was William Logan, elected to the convention as George Nicholas's protégé and now turning his attack upon the independent Senate deemed essential by the Breckinridge-Nicholas clique. The Senate had been the main target of public fury before the election, he thought, and it must be altered to fit the popular preference. He would prefer the old mode himself, but he believed the people would not tolerate it. Government would not attain stability without the confidence of the people, and a new convention would soon be demanded if the second constitution did not eliminate that odious feature. As to theoretical doctrines and lessons drawn from the past, he believed that "Antient History don't apply to us." Nicholas had clearly mistaken young Logan's views, but he was correct in assuming that William Logan would carry his influential father with him: Benjamin Logan announced that he held the same opinion and felt obliged to vote for direct election.[60]

Samuel Taylor and John Bailey joined in the general attack upon the indirect election of senators. Arguing from a doctrinaire democratic position, the two insisted that either the people were trusted with self-government or they were not. Anyway, Taylor indicated, he would trust people with no property sooner than people of substance. He conceded that the Senate provided a check but maintained that it "may sometimes check good." Breckinridge attempted desperately to meet and match every argument. He employed the tactic used successfully in the spring election, linking those who attacked the Senate with emancipation. Those who wanted a directly elected Senate planned to free the slaves and destroy property rights; only an indirectly elected Senate, he asserted, would protect property against the majority of the voters who owned none. To Taylor's argument that the convention ought to satisfy "those who ought to govern," Breckinridge agreed but rejoined, "*who* are those who *ought* to *govern?*" As before, he ridiculed the abilities of his opponents. He regretted that "precedents seem of no account here."[61]

A few joined Breckinridge in his opposition to the motion. Senate Speaker Alexander Bullitt spoke, probably from a prepared speech, lauding the existing Senate, its means of election, and the four-year term. Senators so chosen were likely to be men of integrity; those possessing only "talents for low intrigue and little arts of popularity" might win at an election but would fail in the electoral college. The length of service protected senators from immediate retaliation for wise but unpopular moves. Another senator, William Henry, added his voice with what Breckinridge defined as "considerable strength & cleverness." But these men failed to convince their fellow delegates, and the convention adopted a direct-election provision without a division.[62]

Once this fundamental question was settled, the convention turned to the details of the senatorial election and the qualifications for the office. So important was the Senate considered that a motion by William Bledsoe that only men married or widowed should be eligible provoked some fifty speeches before being rejected. But more basic were questions on the size of the Senate and the apportionment of its members. Breckinridge suggested a Senate initially composed of twenty-four, with one to be added for each five representatives added to the House. The senators should be chosen from districts established by the legislature upon the basis of the number of voters. Two senators were to be drawn from each district, which was to be composed of one or several contiguous counties.[63] It was a plan which would allow some counties to have two senators while others had none.

In the convention, delegates who had earlier supported representation by county in the House opposed this plan. Now they attempted to gain representation by county in the Senate, this time with more support. As with representation in the House, there were two objectives: to diffuse representation throughout the state and to minimize the dominance of large counties. William Logan led the fight. With the figure of twenty-four agreed upon, Logan argued that the state ought to be divided into twelve districts by counties. If there were only twenty-four counties, it would be proper to draw one senator from each county. Since more than twenty-four counties existed, his plan would be fair to all sections of the state. Minorities could hinder majorities from crushing them. As before, young Logan carried his father with him. Benjamin Logan commented that he had supported representation by county in the Senate during the 1792 convention and he still did.[64]

The young lawyer jumped up four more times to reiterate his arguments, but the principle of representation by numbers prevailed for the Senate as well as for the House. However, the convention rejected the Breckinridge plan for twelve districts – and other proposals for eight, four, and two districts – and adopted single-man districts instead. As Logan pointed out, if a large county were placed in a district with a small county, the larger one would dominate the election. John Adair agreed, insisting that a large county be able to send no more than one senator. Young Logan also introduced a motion, accepted by the convention, to add a new seat in the Senate for each three in the House, instead of one senator for each five representatives. The 1799 constitution broadened representation in the Senate as well as in the House.[65]

The decision to shift to direct election of the Senate created a new dilemma for the convention. Some of the delegates accepted the republican axiom that the two houses of assembly ought to differ in some respect, so that a real check would exist within the legislative branch. Some of those who had urged direct election were willing to insert a property qualification for the upper house. Philemon Thomas, who had introduced the intitial resolution eliminating the electoral college, proposed a land-property qualification, and Robert Johnson and Caleb Wallace supported a proposal requiring that senators "be citizens & own land," but the convention failed to incorporate either provision in the draft constitution. As the delegates reviewed the draft during the last few days of the meeting, an effort was made to set as a qualification the payment of taxes equal to the tax upon 500 acres of first-rate land. The requirement was a stiff one, and the convention rejected it, 11 to 41.[66]

Although this vote (Issue 11) intercorrelates with the votes on the ballot and widened representation in the factor analysis and is thus identified as being related to democracy, surprises appear in the roll call. Members of the Breckinridge clique provided most of the votes for the property qualification, but Breckinridge and Wallace rejected this high requirement despite their previous interest in a limitation of some sort. On the other hand, Thomas supported the qualification even though he was most closely allied to the democratic camp.[67]

With the convention declining to incorporate a property qualification for officeholders, attention turned to another means of limiting popular control over the legislature. John Breckinridge had admitted in debate that he would have no objection to a directly elected Senate if the constitution included a property qualification for voting. His ally, John Price, moved to limit suffrage to those who had paid *taxes or livery.* Wallace and Johnson supported Price, but he withdrew his motion after it met strong opposition. The convention then rejected a substitute motion, requiring only that the voter "have residence."[68]

Neither the convention's deliberations on the legislature nor the outcome could have satisfied Breckinridge and Wallace. The convention had breached the doctrine of separation of power, while demonstrating real hostility toward the present upper house. The same people would elect senators and representatives, and the upper and lower houses possessed precisely the same qualifications, except for age and length of residence. Furthermore, the 1799 constitution continued universal suffrage, except for the exclusion of free blacks and mulattoes. The judicial or the executive branches would have to provide any checks and balances within the system. The convention considered the sections on the executive first.

Since the second constitution eliminated the electoral college in the choice of senators, the convention made no effort to maintain it to select a governor. The choice was between direct election and election by the assembly. Green Clay offered a resolution that the legislature elect the governor by joint ballot. In a direct election, one county would dominate the vote and thus, in effect, choose the executive. The assembly would make the best choice because the best-informed citizens served there. Robert Johnson agreed, arguing that the legislature elected the governor in most states. The governor would not be dependent on the assembly even though it appointed him and paid his salary.[69]

Breckinridge wasted no time defending the electoral method he had originally supported but shifted to a popular election; like Nicholas in 1792, he wanted to bypass the legislature. He contradicted Johnson's assertion that the assembly elected the governor in most states: eight states provided for popular election, in six the assemblies acted, and in two there were electors. He denied that a governor whose salary and appointment depended upon the assembly could be independent of it; nor did he agree that those in the assembly were best informed. Harry Innes and Caleb Wallace supported him, equally intent upon avoiding assembly domination. Independent-minded John Adair denied the importance of the decision, since the governor would court the people if elected by them or the assembly if elected by it. Only a provision making the executive ineligible for re-election would render him truly independent. But others did not share Adair's indifference; John Bailey supported direct election, not because of a fear of assembly control but because the people should have the power. Probably the combination of republican and democratic arguments proved persuasive, and the delegates accepted election.[70]

Assembly domination over the governor was also at stake in a hassle over the appointive power. The 1792 constitution vested the general power of nomination in the governor except for those officials for whom the constitution made specific provision. Breckinridge defended executive choice, even of local officials, despite the fact that his draft resolutions had conceded county court nomination in that area. The governor had fewer favorites than all the assemblymen and thus would make a more impartial choice, Breckinridge insisted, using an argument advanced by Nicholas in 1792. As administrator of government, the executive suffered when bad men were selected and thus would choose well.[71]

Robert Johnson attempted to vest this general power in the assembly. He preferred that the lower house recommend judges and other officials, the upper house confirm them, and the governor issue the commissions. Samuel Taylor approved Johnson's plan, since he thought the governor received all his information on appointments from men in the assembly; those giving the information ought to be responsible for the appointments. Eventually, however, in the face of opposition, Johnson withdrew his motion. Authority to name state officials remained with the governor, with the Senate continuing to possess the right to confirm. Only two officials were excluded, the state treasurer and the public printer. Since the first constitution provided for assembly choice of the state treasurer, and a law of 1794 did the same for the printer, the second constitution merely codified current practice.[72] The nomination of county officers however, was later turned over to the county court.

With respect to his election and appointive powers, the attempt to place assembly over governor had failed. The last test of strength between the two branches regarded the veto power, and here advocates of legislative supremacy were more successful. The convention was troubled on the point: although the delegates proceeded through the constitution systematically, clause by clause, as they had originally determined to do, the sections dealing with the veto were tabled two days in a row with only brief debate. The question was only decided on the third day, after the convention had settled upon a popularly elected governor. Then William Bledsoe reiterated the argument that one man's opinion should not be able to outweigh the will of a large number. Breckinridge responded that the veto was not absolute, that it only allowed the assembly an opportunity to reconsider its action. Unquestionably Breckinridge, Innes, and Wallace – all supporters of executive independence – desired to retain the provision requiring a two-thirds vote to override a veto; but they apparently recognized that the convention would not tolerate this proposition. As a compromise, Innes offered a motion to substitute "a majority of all elected" for "two-thirds," and Wallace seconded this proposal. To this limited veto power, which literally gave the assembly the opportunity to reconsider its previous action, the convention agreed.[73]

The convention's encroachment upon the executive authority was unquestionably a reflection of the thrust toward legislative supremacy. However, it was probably intensified by the incumbent, James Garrard, who had been a more forceful governor than Isaac Shelby and, thereby, may have aroused both latent fears of executive authority and anger at his actions. Subsequent events suggest some personal animosity toward Garrard. The convention specifically excluded ministers from the office of governor, perhaps a jab at him or perhaps only an extension of the already existing exclusion of ministers from the assembly. During his reelection campaign in 1800, critics attacked his emancipationist activity in 1799 and his refusal to pardon the convicted murderer Henry Field. His reelection was followed by several sharp clashes with the legislature. Garrard vetoed a bill eliminating his fuel allowance, contending that the assembly could not constitutionally reduce his pay; the assembly failed to override only by a narrow margin. In 1803 the Senate rejected four nominees for the post of state register because it had its own preferred candidate; the impasse was only broken by the impending end of Garrard's term of office.[74]

With regard to the executive and the legislature, Breckinridge had lost almost as much as he had gained in his efforts to maintain a balanced government. The convention turned last to the judiciary, about which he had particularly strong opinions. These debates, the last ones he recorded, were as protracted as those on the Senate. Breckinridge hoped only to retain the existing system: the "original jurisdiction" proviso of 1792 was defunct, but the first constitution included reasonably strong guarantees of judicial independence. The legal establishment considered this security essential.[75]

In the convention, the judiciary was subjected to a two-pronged assault, upon its centralized structure and upon its independence. One delegate proposed to break up the district court system established in 1795 by limiting jurisdiction of lower courts to the county. Samuel Taylor supported the motion, claiming that the requirement that the people be "dragged into centre of 4 Counties to meet Courts & Lawyers" was oppressive. Justice would be nearer at hand with a circuit court meeting in each county. According to the plan Taylor offered, money would be saved since 114 quarter sessions justices and six district court judges would be replaced by ten circuit court judges. Eventually Green Clay offered an alternative, a smaller number of judges riding circuit, with court in each county consisting of one circuit judge and two "associates" from the county. Clay suggested that the judges presently serving in the district courts could continue to hold office but be required to ride circuit. The state would save the expense of one quarter sessions justice in each county; the witnesses would be spared the long trip presently required; and prosecution costs would be smaller.[76]

Two of the young lawyers ardently supported circuit courts. Felix Grundy, fairly silent until this time, made a lengthy and impassioned speech attacking the existing system. He agreed with Clay and Taylor that district courts were insufficiently numerous. The quarter sessions courts – the only courts easily available – were inadequate to the business before them; the justices of the quarter sessions had no legal knowledge and could not be trusted. A court composed of one judge with legal knowledge and two local associates would solve all these problems. Their convenience would provide equal justice for rich and poor alike. William Bledsoe confessed that he had little experience in the courts. But he too approved the plan and denounced regulation of the court system by "Legislating lawyers," probably a jibe at Breckinridge who had successfully fended off attempts at a localized judiciary during the 1797-1798 legislative assembly. Impatient of fluctuations in the judicial system, he insisted that "WE are now going to stop this fluctuating pendulum; & pin it down forever."[77]

The attack upon the judiciary and the demands of Grundy and Bledsoe that the convention ought to fix the outlines of the department were founded in a widespread dislike of "Legislating lawyers." The dominance of a few lawyers and judges over the state judiciary had caused much resentment; in an attempt to eliminate such influence in the convention, Taylor asked, midway in the debate, if all those gentlemen who were "INTERESTED" ought not to retire. Green Clay had earlier threatened to offer a motion excluding lawyers from the assembly. Before the convention ended, two roll calls were taken on that question; in each case the exclusion was rejected, but a third of the convention favored it.[78]

In his counterattack, Breckinridge belittled his opponents. He was not, he commented, acquainted with Taylor's "*legal* skill & sagacity." Bledsoe, who admitted his inexperience at the law, was asking the convention to try something completely new and untried. Breckinridge maintained that the constitution should only provide a judicial framework to be filled in by the legislature. The designation of a circuit court system with one judge and two associates went far beyond such outlines, he believed. Breckinridge was on the defensive about past legislation; he suspected that many delegates wanted to include specific provisions in the constitution because of "corruption of the Legislature in establishing courts of Justice." The convention delegates were so determined to avoid the "awkward regulations" previously enacted that they proposed to give the assembly no discretion at all in the formation of the state judiciary. Faced with the hostility of the delegates, Breckinridge finally conceded that the district court system was imperfect and disclaimed any responsibility for its formation. Future legislatures could make any modifications required.[79]

Breckinridge's plea for legislative discretion prevailed, although a majority of the delegates had originally favored filling in the details of the judiciary. The circuit court plan was defeated by a 23 to 30 vote. The narrow margin could hardly have been comforting to Breckinridge and the judges, since they must have anticipated pressure in future legislatures to localize the judiciary. Such pressure began in 1800, and the victory was of short duration. In 1802, in an effort led by Felix Grundy, the legislature replaced the district courts and quarter sessions courts with the convenient and popular circuit courts, described by most educated observers in extremely unflattering terms. The court was "three Judges; one *pretendedly* learned, . . . and the other two as avowedly ignorant." The judge in the middle was "an organ pipe through which the other two speak their unlettered decisions."[80]

Following this uncertain victory of Breckinridge, discussion turned to the separation between assembly and judiciary. Breckinridge and Nicholas had feared an assault upon judicial independence and had included in their platform an unequivocal support of the principle. Earlier in the convention, Breckinridge had resisted an effort to require a legislative appointment of judges; now he attempted to defend the clauses of the constitution which protected them. By the 1792 document, judges held office during good behavior and could only be removed by impeachment or upon the address of two-thirds of each legislative branch. The assembly fixed their pay and could not diminish it during their continuance in office. Although the judges were not completely protected from legislative interference, the legal establishment apparently considered this portion of the constitution adequate when the convention opened. However, the venomous attack caused Breckinridge and his cohorts to attempt to buttress independence with additional safeguards.[81]

The debates exhibited no single motive behind the vehement assault upon the judiciary. The memory of the 1794 *Kenton* v. *McConnell* decision by which the Court of Appeals had cast doubt upon the validity of many of the land titles obtained from Virginia strongly influenced the discussion and added to its bitter tone. Amidst the furor raised by that decision, the House had summoned the judges to appear before it, the judges had declined to appear, and the assembly had subsequently censured them. In retaliation, the two judges had published a pamphlet denouncing the assembly and singling out several assemblymen for particular criticism. In 1799 two of the three men whom the judges had publicly excoriated – Alexander Bullitt and Benjamin Logan – were in the convention and thus in a position to retaliate.[82]

Much of the convention debate turned upon such considerations. Alexander Bullitt, who did not often participate in the proceedings except in defense of the Senate, took the lead. He believed that judges sometimes interpret the laws improperly, and the assembly ought to be empowered to "decide on their decisions." Indeed, in the past, "Judges have given such erroneous *opinions* that they ought to be removed." His strongest supporter was Robert Johnson, who asked the convention, "How are you to get at him for a wrong ju[d]g[men]t," if you cannot remove him for "misconstruing the law"?[83]

The rhetoric seemed to demonstrate that the effort to limit judicial independence was solely a reprisal for past decisions. But a comparison of the votes taken in 1794 to remove or censure the judges with the votes in 1799 to limit future independence suggests that such an assumption is an oversimplification. John Breckinridge and John McDowell had disapproved the 1794 *Kenton* decision. Breckinridge had circulated a petition sent into the assembly protesting the verdict, although he had not asked for the removal of the judges;

McDowell had voted for their removal and for their censure. In 1799 both these men were members of the Bryan's Station party, and any temporary unhappiness over one previous decision was overshadowed by the need to protect the court's independence.[84]

Nine other delegates had sat in either the House or Senate in 1794. Three of them had not voted on court issues: Senate Speaker Bullitt customarily did not vote, and Robert Johnson and Benjamin Logan either abstained or were absent. Six had voted against removal and/or censure. Yet in convention all nine of them favored limitations upon judicial independence. The situation was different: in 1794, when one specific case caused the outburst, assemblymen might easily differ upon whether the verdict warranted removal or a harshly worded censure. That verdict may not have affected them personally. Whatever the reaction to the earlier opinion had been, however, all were prepared to reshape the constitution so that in any future circumstance the judiciary could be forced to accede to the legislative will.[85]

These veteran assemblymen increasingly believed that separation of powers was neither desirable nor even possible. Bullitt stressed that "departments [were] distinct in theory; but impossible in practice." The assembly was the proper body to investigate the conduct of a judge, and it would certainly give the judge a fair hearing. Samuel Taylor agreed, proposing that the assembly also ought to have the right to lower salaries as well as to raise them. The young lawyers espoused this philosophy of legislative supremacy. Indeed, on this point, the polarity between the senior lawyers and judges and the junior barristers was almost complete. The young men supported Johnson, Bullitt, and Taylor in demands for accountability, William Bledsoe and John Rowan in such insistent tones that Breckinridge commented, "See how soon Gent[leme]n fire at the idea of any branch being independent of Legislature."[86]

The motives for the attack were apparently mixed, including an element of revenge for one past decision, a desire to avoid any similar actions in the future, and a strong effort to gain absolute assembly dominance over the state government. Whatever the cause, the result was a total defeat for Breckinridge and the legal establishment. The convention considered the topic for two days. During the first day, judicial salaries were discussed, and, although nothing was decided, opinion generally favored the assembly's right to lower as well as raise the pay. In the last action of the day, the convention, upon the motion of William Logan, revised the language of the removal provision, so that the governor *shall* rather than *may* remove judges, upon address by the legislature.[87]

Overnight the Breckinridge-Wallace strategy shifted, occasioned by the strong attack. Next day they made two efforts to provide additional protection from the assembly. Caleb Wallace moved that no judge could be removed by the assembly before the facts upon which the removal was based were proved by the verdict of a competent jury. The motion provoked lengthy dissent. Philemon Thomas asserted that "If a Judge had not sense enough to be a Judge he would remove him." Bullitt argued that a judge might be "*suspected* of corruption." The convention rejected Wallace's motion, whereupon Buckner Thruston offered a resolution that no judge should be removed for an official act. Again protracted debate ensued and again the delegates rejected the motion. The final convention action recorded by Breckinridge was upon a proposal by Robert Johnson to delete the clause forbidding the assembly to lower judicial salaries. It was adopted, Breckinridge noted, "after much argument."[88]

Last-minute efforts in the convention to build in some protection for judges demonstrated even more clearly the delegates' intense dislike of the judiciary and their desire to bring the judges to account. A motion to require jury determination of the facts before removal was rejected 9 to 42. Then the convention refused by a 17-to-36 vote to stipulate that judges' salaries could not be diminished below the level they received at the time of their appointments. Finally the delegates were asked to insert a provision that judges could not be removed for "official act or judicial opinion." On this they voted 12 to 40.[89]

The 1799 convention action laid the groundwork for a prolonged controversy between the Court of Appeals and the General Assembly in the 1820s. With Kentucky hard hit by the panic of 1819, the assembly passed a law in 1820 which permitted debtors under certain circumstances to replevy for two years. The Court of Appeals declared the law unconstitutional, whereupon the "relief party" controlling the legislature and supported by Governor John Adair attacked the court. The effort to remove the judges failed to gain the requisite two-thirds vote. The House then passed a bill lowering the salary of the judges to twenty-five cents a year, but the bill failed in the Senate. The two houses finally agreed upon a "reorganization" bill shepherded through the assembly by John Rowan, which replaced the acting Court of Appeals with another. The judges refused to acquiesce in the move, and for two years Kentucky possessed an "Old Court" and a "New Court." The dilemma was resolved when the voters returned an anti-relief majority to the assembly and the New Court was abandoned.[90]

John Breckinridge had not obtained several of his major objectives: a guarantee of judicial independence; an indirectly elected Senate; an effective executive veto; limited representation; possible future restriction of slave imports. But, despite such failures, Breckinridge was anxious to avoid another convention. He shared with Nicholas a deep pessimism about Kentucky society. Nicholas had predicted in January of 1799, "We shall never have as good a constitution again," and convention debates further corroborated that opinion.[91] But worse still might follow. Breckinridge had at least avoided representation by county; the executive continued to possess extensive appointment powers; a Senate still existed. Another convention might begin where the 1799 gathering left off, further dismantling the system of checks and balances.

The resolutions prepared by Breckinridge and Nicholas before the convention testify to this fear of the future. They offered no method of amending the constitution; only a convention could effect any change. Breckinridge's plan required an attenuated process initiated by the legislature. A majority of each house must concur within fifteen days after the beginning of a legislative session in a law calling for a vote on the convention. A majority of all citizens casting votes must vote for a convention two years in a row, whereupon a convention would be called. No man who had been a member of the assembly which called for the popular vote could serve in the convention. George Nicholas made two revisions in this draft, both intended to make the process even more difficult. The first change would require two-thirds of each house – instead of a majority – to concur in the law calling for a referendum. By the second, a majority of those holding the franchise would be required to approve the convention for two years, rather than a majority of those actually voting.[92]

Breckinridge and Nicholas supported these stringent requirements because of apprehensions about what future conventions would do. The majority of the delegates probably concurred with the general intent because of satisfaction with the constitution itself. The convention accepted the Breckinridge-Nicholas proposal, only altering it to allow a simple majority of both houses of assembly to initiate the procedure. An attempt to eliminate the necessity of assembly action to call for the referendum failed. The convention did, however, delete the clause forbidding assemblymen who had voted to call the referendum from serving in the convention.[93]

The convention had finished its work. Whatever their reasons for doing so, the delegates voted overwhelmingly to adopt the draft constitution, 53 to 3. The trio of dissenters had no common motive. Patrick Brown was apparently distressed by the protection of slavery. When the convention adopted the constitution, Brown alone refused to sign. Thomas Clay, less voluble and more radical than his brother, Green, protested that natural rights contained in the Bill of Rights were contravened. He singled out the schedule for carrying the constitution into effect, which allowed the first officers an extended period in office. The third, Nathan Huston of Lincoln County, who had most often voted with the Breckinridge camp, did not record his motive.[94]

As in 1792, the new constitution was not submitted to the electorate. There was apparently no feeling among the delegates that popular ratification was necessary. However, it went into effect with so little reaction that it seems likely that a referendum would have produced a favorable vote. The document was close enough to the de facto arrangements which had been worked out between 1792 and 1799 so that it seemed little changed. The shifts in power were satisfactory to most Kentuckians: the populace obtained, by the constitution and the circuit court law of 1802, the locally controlled government it had desired. And the legislature obtained a greater share of the power within the state government. One provision which did provoke a flurry of activity was the shift from popular election of militia officers. Conscious of the deadline after which officers would be appointed by fellow officers, militia companies hurriedly held elections and forwarded election certificates to the governor's office, several carefully specifying that the elections were held before the new constitution took effect.[95]

Among Kentucky conservatives who had been engaged in the political turmoil of the late 1790s, there was a sense of relief. One listed several features of which he disapproved but thought it was nonetheless "miraculously perfect." Without despairing of his defeats, John Breckinridge could even find virtue in the direct election of senators. Showing the ambivalence of the Kentucky Jeffersonian Republicans, Breckinridge the Kentucky politician had desperately sought to retain the electoral college, but Breckinridge the Democratic Republican could report to Jefferson that direct election would have salutary effects. The Kentucky Senate had been divided over the 1799 Kentucky Resolutions because there was some "federal influence" there, but the direct election would eliminate this pocket of federalism, since the people were "uncontaminated & firm."[96]

These were practical men. To those still focusing upon theoretical principles of republicanism, the constitution was badly flawed. Humphrey Marshall, who had considered the 1792 constitution faulty but with an admirable effort to check the popular branch of legislature, believed that the second constitution surrendered the principle entirely. Young lawyer Ninian Edwards, describing the convention, thought the constitution "worse instead of better" because the delegates were "ignorant of the history of human events, ignorant of the fundamental principles of civil Society, and still more so of the Science of government."[97] Edwards's assessment that the "Science of government" had not been considered in recasting Kentucky's political tradition was by-and-large correct, but the omission resulted more from indifference and impatience with theory than from ignorance. Pragmatism had prevailed.

Much more deeply disturbed by the culmination of Kentucky constitutionalism were the antislavery proponents. The 1799 convention ended their incursion into political antislavery. Several of the men who had engaged in the emancipationist effort in 1799 were active and practiced politicians who had accepted the challenge of attempting slavery limitation. In losing, they incurred a personal loss as well. Most of them were eliminated from politics thereafter, including Edmund Bullock, previously Speaker of the House of Representatives. The only antislavery activists who regained political stature were those who retreated from their antislavery posture, such as Henry Clay and Governor James Garrard. Nonpoliticians were equally disillusioned. David Rice, in the aftermath of the convention, thought there was little chance to obtain emancipation through civil authority. Only moral suasion, he had finally decided, would accomplish the difficult task.[98]

EPILOGUE

WITH THE implementation of its second constitution, Kentucky concluded its evaluation of eighteenth-century political institutions. The constitution which George Nicholas and the 1792 convention had fashioned conformed to eastern republican standards in many respects. However, Nicholas and other members of Kentucky's elite distrusted the abilities and intentions of the citizens, and the constitution carefully consolidated power in the hands of a few – the governor, the Senate, and the Court of Appeals. Those authorities, Nicholas hoped, would give enlightened direction to Kentucky's development as well as provide needed checks to an unruly democracy.

However, in the seven years before the second convention, a generation came of age with very different expectations and very little interest in the "science of government" which had so preoccupied its predecessors. Kentuckians – rich and not-so-rich – were exhilarated by opportunities arising in the rapidly developing society, and legislators responded with expansionary policies. In 1799 convention delegates measured existing constitutional tenets, not by theoretical precepts of republicanism or democracy, but by practical workability and by usefulness in enhancing opportunity. The delegates included farmers and planters, lawyers and politicians, who disagreed upon many details of the political system but concurred in rejecting the paternalistic features of the 1792 constitution. Impatient of restraints – potential or existing – upon their ambitions, they worked out a settlement which maximized their access to economic and political opportunity.

The constitutionalists reestablished the powerful county court system Virginia had originally installed, erasing Nicholas's experiment in limiting such independent oligarchies. By the delegates' evaluation in 1799, autonomous county courts would provide cheaper and more efficient government than Nicholas's plan had given. They were unworried about the undemocratic selection of justices, and, in fact, criticism had been muted in the 1790s by the multiplication of county units, which had opened office to aspiring local politicians.

The convention partially dismantled the careful separation of powers built into the first constitution. The delegates did not believe the principle worked, insisting that there must be a single locus of power and that it ought to be the assembly, the branch most sympathetic to their aspirations. But the settlement worked out in the convention was a nice balance, suggesting that Kentuckians did not want to eradicate the principle of separation of powers but to circumscribe the executive and judiciary so that, in any head-to-head clash, legislative intent would prevail. The constitution continued an independently appointed judiciary but deleted a guarantee of a secure and settled salary. It recognized the principle of the executive veto, but eliminated its efficacy in nullifying legislation by permitting a simple majority of each house to override rather than the customary two-thirds. This nice amalgamation of the theory of checks and balances and the democratic thrust toward legislative primacy was incorporated in the constitutions of a dozen other states in the early nineteenth century.[1]

During the 1790s, the institution of slavery in Kentucky underwent perhaps the sharpest challenge it faced anywhere in the South. Kentucky appeared to offer emancipators a good chance of success, since there was a diverse population and a good deal of antislavery sympathy. During the decade, antislavery advocates attempted to transform that sympathy into a political program of emancipation or slave limitation. In 1792, the effort was a largely unorganized religious and moral appeal for support; in 1798-1799, it was a carefully orchestrated campaign by publicists and practical politicians. No matter what the tactics, efforts were thwarted and slavery remained secure. Kentuckians were quite reticent in approving or justifying slavery, but they could not overcome ambitions, both for themselves and for Kentucky, which required a continued expansion of the economy and of the labor force to work it. The 1799 constitution guaranteed both slavery and its essentially unlimited importation.

During the decade, in the midst of debates upon such concrete issues as separation of powers, local government, and slavery, the erosion of deferential politics continued. The process had been under way before 1790 and was by no means complete by 1800 – indeed, the 1799 constitution reinstituted viva voce voting and reinvigorated county court oligarchies – but in the 1790s several forces clearly combined to undermine traditional political behavior. National politics played little part, for Kentucky was too united in support of Jeffersonian principles to invite partisan competition for votes. However, within Kentucky, intensely parochial issues involved the electorate and compelled politicians to engage in active competitive politics. Conservatives in 1791-1792 had exhorted against electioneering and appealed for the election of the best men to the convention, but they could not stand aloof when their opponents were organized without disastrous defeats. In 1798-1799, anti-convention forces marshaled the weapons of political organization to rout the emancipators, but in doing so ignored their own previous admonitions against platforms, slates of candidates, and electioneering. The 1799 convention simply acknowledged reality when it deleted the prohibition of canvassing which Nicholas had written into the 1792 constitution.

Issue-oriented campaigns undercut deferential politics, but a deeper cause of the malaise was the deterioration of the tradition of disinterested civic service upon which it depended. Both as justices and as representatives, political leaders were expected to act for the good of the community, with personal gain at most a subsidiary motive. Signs of crumbling showed as particular parts of the county court jurisdiction were handed to more competent – or better paid – elements. Men jostled for office in the county and in the legislature, then used office for personal advantage. After 1799 justices did not give their services gratis in return for two-year stints as sheriff, as had been implicitly promised in convention, but instead took the benefits of the sheriffalty, while demanding large fees as justices. As officeholding yielded rewards, however, it increasingly did not demand respect.[2]

The second constitution probably accommodated the ambitions of most settled and politically active Kentuckians when it was written in 1799. Implemented with scarcely a ripple of interest, it remained in force fifty years, a testimonial both to its general acceptability and to the compounded difficulties in its amendment. A major target of the criticism which did mount over the years was the county court system. Counties became fiefdoms, dominated by the justices. The courts' egregiously undemocratic features were increasingly out of line with nineteenth-century egalitarianism, and blatant office-selling no doubt exacerbated complaint. In the 1790s, criticism had been lessened because the rapid growth of county government offered a share of power to political upstarts. As the pace of county formation slowed sharply after 1800, such accessibility necessarily diminished, leaving the courts even more vulnerable to the charge of exclusivity.[3]

The constitutionalists in 1799 had been intensely introspective, writing a document to suit their needs and dismissing the claims of either precedent or posterity. However, the history of American constitutionalism is a story of massive plagiarism, and other states sometimes borrowed from Kentucky. In most cases, the duplication represented only a convenient appropriation of existing language, but in one respect Kentucky's constitution provided a significant turning point in legal doctrine. The first state constitutions had not mentioned slavery. Southern states were silent either because they did not feel threatened or because they preferred to preserve flexibility upon the future of the institution. But slavery supporters in Kentucky had felt distinctly threatened by 1792, and George Nicholas had prevailed upon the convention to adopt positive guarantees, which were continued in the 1799 document. Kentucky's proslavery constitutionalism included a formulation of the social contract in the Bill of Rights which specifically excluded slaves and a separate section of the constitution prohibiting legislative emancipation or the limitation of slave imports, except under very specific conditions. Other slave states found Kentucky's model so useful that virtually every southern state that joined the Union after 1800 contained both Kentucky's version of the Bill of Rights and Kentucky's section on slave emancipation. Kentucky's antislavery activists had accomplished nothing positive but instead had bequeathed to states as distant as Texas ironclad guarantees of slavery and an intellectual justification that slaves had not participated in the social compact. It was a bitter legacy.[4]

The legacy to Kentucky politics was more positive. The 1799 convention delegates had virtually ignored the arguments of the few vociferous democrats in the convention, and they incorporated certain features of oligarchic government – such as the self-perpetuating county courts – in the constitution. But a majority of the delegates were realists, and they recognized that the constitution would not long survive if it contained unpopular features. Further, many of them were practiced and successful politicians who were willing to entrust their own and Kentucky's political future to a broad electorate. Consequently, the political settlement included direct election of state officers, universal white male suffrage, no property qualifications for officeholding, and no prohibition on campaigning. Representation was broadened, and the Kentucky constitution was the first state charter to define precisely how the principle of representation by numbers could be implemented. Critics in the future still complained that representation was not apportioned fairly and that there remained "slavish appendages and aristocratic features." Nonetheless, Kentucky, by 1800, had shed much of the paternalism of its Virginia origins and moved toward a competitive nineteenth-century politics.[5]

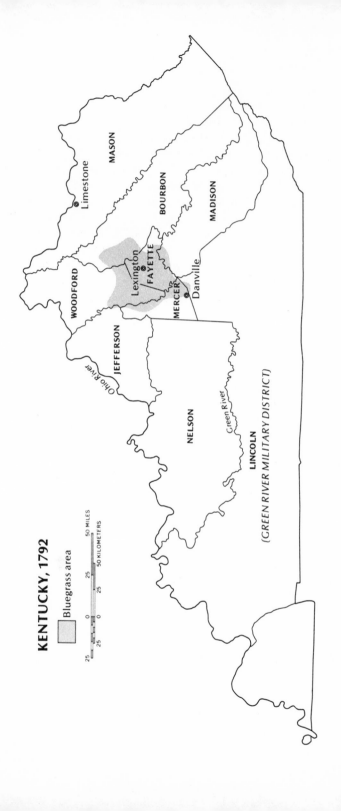

KENTUCKY, 1792

Bluegrass area

Limestone

MASON

BOURBON

MADISON

WOODFORD

Lexington
FAYETTE

MERCER
Danville

JEFFERSON

Ohio River

NELSON

Green River

LINCOLN

(GREEN RIVER MILITARY DISTRICT)

25   0   25   50 MILES

25   0   25   50 KILOMETERS

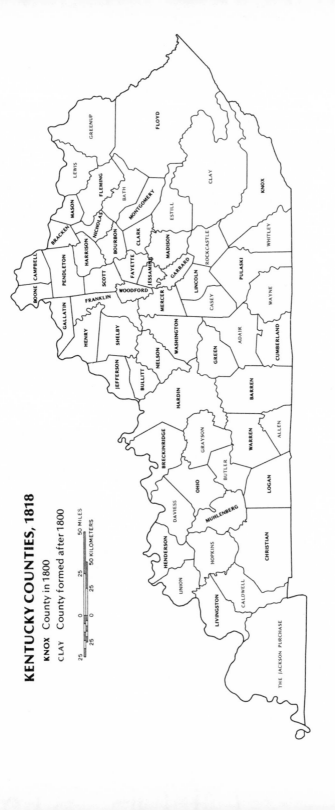

KENTUCKY COUNTIES, 1818

KNOX County in 1800

CLAY County formed after 1800

50 MILES

25   0

50 KILOMETERS

25   0

25

GREENUP

FLOYD

LEWIS

CLAY

KNOX

MASON

FLEMING

BATH

MONTGOMERY

ESTILL

BRACKEN

NICHOLAS

BOURBON

CLARK

MADISON

WHITLEY

CAMPBELL

HARRISON

FAYETTE

GARRARD

ROCKCASTLE

PENDLETON

SCOTT

JESSAMINE

PULASKI

BOONE

FRANKLIN

WOODFORD

MERCER

LINCOLN

WAYNE

GALLATIN

CASEY

HENRY

SHELBY

WASHINGTON

GREEN

ADAIR

CUMBERLAND

JEFFERSON

NELSON

BULLITT

HARDIN

BARREN

ALLEN

BRECKINRIDGE

GRAYSON

WARREN

BUTLER

OHIO

LOGAN

DAVIESS

MUHLENBERG

HENDERSON

HOPKINS

CHRISTIAN

UNION

CALDWELL

LIVINGSTON

THE JACKSON PURCHASE

NOTES

Chapter 1

1. *American Museum* 1 (1787): 159-60.

2. William W. Hening, ed., *The Statutes at Large: Being a Collection of All the Laws of Virginia, from the First Session of the Legislature, in the Year 1619* (Richmond, 1810-1823), 13: 17-20.

3. U.S. Department of Commerce and Labor, Bureau of the Census, *A Century of Population Growth from the First Census of the United States to the Twelfth, 1790-1900* (Washington, D.C., 1909), p. 207; John Joyce to the Reverend Robert Dickson, 24 March 1785, *Virginia Historical Magazine* 23 (1915): 413; Francis S. Philbrick, *The Rise of the West, 1754-1830*, in *The New American Nation Series*, ed. Henry S. Commager and Richard B. Morris (New York, 1965), pp. 303-21.

4. Gordon S. Wood, *The Creation of the American Republic, 1776-1787*, Institute of Early American History and Culture (Chapel Hill, N.C., 1969), passim, especially pp. 127-255, 393-518; Fletcher M. Green, *Constitutional Development in the South Atlantic States, 1776-1860: A Study in the Evolution of Democracy* (Chapel Hill, N.C., 1930), pp. 83-91, 101-29. Constitutional comparisons here and throughout this book are based upon detailed examination of all state and national constitutions written in the United States through 1850: Francis N. Thorpe, ed., *The Federal and State Constitutions, Colonial Charters, and Other Organic Laws of the States, Territories, and Colonies* (Washington, D.C., 1909), vols. 1-7. Actually, two states – Rhode Island and Connecticut – continued to use colonial charters in which references to royal authority were deleted.

5. Wood, *Creation of the American Republic*, pp. 70-75, 173-81, 476-83.

6. Ibid., pp. 70-90, 162-96, 476-83; Ronald P. Formisano, "Deferential-Participant Politics: The Early Republic's Political Culture, 1789-1840," *American Political Science Review* 68 (1974): 483-84; Richard R. Beeman, *The Old Dominion and the New Nation, 1788-1801* (Lexington, Ky., 1972), pp. 33-41.

7. Humphrey Marshall, *The History of Kentucky, Exhibiting an Account of the Modern Discovery, Settlement, Progressive Improvement, Civil and Military Transactions, and the Present State of the Country*, 2d ed. (Frankfort, 1824), 1: 441-42, 444; *Calendar of Virginia State Papers and Other Manuscripts*, ed. William P. Palmer et al. (Richmond, 1875-1893), 4: 191 (hereafter *CVSP*). Precise figures on the migration do not exist and estimates vary, Marshall, *History of Kentucky*, 1: 441-42; Theodore Roo-

sevelt, *The Winning of the West* (New York, 1889), 1: 102-8; Robert S. Cotterill, *History of Pioneer Kentucky* (Cincinnati, 1917), p. 24. For comment upon the fragmented population, see also interview with John Hedge, Kentucky Papers, XI, 19, of the Lyman C. Draper Collection, Wisconsin Historical Society, Madison (the Draper Collection is organized into groups, then into volumes. References give the volume number, then the letter designation of the group, then the page. The above is Draper 11 CC 19); Caleb Wallace to James Madison, 12 July 1785, George Nicholas to Madison, 5 September 1792, James Madison Papers, Library of Congress (hereafter Madison MSS).

8. Hening, ed., *Statutes at Large*, 9: 355-56, 10: 35-50. A convenient compilation of land law is in *Acts Passed at the First Session of the Fifth General Assembly for the Commonwealth of Kentucky*, [Chapt. XXXIX] (hereafter *Session Laws*, 1796 session). An excellent summary and discussion of Virginia land law is in Patricia Watlington, *The Partisan Spirit: Kentucky Politics, 1779-1792*, Institute of Early American History and Culture (New York, 1972), pp. 11-30; see also Thomas P. Abernethy, *Western Lands and the American Revolution* (New York, 1937), pp. 217-29.

9. Marshall, *History of Kentucky*, 1: 153; Watlington, *Partisan Spirit*, pp. 13-27; Hening, ed., *Statutes at Large*, 10: 55-56.

10. Willard R. Jillson, *The Kentucky Land Grants*, Filson Club Publications No. 33 (Louisville, 1925); Thomas Marshall to Michael Gratz, 23 April 1783, William V. Byars, ed., *B. and M. Gratz: Merchants in Philadelphia, 1754-1798* (Jefferson City, Mo., 1916), p. 212; "History in Circuit Court Records," ed. Charles R. Staples, *Kentucky Historical Society Register* 32 (1934): 7 (hereafter *KHSR*). For information on land ownership, see George Nicholas, "The expences of government," George Nicholas Papers, Reuben T. Durrett Collection, University of Chicago Library (hereafter Nicholas MSS, Durrett); Harry Toulmin, *The Western Country in 1793: Reports on Kentucky and Virginia*, ed. Marion Tinling and Godfrey Davis (San Marino, Calif., 1948), p. 80; "A Real Friend to the People," *Kentucky Gazette*, 15 August 1789; Lincoln and Madison County Tax Lists, Kentucky Historical Society (hereafter KHS); Watlington, *Partisan Spirit*, pp. 22-23.

11. Albert O. Porter, *County Government in Virginia: A Legislative History, 1607-1904*, Studies in History, Economics and Public Law, ed. Faculty of Political Science of Columbia University, No. 526 (New York, 1947), pp. 105-6.

12. Ibid., pp. 107-24; Charles S. Sydnor, *Gentlemen Freeholders: Political Practices in Washington's Virginia* (Chapel Hill, N.C., 1952), pp. 78-93; Beeman, *Old Dominion and the New Nation*, pp. 28-30; List of county officials in Kentucky counties before statehood, 1780-1792, see Appendix for sources.

13. List of county officials in Kentucky counties before statehood, 1780-1792, see Appendix for sources; county court order books, University of Kentucky Library, Lexington, see, for example, Mercer County Court Order Book, April 1787; Jefferson County Court Order Book, April 1784, August 1785 (hereafter UK).

14. "Poplicola," *Kentucky Gazette*, 20 September 1788; Earl G. Swem and John W. Williams, *A Register of the General Assembly of Virginia, 1776-1918, and of the Constitutional Conventions*, Fourteenth Annual Report of the Library Board of the Virginia State Library, 1916-1917 (Richmond, 1917-1918). Leadership is measured by committee assignments: Jack P. Greene, "Foundations of Political Power in the Virginia House of Burgesses, 1720-1776," *William and Mary Quarterly*, 3d ser., 16

(1959): 485-506, and Robert Zemsky, *Merchants, Farmers, and River Gods: An Essay on Eighteenth-Century American Politics* (Boston, 1971), especially pp. 287-94, both use such measurements though with somewhat different techniques. This study follows Greene, since Virginia and Kentucky committee structures were similar; List of leaders in Kentucky House of Representatives, 1792-1798, see Appendix for note on methodology.

15. List of delegates to Kentucky statehood conventions, 1784-1790, see Appendix for sources; manuscript journal of Kentucky conventions, KHS.

16. Watlington, *Partisan Spirit*, pp. 47-132, especially pp. 50-52, 83-84, 108. Watlington defines the groups as parties but concedes a transitory membership; only three men signed both of two partisan petitions sent east in 1782 and 1789: petitions # 15 and # 58 in James R. Robertson, *Petitions of the Early Inhabitants of Kentucky to the General Assembly of Virginia, 1769-1792*, Filson Club Publications No. 27 (Louisville, 1914).

17. "A Real Friend to the People," *Kentucky Gazette*, 25 April 1789; Marshall, *History of Kentucky*, 1: 195; George Muter to James Madison, 20 February 1787, Madison MSS: "A Virginian," *Kentucky Gazette*, 13 October 1787.

18. Caleb Wallace to William Fleming, 13 July 1786, Fleming-Christian Letters, in the Hugh Blair Grigsby Collection, Virginia Historical Society, Richmond (hereafter Fleming-Christian MSS); Wallace to James Madison, 30 September 1786, George Muter to Madison, 23 September 1786, 20 February 1787, Madison MSS; "A Real Friend to the People," *Kentucky Gazette*, 25 April 1789; "A Virginian," ibid., 13 October 1787; "A Farmer," ibid., 2 February, 18 October 1788; Dwight L. Mikkelson, "*Kentucky Gazette*, 1787-1848: 'The Herald of a Noisy World' " (Ph.D. diss., University of Kentucky, 1963).

19. Watlington, *Partisan Spirit*, pp. 100-109.

20. Manuscript journal of Kentucky conventions, KHS; Watlington, *Partisan Spirit*, pp. 159-87; editorial note on "The Threat of Disunion in the West," *The Papers of Thomas Jefferson*, ed. Julian P. Boyd et al. (Princeton, N.J., 1950-   ), 19: 469-74. There is a voluminous polemic literature upon these transactions, much of which was written by men related to participants in the events: Marshall, *History of Kentucky*, vol. 1; John M. Brown, *The Political Beginnings of Kentucky*, Filson Club Publications No. 6 (Louisville, 1889); Thomas M. Green, *The Spanish Conspiracy* (Cincinnati, 1891); William Littell, *Political Transactions in and concerning Kentucky*, reprinted with introduction by Temple Bodley, Filson Club Publications No. 31 (Louisville, 1926).

21. Watlington, *Partisan Spirit*, pp. 174-87; Boyd et al., ed., *Papers of Thomas Jefferson*, 19: 470-72; List of delegates to Kentucky statehood conventions, 1784-1790, see Appendix for sources. John Brown was easily reelected to the United States House of Representatives in 1790, after the publication of a letter which implicated him in the Conspiracy, suggesting that the absence from local politics was voluntary.

22. James Brown to John Preston, 3 September 1789, Draper 5 QQ 122; Samuel Terrell to Garritt Minor, 7 July 1790, Terrell-Carr Papers, University of Virginia Library, Charlottesville (hereafter Terrell-Carr MSS); John Brown to Harry Innes, 13 September 1789, Harry Innes Papers, LC (hereafter Innes MSS); Joel Watkins Diary, 23 July 1789, Durrett Collection; Robertson, *Petitions of the Early Inhabitants*, Petition # 58; manuscript journal, ninth convention, KHS.

23. "A Farmer," *Kentucky Gazette*, 2 February 1788; "Republicus," ibid., 12 February 1788; "Mancipium," ibid., 23 February 1788; "A Citizen of Kentucky," ibid., 10 May 1788; "Cornplanter," ibid., 12 July 1788; "Philopatria," ibid., 23 August, 6 September 1788; "Theologues," ibid., 4 October 1788.

24. Political Club Papers, Filson Club, Louisville (hereafter Political Club MSS). Most of the material in the manuscript collection has been published in Thomas Speed, *The Political Club, Danville, Kentucky, 1786-1790*, Filson Club Publications No. 9 (Louisville, 1894).

25. George Nicholas to James Madison, 5 September 1792, Madison MSS. See the following justifications for separation: Extract from *Maryland Gazette*, 1 July 1785, Draper 3 JJ 138-39; Harry Innes to John Brown, 7 December 1787, Harry Innes Papers, KHS; Caleb Wallace to James Madison, 12 July, 8 October 1785, 30 September 1786, 12 November 1787, Madison MSS; George Nicholas to John Brown, 31 December 1790, George Nicholas Papers, KHS (hereafter Nicholas MSS, KHS). James Speed to Governor Harrison, 22 May 1784, *CVSP*, 3: 588-89; "Cornplanter," *Kentucky Gazette*, 13 September 1788; Samuel Terrell to Garritt Minor, 7 July 1790, Terrell-Carr MSS, all oppose statehood and cite unreadiness as the reason. Caleb Wallace to James Madison, 12 July 1785, 30 September 1786, Madison MSS; Wallace to William Fleming, 11 August 1792, Fleming-Christian MSS; George Nicholas to James Madison, 5 September 1792, Madison MSS; and Marshall, *History of Kentucky*, 1: 441-42, concede lack of readiness but support statehood.

26. George Muter to James Madison, 6 January 1785, Caleb Wallace to Madison, 12 July 1785, Madison MSS.

27. John Brown to James Madison, 12 May 1788, ibid.; see also Brown to Madison, 7 June, 26 August 1788, George Muter to Madison, 6 January 1785, Caleb Wallace to Madison, 12 July 1785, Robert Johnson to Madison, 23 September 1786, all in ibid.; James Wilkinson to James Hutchinson, 20 June 1785, *Pennsylvania Magazine of History and Biography* 12 (1888): 60-61; George Nicholas to Wilkinson, 23 January 1788, Nicholas MSS, Durrett; Edmund Pendleton to Harry Innes, 9 November 1791, *The Letters and Papers of Edmund Pendleton*, ed. David J. Mays (Charlottesville, Va., 1967), 2: 579-81; Innes to Thomas Jefferson, 27 August 1791, Thomas Jefferson Papers, LC (hereafter Jefferson MSS).

28. Harry Innes to Thomas Jefferson, 27 August 1791, Jefferson MSS; James Madison to Caleb Wallace, 23 August 1785, Madison MSS.

Chapter 2

1. Caleb Wallace to [Thomas Madison], 28 June 1785, Draper 5 ZZ 80; see also James Brown to James Breckinridge, 30 September 1788, James Breckinridge Papers, University of Virginia, which reported so many lawyers that "they must hunt Buffallo or starve." For information on Nicholas, see manuscript biographical sketch of him, written by his brother, Wilson Cary Nicholas, Thomas Jefferson Papers, Massachusetts Historical Society; Hugh B. Grigsby, *The History of the Virginia Federal Convention of 1788*, Collections of the Virginia Historical Society, n.s., 9 and 10 (Richmond, 1890), 2: 281-98; Richard H. Caldemeyer, "The Career of George Nicholas" (Ph.D. diss., Indiana University, 1951), pp. 2-6; Thomas P. Abernethy, "George Nicholas," *Dictionary of American Biography*, ed. Allen Johnson and Dumas Malone (New

York, 1928-1936), 13: 482-83 (hereafter *DAB*); Dumas Malone, *Jefferson and His Time* (Boston, 1948-   ), 1: 361-66; Swem and Williams, ed., *Register of the General Assembly*.

2. Caldemeyer, "Career of George Nicholas," pp. 9-11; Irving Brant, *James Madison* (Indianapolis, Ind., 1941-1961), 2: 348-50; Jonathan Elliot, *The Debates in the Several State Conventions on the Adoption of the Federal Constitution . . .* , 2d ed. (Washington, D.C., 1836), vol. 3, passim. Only one Kentuckian is recorded as speaking.

3. Grigsby, *Virginia Federal Convention*, 1: 79, see also pp. 73, 78, 140-43; Elliot, *Debates in the Several State Conventions*, 3: 103; Robert Wickliffe, "Sketch of George Nicholas," p. 12, Carter-Smith Family Papers, University of Virginia.

4. Elliot, *Debates in the Several State Conventions*, 3: 360-61, see also pp. 238-41, 356-60; George Nicholas to James Madison, 9 May 1788, and Madison to Nicholas, 17 May 1788, both in Madison MSS; Charles G. Talbert, "Kentuckians in the Virginia Convention of 1788," *KHSR* 58 (1960): 187-93. One delegate did not vote.

5. John Hoomes to James Madison, 27 July 1789, George Nicholas to Madison, December 1788, Madison MSS; Nicholas to Harry Innes, 4 May 1789, Innes MSS; John T. Mason to John Breckinridge, 1 February 1793, John Tyler to Breckinridge, September 1795, Breckinridge Family Papers, LC (hereafter Breckinridge MSS); Caldemeyer, "Career of George Nicholas," pp. 29-36.

6. George Nicholas to James Madison, 2 January, 8 May 1789, Madison MSS; Nicholas to Wilson Cary Nicholas, 1 May 1790, Samuel Smith Papers, University of Virginia (hereafter Smith MSS); Nicholas to James Wilkinson, 23 January 1788, Nicholas MSS, Durrett; Nicholas to John Brown, 2 November 1789, Nicholas MSS, KHS.

7. George Nicholas to John Brown, 31 December 1790, Nicholas MSS, KHS; Harry Innes to William Fleming, 14 August 1791, William Fleming Papers, Washington and Lee University (hereafter Fleming MSS); "A.B.C.," *Kentucky Gazette*, 8 October 1791.

8. Wood, *Creation of the American Republic*, pp. 320-28; H. J. Eckenrode, *The Revolution in Virginia* (New York, 1916), pp. 43-45, 96-122; Porter, *County Government in Virginia*, pp. 101-5; Watlington, *Partisan Spirit*, pp. 77, 123; Caleb Wallace to James Madison, 12 November 1787, Madison MSS.

9. "H.S.B.M.," *Kentucky Gazette*, 24 December 1791; "An Address to the free men of the district of Kentucky," ibid., 15 October 1791. Only seven members of the committees can be identified, two of whom signed an anti-statehood petition and one of whom voted for statehood: see ibid., 8, 22 October 1791, 11 February, 3 March 1792; Robertson, *Petitions of the Early Inhabitants*, # 58; manuscript journals of eighth and ninth conventions, KHS.

10. "An Address to the free men of the district of Kentucky," *Kentucky Gazette*, 15, 22 October 1791; "H.S.B.M.," ibid., 19 November 1791.

11. "An Address to the free men of the district of Kentucky," ibid., 15 October 1791; "H.S.B.M.," ibid., 26 November 1791; Bourbon County committee proposals, ibid., 11 February 1792.

12. James Hughes to Charles Simms, 30 March 1792, Charles Simms Papers, LC (hereafter Simms MSS).

13. "The disinterested Citizen," *Kentucky Gazette*, 5, 12 March, 2 July, 22, 29 October, 31 December 1791, 25 February 1792.

14. "A.B.C.," ibid., 24 September, 1, 8 October, 10 December 1791; Harry Innes to William Fleming, 14 August 1791, Fleming MSS; Innes to Thomas Jefferson, 27 August 1791, Jefferson MSS.

15. "A.B.C.," *Kentucky Gazette*, 8 October 1791; "A Citizen," ibid., 17 December 1791.

16. "A.B.C.," ibid., 24 September, 8 October, 3, 10 December 1791; "Philanthropos," ibid., 14 January 1792; "X.Y.Z.," ibid., 14 January, 18 February 1792. Instructions were defended by William Henry, ibid., 22 October 1791; "Torismond," ibid., 28 January 1792. See also Wood, *Creation of the American Republic*, pp. 189-96.

17. Harry Innes to Thomas Jefferson, 27 August 1791, Jefferson MSS; Thomas Lewis, *Kentucky Gazette*, 12 March 1791; "A.B.C.," ibid., 10 December 1791; "Felte Firebrand," ibid., 12 November 1791; "Torismond," ibid., 28 January 1792; "Philip Philips," ibid., 26 November 1791.

18. "Philip Philips," *Kentucky Gazette*, 26 November 1791; David B. Davis, *The Problem of Slavery in the Age of Revolution, 1770-1823* (Ithaca, N.Y., 1975), pp. 84-89, 312-21; Winthrop D. Jordan, *White over Black: American Attitudes toward the Negro, 1550-1812* (Chapel Hill, N.C., 1968), pp. 342-74; Arthur Zilversmit, *The First Emancipation: The Abolition of Slavery in the North* (Chicago, 1967), pp. 153-56, 169-222; Asa E. Martin, *The Anti-Slavery Movement in Kentucky prior to 1850*, Filson Club Publications No. 29 (Louisville, 1918), pp. 18-25. Missing issues of the *Gazette* include those from 30 July to 17 September 1791; "Henry Hudibras," *Kentucky Gazette*, 10 December 1791, refers to an emancipation argument in a missing issue.

19. "H.S.B.M.," *Kentucky Gazette*, 25 February 1792; "The disinterested Citizen," ibid., 31 December 1791. Upon the relationship of antislavery activity to the committees, see James Hughes to Charles Simms, 30 March 1792, Simms MSS. One committeeman voted for emancipation in the 1792 convention (*Journal of the First Constitutional Convention of Kentucky, Held in Danville, April 2 to 19, 1792* [Lexington, 1942], p. 10); another was an emancipation candidate to the 1799 convention (*Kentucky Gazette*, 28 March 1799); correspondence of two others affirms their connection (William Henry to James H. Dickey, 19 February 1814, James H. Dickey Papers, Shane Collection, Presbyterian Historical Society, Philadelphia [hereafter Dickey MSS]; John Boyd to Dickey, 1 August 1807, ibid.).

20. Hubbard Taylor to James Madison, 16 April 1792, Madison MSS; Samuel McDowell to Arthur Campbell, 22 June 1796, Draper 9 DD 61.

21. James Hughes to Charles Simms, 30 March 1792, Simms MSS; Marshall, *History of Kentucky*, 1: 389; "X.Y.Z.," *Kentucky Gazette*, 14 January, 18 February 1792; *Journal of the First Constitutional Convention*, p. 10.

22. John Brown to Harry Innes, 13 April 1792, Innes MSS; Marshall, *History of Kentucky*, 1: 394; James Wilkinson to John Brown, 3 January 1792, John Mason Brown Collection, Yale University (hereafter Brown MSS).

23. Robert Johnson to Benjamin Johnson, 18 January 1792, Barbour Papers, University of Virginia. The biographical composite is drawn from a wide variety of sources: Mrs. William P. Drake et al., *Kentucky in Retrospect: Noteworthy Personages and Events in Kentucky History, 1792-1942* (n.p., 1942); supplemented by numerous county histories, genealogies, articles in the *KHSR* and the *Filson Club Quarterly;* county court order books, UK; county deed books, UK; landholding figures based

upon Kentucky County Tax Lists, KHS; Virginia and Kentucky land grants found in Jillson, *Kentucky Land Grants;* List of county officials in Kentucky counties before statehood, 1780-1792, and List of delegates to Kentucky statehood conventions, 1784-1790, see Appendix for sources.

24. Ibid.

25. Ibid.; List of Kentucky delegates to Virginia House of Delegates, see Appendix for sources. Included is service in the assembly from another Virginia county before moving to Kentucky, see William G. Stanard and Mary N. Stanard, comps., *The Colonial Virginia Register: A List of Governors, Councillors and Other Higher Officials, and Also of Members of the House of Burgesses, and the Revolutionary Conventions of the Colony of Virginia* (Albany, N.Y., 1902); William and Mary College, *A Provisional List of Alumni* (Richmond, Va., 1941). At least thirty-nine lawyers had been admitted to practice before county courts before 1792, see county court order books, UK.

26. "Salamander," *Kentucky Gazette*, 24 December 1791; Wood, *Creation of the American Republic*, pp. 300-301; Richard E. Ellis, *The Jeffersonian Crisis: Courts and Politics in the Young Republic* (New York, 1971), pp. 111-22; Marshall, *History of Kentucky*, 1: 394.

27. Wood, *Creation of the American Republic*, pp. 226-37, 438-46; Robert L. Brunhouse, *The Counter-Revolution in Pennsylvania, 1776-1790* (Harrisburg, Pa., 1942), especially pp. 13-15, 225; Robert A. Dahl, *Pluralist Democracy in the United States* (Chicago, 1967), pp. 30-31; Carl R. Fields, "Making Kentucky's Third Constitution, 1830-1850" (Ph.D. diss., University of Kentucky, 1951), p. 190; John D. Barnhart, *Valley of Democracy: The Frontier versus the Plantation in the Ohio Valley, 1775-1818* (Bloomington, Ind., 1953), pp. 111-18, 150-55.

28. Samuel M. Wilson, "Isaac Shelby," *DAB*, 17: 60-62; Robert S. Cotterill, "Benjamin Logan," ibid., 11: 356-57; Charles G. Talbert, *Benjamin Logan: Kentucky Frontiersman* (Lexington, Ky., 1962), especially p. 129; Thomas M. Green, *Historic Families of Kentucky* (Cincinnati, 1889), pp. 31-39; George Nicholas to James Madison, 5 September 1792, Madison MSS; Caleb Wallace to William Fleming, 28 May 1792, Fleming-Christian MSS; Samuel McDowell to Arthur Campbell, 21 May 1792, Draper 9 DD 69; Political Club MSS.

29. Alexander S. Bullitt to George Nicholas, 15 August 1792, Nicholas to Bullitt, 30 July 1791, 19 August 1792, Bullitt Family Genealogy and Papers, Filson Club (hereafter Bullitt MSS); Robert S. Cotterill, "Alexander Scott Bullitt," *DAB*, 3: 255-56; Jefferson County Tax List, KHS; Toulmin, *Western Country in 1793*, pp. 84-88; Harry Innes to William Fleming, 31 July 1790, Fleming MSS; Caleb Wallace to Mrs. Elizabeth Christian, 1 January 1788, Fleming-Christian MSS.

30. Robert S. Cotterill, "James Garrard," *DAB*, 7: 159-60; J. H. Spencer, *A History of Kentucky Baptists* (Cincinnati, 1886), 1: 133-34; James Wilkinson to John Brown, 12 September 1790, Brown MSS, reported Brown could expect no political help from Garrard but prayer.

31. Robert H. Bishop, *An Outline of the History of the Church in the State of Kentucky . . . Containing the Memoirs of Rev. David Rice* (Lexington, 1824); see also Marshall, *History of Kentucky*, 1: 394; interview with B. Snelling, Draper 12 CC 111; Vernon P. Martin, "Father Rice, the Preacher Who Followed the Frontier," *Filson Club Quarterly* 29 (1955): 324-30.

32. Edward Weist, "Harry Innes," *DAB*, 5: 485-86; Speed, *Political Club*, pp. 42-

45; Harry Innes to Thomas Jefferson, 27 August 1791, Jefferson MSS. Innes proved his antislavery credentials by his decade-long guardianship of three freed underage slaves, resisting both the efforts of Bourbon County to have them bound out and the efforts of the heirs to restrict the money spent for their education: Edmund Lyne Estate Papers, 1774-1804, Durrett; Bourbon County Court Order Book, December 1795 and October 1796, UK; *Journal of the First Constitutional Convention*, especially p. 10.

33. James Brown to John Preston, 3 September 1789, Draper 5 QQ 122; Marshall, *History of Kentucky*, 1: 395; "Philip Philips," *Kentucky Gazette*, 26 November 1791; "A Real Friend to the People," ibid., 25 April, 15 August 1789; Neva Lillian (Long-fellow) Williams, "Samuel Taylor," paper read before the Harrodsburg Historical Society, 7 April 1932 (original owned by George Chinn). For political service, see List of Kentucky delegates to Virginia House of Delegates, 1776-1791, List of members of Kentucky House of Representatives, 1792-1799, and List of delegates to Kentucky statehood conventions, 1784-1790, see Appendix for sources; see also poem on election of 1787, describing his supporters as "ragged ruffians": Thomas Johnson, *The Kentucky Miscellany*, 4th ed. (Lexington, 1821, reprinted Lexington, 1949), pp. 13-14.

34. Samuel M. Wilson, "James Smith," *DAB*, 9: 284-85; James M. Smith, *An Account of the Remarkable Occurrences in the Life and Travels of Colonel James Smith* (Philadelphia, 1831).

35. James Brown to John Brown, 20 October 1790, Brown MSS; Grigsby, *Virginia Federal Convention*, 1: 246-47; George Nicholas to Wilson Cary Nicholas, 1 May 1790, Smith MSS.

36. George Nicholas to James Madison, 5 September 1792, Madison MSS; Marshall, *History of Kentucky*, 1: 395-96.

37. George Nicholas to Alexander S. Bullitt, 30 July 1791, Bullitt MSS; "The disinterested Citizen," *Kentucky Gazette*, 11 February 1792 (this assumes he, in fact, did write this series); George Nicholas to Wilson Cary Nicholas, 1 February 1792, Wilson Cary Nicholas Papers, University of Virginia; Hubbard Taylor to James Madison, 17 December 1791, Madison MSS; James Wilkinson to John Brown, 3 January 1792, Brown MSS.

38. *Journal of the First Constitutional Convention*, especially p. 3. He was re-elected.

39. The Nicholas MSS, Durrett, contain the convention materials. They include reading notes; drafts of speeches in his handwriting (hereafter cited by title); final drafts of some speeches in another, more legible handwriting (hereafter "Speech"); and a series of resolutions he had readied to present to the convention, embodying his ideas (hereafter "Nicholas Resolutions"). Caldemeyer, "Career of George Nicholas," pp. 73-74, and Barnhart, *Valley of Democracy*, p. 102, assumed these resolutions were the work of the convention and that Nicholas merely acted as a secretary when he copied them down. Internal evidence supports the assumption that the resolutions were presented by Nicholas to the convention; the "Nicholas Resolutions" differ from the published resolutions of the convention committee of the whole and from the convention resolutions sent east during the proceedings: *Journal of the First Constitutional Convention*, pp. 4-9; Hubbard Taylor to James Madison, 16 April 1792, Madison MSS. Watlington, *Partisan Spirit*, p. 218, and Ellis, *Jeffersonian Crisis*, p. 128, also identify the resolutions as those of Nicholas rather than the convention. George Nicholas to James Madison, 2 May 1792, Madison MSS.

40. Thorpe, ed., *Federal and State Constitutions*.

41. George Nicholas to James Wilkinson, 23 January 1788, Nicholas MSS, Durrett; Wood, *Creation of the American Republic*, pp. 180, 393-463, especially pp. 403-13.

42. Hubbard Taylor to James Madison, 8 May 1792, Madison MSS; George Nicholas to John Brown, 2 November 1789, Nicholas MSS, KHS; Nicholas to Alexander S. Bullitt, 30 July 1791, Bullitt MSS. On suffrage, see Thorpe, ed., *Federal and State Constitutions;* Wood, *Creation of the American Republic*, pp. 167-69; Marshall, *History of Kentucky*, 1: 197-98; petition of John Waller, 28 October 1789, Bourbon County Legislative Petitions, Virginia State Library; by the terms of the separation in the Virginia Compact, the election for the 1792 constitutional convention permitted universal suffrage: Hening, ed., *Statutes at Large*, 13: 17.

43. "Nicholas Resolutions," Nicholas MSS, Durrett.

44. Ibid.; see also his speeches, ibid.

45. Ibid.; George Nicholas to James Wilkinson, 23 January 1788, ibid.

46. George Nicholas to James Madison, 2 May 1792, Madison MSS; "Nicholas Resolutions" and "Speech on Senate," Nicholas MSS, Durrett; compared with convention resolutions, *Journal of the First Constitutional Convention*, p. 5; Wood, *Creation of the American Republic*, pp. 206-16, especially p. 214.

47. "Speech on Senate," Nicholas MSS, Durrett; convention resolutions, *Journal of the First Constitutional Convention*, p. 5; George Nicholas to James Madison, 2 May 1792, Madison MSS.

48. "Nicholas Resolutions" and "Speech on Governor," Nicholas MSS, Durrett; compared with convention resolutions, *Journal of the First Constitutional Convention*, p. 5; George Nicholas to James Madison, 5 September 1792, Madison MSS.

49. George Nicholas to James Wilkinson, 23 January 1788, "Nicholas Resolutions," and "Speech on Governor," all in Nicholas MSS, Durrett. Republicans elsewhere were having the same sort of second thoughts about the virtue of rotation in office: Wood, *Creation of the American Republic*, pp. 140-41, 436.

50. James Madison to John Brown, [October 1788], Madison MSS; "Appointments to Office," Nicholas MSS, Durrett; Wood, *Creation of the American Republic*, pp. 143-49, 435.

51. George Nicholas to James Wilkinson, 23 January 1788, Nicholas MSS, Durrett; James Madison to John Brown, [October 1788], Madison MSS.

52. "Appointments to Office," Nicholas MSS, Durrett.

53. Ibid.

54. Ibid.; "Nicholas Resolutions" and Nicholas to James Wilkinson, 23 January 1788, ibid. The quote, in Nicholas to David Stewart, 9 April 1788, C. E. French Papers, LC, discusses the inclusion of a Bill of Rights in the United States Constitution, but it is revealing of Nicholas's thinking generally.

55. "Appointments to Office" and "Nicholas Resolutions," Nicholas MSS, Durrett; convention resolutions, *Journal of the First Constitutional Convention*, p. 4; George Nicholas to James Madison, 5 September 1792, Madison MSS.

56. "Nicholas Resolutions," Nicholas to James Wilkinson, 23 January 1788, and "Suffrage," all in Nicholas MSS, Durrett; James Madison to John Brown, [October 1788], Madison MSS; Wood, *Creation of the American Republic*, pp. 169-70.

57. "Suffrage," Nicholas MSS, Durrett; Nicholas to James Madison, 2 May 1792, Madison MSS.

58. "Suffrage," Nicholas MSS, Durrett; Wood, *Creation of the American Republic*, pp. 517-18. Nicholas's comment upon the virtues of a large electorate parallels the argument of James Madison in *The Federalist* No. 10 upon the value of an extended republic: *The Federalist Papers*, ed. Clinton Rossiter (New York, 1961).

59. Thorpe, *Federal and State Constitutions;* "Nicholas Resolutions," Nicholas MSS, Durrett; convention resolutions, *Journal of the First Constitutional Convention*, p. 8; Kentucky, *Constitution* (1792), Art. I, Sect. 27.

60. List of county officials in Kentucky counties before statehood, 1780-1792, and List of Kentucky delegates to Virginia House of Delegates, 1776-1791, see Appendix for sources.

61. Alexander S. Bullitt to George Nicholas, 15 August 1792, Bullitt MSS.

62. George Nicholas to James Wilkinson, 23 January 1788, Nicholas MSS, Durrett; Nicholas to Alexander S. Bullitt, 30 July 1791, Bullitt MSS; Nicholas to John Brown, 2 November 1789, Nicholas MSS, KHS; James Hughes to Charles Simms, 30 March 1792, Simms MSS; "Nicholas Resolutions" and "Speech on Courts," Nicholas MSS, Durrett; Ellis, *Jeffersonian Crisis*, pp. 119-21; Wood, *Creation of the American Republic*, pp. 452-56.

63. "Speech on Courts," Nicholas MSS, Durrett; *Journal of the First Constitutional Convention*, pp. 3, 8; Marshall, *History of Kentucky*, 1: 395-96; estimate on landholders in "Journal of General [Richard] Butler," 2 January 1786, in Neville B. Craig, ed., *The Olden Time* (Pittsburgh, Pa., 1847), 2: 509.

64. Marshall, *History of Kentucky*, 1: 396. However, Alexander S. Bullitt to George Nicholas, 15 August 1792, Bullitt MSS, begrudgingly admitted that Nicholas had no difficulty in inserting the provision.

65. "The expences of government," Nicholas MSS, Durrett. For expression of concern over adequate governmental expenditure, see George Nicholas to Alexander S. Bullitt, 30 July 1791, Bullitt MSS; James Hughes to Charles Simms, 30 March 1792, Simms MSS; John Brown to Harry Innes, 13 April 1792, Innes MSS; James McDowell to John McDowell, 27 September 1792, John McDowell Papers, Shane Collection, Presbyterian Historical Society. Kentuckians used the two monetary systems during the 1790s, sometimes including both within the same law. For convenience, hereafter, all figures have been translated into dollars. The exchange rate was six shillings to the dollar.

66. "The expences of government," Nicholas MSS, Durrett.

67. Ibid.

68. Ibid.; material on education in reading notes, ibid., but it was not included in any speech. His ideas upon the support of manufacturing are found in "The disinterested Citizen," *Kentucky Gazette*, 21 December 1790.

69. Convention resolutions, *Journal of the First Constitutional Convention*, pp. 4-9.

70. Ibid., p. 10; Davis, *Problem of Slavery*, pp. 84-89, 164-84; Jordan, *White over Black*, pp. 269-311; Zilversmit, *First Emancipation*, pp. 153-56, 169-222.

71. Davis, *Problem of Slavery*, pp. 196-212; Jordan, *White over Black*, pp. 342-74.

72. Joseph Ficklin interview, Draper 16 CC 259; Colonel John Graves interview, ibid., 11 CC 121-22; Toulmin, *Western Country in 1793*, pp. 68, 115, 125; Daniel Drake, *Pioneer Life in Kentucky, 1785-1800*, ed. Emmet F. Horine (New York,

1948), pp. 207-8; Charles R. Staples, *The History of Pioneer Lexington, Kentucky, 1779-1806* (Lexington, 1939), pp. 27-30.

73. "Original Records of the Phi Beta Kappa Society," *William and Mary Quarterly*, 1st ser., 4 (1896): 295; Thomas B. Craighead to John Brown, 1 May 1787, Brown MSS; Political Club MSS; Davis, *Problem of Slavery*, pp. 196-200; Jordan, *White over Black*, pp. 342-74.

74. Martin, *Anti-Slavery in Kentucky*, pp. 18-25.

75. Elkhorn Association Minutes, 26-27 August 1791, published in William W. Sweet, ed., *Religion on the American Frontier: The Baptists, 1783-1830. A Collection of Source Material* (New York, 1931), pp. 440-44.

76. Ibid., 26 December 1791, pp. 446-47. On divisions among Baptists, see East Hickman Baptist Church Minutes, Southern Baptist Theological Seminary, Louisville; David Benedict, *A General History of the Baptist Denomination in America, and Other Parts of the World* (Boston, 1813), 1: 207; David Rice to William Rodgers, 4 November 1794, Committee of Correspondence Letter Book, Pennsylvania Abolition Society Papers, Pennsylvania Historical Society, Philadelphia (hereafter Pennsylvania Abolition Society MSS).

77. *Journal of the First Constitutional Convention*; Robert Johnson to Benjamin Johnson, 18 January 1792, Barbour Papers, University of Virginia; "Philanthropos," *Slavery Inconsistent with Justice and Good Policy* (Lexington, Ky., 1792), reprinted in Bishop, *History of the Church*, pp. 385-418; David Rice, *Slavery Inconsistent with Justice and Good Policy, Proved by a Speech Delivered in the Convention, Held at Danville, Kentucky* (Philadelphia, 1792).

78. "Philanthropos," *Slavery Inconsistent with Justice*, p. 43 and passim.

79. Toulmin, *Western Country in 1793*, p. 79, reports that the advocates cannot "digest any plan which has general concurrence among themselves"; Hubbard Taylor to James Madison, 16 April 1792, Madison MSS.

80. "Philanthropos," *Slavery Inconsistent with Justice*.

81. Ibid.; memoir of Rev. James Gallaher, Draper 15 CC 224; Jordan, *White over Black*, pp. 544-69.

82. "Speech on Slaves," Nicholas MSS, Durrett.

83. Ibid.

84. Ibid.; compare with "Suffrage," ibid.

85. "Speech on Slaves," ibid.

86. *Journal of the First Constitutional Convention*; George Nicholas to James Madison, 2 May 1792, Madison MSS. The defensive tone of the letter suggests he expected criticism from Madison for the proslavery provisions of the constitution; he advanced an argument which was not mentioned in convention and which was probably specious, that the danger of Indian attack was so great that an immediate population increase must be obtained.

87. "Bill of Rights," Nicholas MSS, Durrett; Robert A. Rutland, *The Birth of the Bill of Rights, 1776-1791*, Institute of Early American History and Culture (Chapel Hill, N.C., 1955), pp. 36, 64, 97-98, 156; see also Davis, *Problem of Slavery*, pp. 317-19.

88. "Philanthropos," *Slavery Inconsistent with Justice*; "Philip Philips," *Kentucky Gazette*, 26 November 1791; "H.S.B.M.," ibid., 25 February 1792; Kentucky, *Constitution* (1792), Art. XII, Sect. 1.

89. Kentucky, *Constitution* (1792), Art. IX, Sect. 1; *Journal of the First Constitutional Convention*, p. 10.

90. Kentucky County Tax Lists, KHS; Jillson, *Kentucky Land Grants*.

91. "Speech on Slaves," Nicholas MSS, Durrett; Hubbard Taylor to James Madison, 16 April 1792, Madison MSS.

92. Bourbon, Franklin, and Nelson County Tax Lists, KHS; Nelson County Court Order Books, UK; Nelson County Deed Books, UK; Nelson County Will Books, UK.

93. James R. Rogers, *The Cane Ridge Meeting-House* (Cincinnati, 1910); interview with Patrick Scott, Draper 11 CC 8; *Journal of the House of Representatives at the Second Session of the General Assembly for the Commonwealth of Kentucky*, p. 19 (hereafter *House Journal*, November 1792 session); ibid., 1794 session, pp. 8-9, 18.

94. East Hickman Baptist Church Minutes, Southern Baptist Theological Seminary, Louisville; Transylvania Presbytery Minutes, 19 April 1796, UK; interview John McKinney's family, Draper 11 CC 25-26; Spencer, *Kentucky Baptists*, 1: 253; Elkhorn Association Minutes, 26-27 August, 26 December 1791, in Sweet, ed., *The Baptists*, pp. 440-44, 446-47.

95. James Madison to Caleb Wallace, 23 August 1785, Madison MSS; George Nicholas to James Wilkinson, 23 January 1788, Nicholas MSS, Durrett.

96. "Speech on Government for Limited Time," Nicholas MSS, Durrett.

97. Ibid.

98. George Nicholas to James Wilkinson, 23 January 1788, ibid.; Nicholas to James Madison, 20 June 1791, Madison MSS.

99. Convention resolutions, *Journal of the First Constitutional Convention*, p. 9; Kentucky, *Constitution* (1792), Art. XI, Sect. 1.

100. George Nicholas to James Madison, 2 May, 5 September 1792, Madison MSS; Caleb Wallace to William Fleming, 28 May 1792, Fleming-Christian MSS; Samuel McDowell to Arthur Campbell, 21 May 1792, Draper 9 DD 69; Joseph Watkins to Nathaniel Massie, 22 February 1793, in David M. Massie, *Nathaniel Massie, A Pioneer of Ohio* (Cincinnati, 1896), p. 120.

Chapter 3

1. G. Glenn Clift, ed., *"Second Census" of Kentucky—1800* (Frankfort, 1954), p. vi.

2. Lowell H. Harrison, *John Breckinridge: Jeffersonian Republican*, Filson Club Publications, 2d ser., No. 2 (Louisville, 1969), pp. 28-33, 114-27; E. Merton Coulter, "John Breckinridge," *DAB*, 3: 6; Walker Daniel to John Breckinridge, 8 August 1784, William Breckinridge to Breckinridge, 9 August 1784, Caleb Wallace to Breckinridge, 9 October 1790, Breckinridge MSS; Fayette County Tax List, KHS.

3. *Kentucky Gazette*, 11 May 1793; John Preston to Francis Preston, 3 May 1793, *William and Mary Quarterly*, 2d ser., 2 (1922): 188-89; Archibald Stuart to John Breckinridge, 10 September 1793, Breckinridge MSS; George Nicholas to Wilson Cary Nicholas, 24 June 1793, Randolph-Nicholas Papers, University of Virginia.

4. John Breckinridge to Archibald Stuart, 14 February 1792, Archibald Stuart Correspondence, Virginia Historical Society; Stuart to Breckinridge, 10 September 1793, Breckinridge MSS; Breckinridge to Adam Guthrie, 19 May 1800, Miscellaneous Manuscripts, Durrett; Harrison, *John Breckinridge*, pp. 49, 63-64, 138. He probably

served as attorney general from 26 January 1795 to 30 November 1797: see Executive Journals, KHS.

5. Harrison, *John Breckinridge*, p. 125.

6. Hening, ed., *Statutes at Large*, 13: 17-21.

7. "Gaius," *Kentucky Gazette*, 7 July 1792; "A Citizen," ibid., 17 May 1794; *House Journal*, November 1792 session, p. 34; ibid., 1793 session, p. 76; ibid., 1795 session, p. 32.

8. Elisha I. Hall to John Breckinridge, 11 March 1796, Breckinridge MSS; Toulmin, *Western Country in 1793*, p. 90.

9. "A Citizen," *Kentucky Gazette*, 17 May 1794; Alexander S. Bullitt, "Fragment of a Treatise Addressed to the Mohawks," Bullitt MSS.

10. Many of the details of this business enterprise were exposed because of a falling out between Elisha Hall and James Brown. Brown accused Hall of stealing some money he carried on his trip east, and the two exchanged charges in a pair of pamphlets: [Elisha I. Hall], *Observations and Documents, Relative to a Calumny, Circulated by John Brown* . . . (N.p., [1802]), especially Doc. VII, p. 34; James Brown, *An Address to the Public, Accompanied by Documents, Exposing the Misrepresentations, Calumnies and Falsehoods, Contained in the Pamphlet of Elisha I. Hall* . . . (Lexington, Ky., [1803]).

11. *House Journal*, 1795 session, pp. 44-45; [Hall], *Observations and Documents*, Doc. VIII, pp. 34-35.

12. *House Journal*, 1795 session, pp. 44-45, 52-53; ibid., February 1797 session, pp. 69, 79, 96; *Senate Journal*, 1795 session, p. 32; [Hall], *Observations and Documents*, Doc. VIII, pp. 34-35, Doc. IX, pp. 35-36, Doc. XIII, pp. 38-39; Brown, *An Address to the Public*, p. 28.

13. *House Journal*, 1793 session, p. 19; ibid., 1794 session, p. 5; *Session Laws*, 1795 session, Chapt. XLIX.

14. *House Journal*, 1796 session, pp. 29-30, 42, 168, 183.

15. *Session Laws*, February 1797 session, [Chapt. LIX].

16. George Nicholas to Isaac Shelby, 29 January 1799, Isaac Shelby Papers, Filson Club (hereafter Shelby MSS, FC).

17. *House Journal*, 1799 session, p. 131; *Session Laws*, November 1798 session, Chapt. LXVIII; ibid., 1800 session, Chapt. LXXIV; William McDowell to John Breckinridge, 8 January 1802, Breckinridge MSS; Marshall, *History of Kentucky*, 2: 177-79.

18. David Meade to Ann Meade Randolph, 1 September 1796, *William and Mary Quarterly*, 2d ser., 21 (1941): 341.

19. John Breckinridge to Samuel Meredith, 7 August 1796, Breckinridge MSS; Harry Innes to James Innes, 23 August 1795, Randolph Family Papers, Virginia Historical Society.

20. *House Journal*, June and November 1792 sessions.

21. Ibid., June 1792 through November 1798 sessions, especially the 1796 session, pp. 100-101; "Quericus," *Kentucky Gazette*, 6 September 1788.

22. Kentucky, *Constitution* (1792), Art. I, Sect. 6. The constitution itself assigned representation initially but required a reapportionment within two years and at four-year intervals thereafter. The assembly passed its first apportionment law in 1793 but obviously keyed the four-year requirement to the date of statehood. The second apportionment law passed in 1795 (to take effect in 1796), the next in 1799.

23. *House Journal*, 1793 session, pp. 69, 87-88, 91-92. Logan County had 289 white males over twenty-one in 1793, Green County had 297, Hardin County had 272 in 1794 (Kentucky County Tax Lists, KHS). "White males over twenty-one" is the only figure available, but it only approximates the number of voters, since free blacks and mulattos could vote.

24. *Session Laws*, 1795 session, Chapt. XVI; Kentucky County Tax Lists, KHS. Campbell County's 1795 white male population was 308, so it may have reached the requisite figure of 330 voters.

25. *House Journal*, 1793, 1794, and 1795 sessions; *Session Laws*, 1796 session, Chapt. III.

26. *House Journal*, November 1797 session, pp. 14-15, 20; ibid., January 1798 session, p. 49; *Senate Journal*, January 1798 session, pp. 24, 44; *Private Session Laws*, January 1798 session, Chapt. VIII.

27. *House Journal*, January 1798 session, passim; *Senate Journal*, January 1798 session, passim; *Private Session Laws*, January 1798 session, Chapt. XXXII.

28. *Session Laws*, November 1798 session, Chapts. I, IV, XLIII, XLVII, XLIX, LIV, LVII, LVIII, LXI, LXII, LXV, LXXIII; Kentucky County Tax Lists, KHS.

29. This feeling was not exhibited in the press during the decade, but the 1799 convention debates demonstrated a pent-up bitterness.

30. *House Journal*, November 1798 session, p. 41.

31. Kentucky County Tax Lists, KHS; George Nicholas to Isaac Shelby, 29 January 1799, Shelby MSS, FC.

32. Enoch Smith to Isaac Shelby, 13 December 1794, Kentucky Governors Papers, Section 1, Box 1, Jacket 4, KHS (hereafter Governors MSS); *Session Laws*, June 1792 session, Chapt. XXXV; petitions in *House Journal*, November 1792 session and in Governors MSS, Section 1, Box 1, Jackets 1, 2, 3, 4; Marshall, *History of Kentucky*, 2: 13.

33. Peter Cartwright, *The Backwoods Preacher: An Autobiography*, ed. W. P. Strickland (London, 1858), p. 5; John Edwards to Isaac Shelby, 24 June 1792, Governors MSS, Section 1, Box 1, Jacket 1; Alexander Barnett to Shelby, 2 April 1796, Shelby Family Papers, LC (hereafter Shelby MSS, LC); John Hall et al. to Shelby, 14 April 1795, Governors MSS, Section 1, Box 1, Jacket 6; letters of resignation are in ibid., Jackets 1, 3, 4, see John Caldwell to Shelby, 9 June 1794, ibid., Jacket 4; Paris (Ky.) *Rights of Man or the Kentucky Mercury*, 30 August 1797.

34. U.S., Bureau of the Census, *Century of Population Growth*, p. 134; Clift, *"Second Census,"* pp. iv-vi.

35. Samuel McDowell to Arthur Campbell, 22 June 1796, Draper 9 DD 61; Kentucky County Tax Lists, KHS.

36. Kentucky County Tax Lists, KHS; Lewis C. Gray, *History of Agriculture in the Southern United States*, Carnegie Institute of Washington Publication No. 430 (Washington, D.C., 1933), 2: 754-55, 837; Toulmin, *Western Country in 1793*, p. 90; *Session Laws*, 1794 session, Chapt. XVI; ibid., 1796 session, Chapt. IX; *Public Session Laws*, January 1798 session, Chapt. LVII, Sect. 3; *Session Laws*, November 1798 session, Chapt. XXXIII; ibid., 1799 session, Chapt. LXXVI.

37. Drake, *Pioneer Life in Kentucky*, pp. 207-8. Among men who supported antislavery in 1792 and subsequently became slaveholders were two delegates to the first constitutional convention, John Wilson and George Lewis: see Mason County Tax List, KHS; see also memoir of Rev. James Gallaher, Draper 15 CC 224.

38. Kentucky, *Constitution* (1792), Art. IX, Sect. 1; Hening, ed., *Statutes at Large*, 12: 182, 713; certificate of John Cromwell, 11 June 1794, in Edward Merritt McEachern Collection, Eastern Carolina Manuscript Collection, Eastern Carolina University, Greenville, N.C.

39. *House Journal*, 1793 session, pp. 29, 56; ibid., 1794 session, passim, especially pp. 28-29; American Convention of Abolition Societies, Minutes of Proceedings, 3 January 1794, in Pennsylvania Abolition Society MSS.

40. *House Journal*, 1794 session, passim, especially pp. 28-29; *Senate Journal*, passim, especially p. 21; *Session Laws*, 1794 session, Chapt. XXVII.

41. *Session Laws*, 1794 session, Chapt. XXVII; compare with Hening, ed., *Statutes at Large*, 11: 39-40. *House Journal*, June 1792 session, p. 9; ibid., November 1792 session, p. 149; ibid., 1794 session, pp. 24-25; ibid., February 1797 session, pp. 46-47; ibid., November 1798 session, p. 40; ibid., 1799 session, p. 22.

42. David Rice to William Rodgers, 4 November 1794, Committee of Correspondence Letter Book, Pennsylvania Abolition Society MSS; Transylvania Presbytery Minutes, UK, especially 15 April 1796; interview with Mrs. Scott, Draper 11 CC 226; Martin, *Anti-Slavery in Kentucky*, pp. 20-25; Marshall, *History of Kentucky*, 1: 444; Randall A. Corkern, "A Study of the Education, Morals, Salary, and Controversial Movements of the Frontier Baptist Preacher in Kentucky from Its Settlement until 1830" (Th.D. diss., Southern Baptist Theological Seminary, Louisville, 1952), pp. 207-9.

43. David Rice to William Rodgers, 4 November 1794, Committee of Correspondence Letter Book, Pennsylvania Abolition Society MSS; Miscellaneous Papers, ibid.; "List of Treatises for D Rice," ibid.; *Kentucky Gazette*, 6 April 1793.

44. David Rice to William Rodgers, 4 November 1794, Committee of Correspondence Letter Book, Pennsylvania Abolition Society MSS; Rice to James Todd, 26 April 1797, Manuscript Collection, ibid.; Samuel Brown to John Brown, 12 January 1798, Brown MSS.

45. J. Watkins to Nathaniel Massie, 27 August 1796, Massie, *Nathaniel Massie*, p. 128; David Meade to Ann Meade Randolph, 6 May 1798, William Bolling Papers, Duke University Library; interview with Patrick Scott, Draper 11 CC 8; Sessional Record of the Miller's Run . . . Churches, 1792-1803, UK; Minutes of the Associate Presbytery of Miami, Wooster College Library, Wooster, Ohio; Rogers, *Cane Ridge*, pp. 14-26; Charlotte R. Conover, *Concerning the Forefathers: Being a Memoir, with Personal Narrative and Letters of Two Pioneers* (Dayton, 1902), p. 268; *Autobiography of Rev. James B. Finley, or Pioneer Life in the West*, ed. W. P. Strickland (Cincinnati, 1853), pp. 99-100; E. B. Welsh, ed., *Buckeye Presbyterianism* (N.p., 1968), Chapt. 2.

Chapter 4

1. *House Journal*, June 1792 session, p. 10; ibid., November 1792 session, pp. 89, 133, 174-76; *Kentucky Gazette*, 28 July, 24 November, 1, 8 December 1792.

2. Samuel McDowell to Arthur Campbell, 21 May 1792, Draper 9 DD 69; Benjamin Howard to John Breckinridge, 22 July 1792, Breckinridge MSS; Hubbard Taylor to James Madison, 8 May 1792, Madison MSS; list of Kentucky delegates to Virginia House of Delegates, 1776-1791, see Appendix for sources.

3. *House Journal*, June and November 1792 sessions, passim. Committee size in

the Virginia House of Delegates has been checked for the 1785 and 1789 sessions: *Virginia House Journal*, 1785 and 1789 sessions.

4. Benjamin Howard to John Breckinridge, 22 July 1792, Breckinridge MSS; *House Journal*, June 1792 session, pp. 9, 11-12, 17; *Senate Journal*, June 1792 session, p. 6; *Session Laws*, November 1792 session, Chapt. XI.

5. George Nicholas to James Madison, 5 September 1792, Madison MSS.

6. *House Journal*, June 1792 session, especially pp. 12, 14, 17-18; *Senate Journal*, June 1792 session, especially pp. 9, 23; *Session Laws*, June 1792 session, Chapt. XXXV.

7. *House Journal*, June 1792 session, passim, especially p. 14; *Senate Journal*, June 1792 session, passim, especially p. 23.

8. George Nicholas to Alexander S. Bullitt, 19 August 1792, Bullitt MSS; Hubbard Taylor to James Madison, 9 July 1792, Madison MSS; *House Journal*, June 1792 session, pp. 14, 29; *Senate Journal*, June 1792 session, passim, especially p. 12; *Session Laws*, June 1792 session, Chapt. [XXXVI].

9. Kentucky, *Constitution* (1792), Art. I, Sect. 8; *Session Laws*, June 1792 session, Chapts. XVI, XX, XXIX, XXXI; John Waller to Isaac Shelby and James Brown to Shelby, both 25 August 1792, Shelby MSS, LC; Marshall, *History of Kentucky*, 2: 29-30.

10. *Session Laws*, June 1792 session, Chapts. XXIX, XXXV, Sect. 12.

11. *House Journal*, June 1792 session, pp. 32-33; ibid., November 1792 session, p. 6; *Session Laws*, November 1792 session, Chapt. XXVIII; James McDowell to John McDowell, 27 September 1792, John McDowell Papers, Shane.

12. *Kentucky Gazette*, 2, 9 June 1792; compare with "The expences of government," Nicholas MSS, Durrett.

13. *House Journal*, June 1792 session, pp. 11, 21, 24-25; *Session Laws*, June 1792 session, Chapt. VII.

14. George Nicholas to Alexander S. Bullitt, 3, 19 August 1792, Bullitt to Nicholas, 15 August 1792, Bullitt MSS; *House Journal*, June 1792 session, pp. 26-27; ibid., November 1792 session, pp. 62-63. The law was passed by the House on November 22; Nicholas resigned before December 7 and probably on November 20, the last day for which he was paid: Executive Journals, KHS; James Wilkinson to John Brown, 11 December 1792, Brown MSS; Richard H. Collins, *Collins' Historical Sketches of Kentucky, History of Kentucky by the Late Lewis Collins, Revised, Enlarged Four-fold, and Brought Down to the Year 1874* (Covington, Ky., 1874), 1: 508.

15. *Session Laws*, 1793 session, Chapt. XXXVII.

16. Kentucky, *Constitution* (1792), Art. I, Sect. 27; Francis G. Slaughter to John Ransdell, 6 June 1792, Virginia State Library, Richmond.

17. List of sheriffs in Kentucky counties, 1792-1799, List of county officials in Kentucky counties before statehood, 1780-1792, and List of county officials in Kentucky counties, 1792-1799, see Appendix for sources; see county court order books, UK, for example, Nelson County Court Order Book, July-August 1795; Campbell County Court Order Book, April 1798; *Guardian of Freedom*, 19 June 1798.

18. *Session Laws*, June 1792 session, Chapt. IV, Sect. 7; ibid., November 1792 session, Chapt. XXVII, Sect. 4; *House Journal*, 1796 session, p. 127; ibid., January 1798 session, p. 27; *Public Session Laws*, January 1798 session, Chapt. LVIII, Sect. 4.

19. *House Journal*, January 1798 session, pp. 26-27; Samuel Brown to John Brown, 12 January 1798, Brown MSS.

20. James Dromgoole to Isaac Shelby, 17 February 1795, Shelby MSS, LC; *House Journal*, November 1797 session, pp. 15, 19-20; *Kentucky Gazette*, 27 December 1797. Robert M. Ireland, in "The Place of the Justice of the Peace in the Legislature and Party System of Kentucky, 1792-1850," *American Journal of Legal History* 13 (1969): 202-22, and *The County Courts in Antebellum Kentucky* (Lexington, 1972), pp. 105-22, comes to somewhat different conclusions, both upon the proportion of assemblymen connected to the local courts and upon their legislative actions upon county court issues.

21. *House Journal*, June 1792 session, pp. 18, 33; ibid., 1795 session, pp. 9, 42; *Senate Journal*, 1795 session, p. 7; "Censor," *Kentucky Gazette*, 11 August, 17 November 1792; "A Farmer," ibid., 8 September 1792; "Peasant," ibid., 27 April 1793; Richard Taylor to Isaac Shelby, 1 December 1792, Shelby MSS, FC.

22. Petition from Jefferson County, 14 May 1793, Governors MSS, Section 1, Box 1, Jacket 3; Nathaniel Richardson to John Breckinridge, 12 August 1794, Breckinridge MSS; *House Journal*, November 1792 session, p. 7; ibid., 1794 session, pp. 42, 48; ibid., 1796 session, pp. 19, 44, 150; ibid., January 1798 session, p. 90; *Session Laws*, June 1792 session, Chapt. XXIX; ibid., November 1792 session, Chapt. VI; ibid., 1793 session, Chapt. XLV; ibid., November 1798 session, Chapt. LXVII, Sect. 12. The 1798 law established fees for over a dozen judicial tasks, ranging from 12.5 cents to 75 cents.

23. *Session Laws*, June 1792 session, Chapt. XXXV; ibid., November 1792 session, Chapt. XLI; ibid., 1796 session, [Chapt. XIV], Sect. 1; *Private Session Laws*, January 1798 session, Chapt. VII; Marshall, *History of Kentucky*, 2: 27; List of county officials in Kentucky counties, 1792-1799, see Appendix for sources.

24. *House Journal*, June 1792 session through 1799 session, see especially 1794 session, p. 14; February 1797 session, p. 52.

25. Ibid., see especially 1795 session, pp. 60-61, 71; "A Farmer," *Kentucky Gazette*, 1, 8 March 1794.

26. *House Journal*, 1796 session, p. 59; *Session Laws*, 1796 session, [Chapts. XXV, XXVII].

27. *Session Laws*, November 1792 session, Chapt. LVII, Sect. 3; ibid., 1794 session, Chapt. XVI; ibid., 1795 session, Chapt. LVI; *Public Session Laws*, January 1798 session, Chapt. XI, Sect. 1, Chapt. LVII, Sects. 6, 21, 23.

28. *House Journal*, November 1792 session, pp. 68, 76, 82, 146; ibid., 1793 session, pp. 34, 54-56.

29. The decision was published in *Kentucky Gazette*, 28 February, 7 March 1795; Hubbard Taylor to James Madison, 3 February 1795, Madison MSS; Mann Butler, *A History of the Commonwealth of Kentucky*, 2d ed. rev. (Cincinnati, 1836), pp. 252-55.

30. *House Journal*, 1794 session, pp. 49, 64, 67, 81-82; *Senate Journal*, 1794 session, p. 63; *Kentucky Gazette*, 6 December 1794; "Tyrannoctonos," ibid., 14, 28 February 1795; Hubbard Taylor to James Madison, 3 February 1795, Madison MSS.

31. Caleb Wallace to William Fleming, 2 March 1795, Fleming-Christian MSS; James Brown to John Brown, 8 April 1795, Brown MSS; *House Journal*, 1794 session, pp. 71, 79; *The Address of George Muter and Benjamin Sebastian, Two of the Judges of the Court of Appeals, to the Free Men of Kentucky* (Lexington, 1795); Butler, *History of the Commonwealth*, p. 255.

32. *House Journal*, 1794 session, pp. 40-41, 78, 81; ibid., 1795 session, p. 41;

Senate Journal, 1794 session, pp. 26, 50, 54; ibid., 1795 session, p. 7; *Session Laws*, 1795 session, Chapts. I, LVII.

33. Levi Purviance, *The Biography of Elder David Purviance, with his Memoirs* (Dayton, 1848), pp. 19-29; Rogers, *Cane Ridge*, pp. 70-73; Nathaniel Hart to John Breckinridge, 19 November 1801, Breckinridge MSS; *Session Laws*, November 1798 session, Chapt. XXXII.

34. *House Journal*, November 1792 session, passim; *Session Laws*, 1793 session, Chapt. XIII; ibid., 1794 session, Chapt. XXX; ibid., February 1797 session, Chapt. LVI; *Public Session Laws*, January 1798 session, Chapt. XV; *Session Laws*, November 1798 session, Chapt. XVIII; ibid., 1799 session, Chapt. XXXVI; Hubbard Taylor to James Madison, 3 January [1793], Madison MSS; *Palladium*, 30 December 1800; Marshall, *History of Kentucky*, 2: 237.

35. *House Journal*, June 1792 session through November 1798 session, see especially November 1798 session, pp. 89-93; *Private Session Laws*, January 1798 session, Chapts. XXIX, XXX.

36. *Senate Journal*, 1795 session, p. 5; "Road," [December 1794], draft in Breckinridge MSS; *Kentucky Gazette*, 21 February 1795; Isaac Shelby to John Grant, 1795, Isaac Shelby Papers, University of Chicago (hereafter Shelby MSS, UC); *Session Laws*, 1795 session, Chapt. XV; ibid., February 1797 session, Chapt. LXXXV; ibid., 1799 session, Chapt. XXV; Thomas Speed, *The Wilderness Road*, Filson Club Publications No. 2 (Louisville, 1886), pp. 47-51.

37. "A Petition drawn for the Democratic Society," November 1793, draft in Breckinridge MSS; "Aristides," *Kentucky Gazette*, 6 July 1793; "A Friend to Justice," ibid., 18 November 1797; John Breckinridge, "Speech on the Penal Laws," [17 January 1798], Breckinridge MSS; *House Journal*, 1796 session, pp. 26-27; ibid., November 1797 session, p. 12; ibid., January 1798 session, p. 60; ibid., November 1798 session, pp. 88, 90; ibid., 1799 session, pp. 122, 133; *Palladium*, 23 December 1800; *Public Session Laws*, January 1798 session, Chapt. IV.

38. "Mohawks My Countrymen," draft in Bullitt MSS; *Session Laws*, June 1792 session through November 1797 session, passim; ibid., November 1798 session, Chapt. XXXV.

39. *Public Session Laws*, January 1798 session, Chapt. LI; *Session Laws*, November 1798 session, Chapts. LVI, LIX, LXXII.

40. *House Journal*, November 1798 session, p. 93; *Session Laws*, November 1798 session, Chapt. LIX, Sect. 3; Marshall, *History of Kentucky*, 2: 336.

41. List of trustees of Kentucky academies, 1798, was compared with List of county officials in Kentucky counties, 1792-1799, see Appendix for sources. For evidence of intrahouse juggling of the lists, the final roster may be compared with the original bill offered to the House, *House Journal*, November 1798 session, pp. 76-77.

42. "Good By'e T'ye," *Palladium*, 15 January 1799; *House Journal*, November 1799 session, pp. 13, 44, 107, 109.

43. *House Journal*, 1792 session; ibid., November 1798 session; List of members of Kentucky House of Representatives, 1792-1799, see Appendix for sources; Greene, "Foundations of Political Power," pp. 485-506; see Appendix for note on the methodology used in ranking leaders. There were nine classified as leaders in 1792; eleven in 1793; eleven in 1794; thirteen in 1795; twelve in 1796; eleven in 1797; thirteen in 1798.

44. E. B. Washburne, ed., *The Edwards Papers* . . . , Chicago Historical Society Collections (Chicago, 1884), 3: 2; *The Biographical Encyclopaedia of Kentucky of the Dead and Living Men of the Nineteenth Century* (Cincinnati, 1878), pp. 717-18; *Kentucky Gazette*, 28 November 1798; *House Journal*, November 1798 session, pp. 12-16; Robert B. McAfee, "The Life and Times of Robert B. McAfee and His Family and Connections," *KHSR* 25 (1927): 223-24.

45. List of leaders in Kentucky House of Representatives, 1792-1798, see Appendix for methodology; Purviance, *Biography of Elder David Purviance*, pp. 19-29; *The B. O. Gaines History of Scott County* (Georgetown, Ky., 1957), 1: 40.

46. All *Senate Journals* are not extant; the only ones located were June 1792 session, 1793 session (incomplete), 1794 session, 1795 session, January 1798 session. Obviously, with its small membership, the Senate did not depend upon a committee system. "An old acquaintance & school fellow" to Alexander S. Bullitt, 10 October 1797, Bullitt MSS.

47. "Cassius," *Kentucky Gazette*, 1 September 1792; "A Freeman," ibid.; "A Plain Republican," ibid., 8 June 1793; William Henry, ibid., 11 October 1794; Kentucky County Tax Lists, KHS; *Senate Journal*, June 1792 session, pp. 21-24; "Reminiscences of Gen. James Taylor of Newport, Kentucky," Taylor-Cannon Papers, Filson Club.

48. *Senate Journal*, 1794 session, pp. 37, 40; ibid., 1795 session, p. 38; *House Journal*, 1793 session, pp. 36, 64, 76; ibid., 1794 session, pp. 47, 58; ibid., 1796 session, p. 149; ibid., February 1797 session, pp. 16, 28-29, 40-41, 51-52; Marshall, *History of Kentucky*, 2: 208; Butler, *History of the Commonwealth*, pp. 261-62.

49. *Session Laws*, June 1792 session through November 1798 session, passim, see especially 1794 session, Chapt. XXXV.

50. Addresses of the governors printed in *House Journal*, except in 1795, when it may be found in *Senate Journal*, pp. 4-6.

51. Ibid.

52. *Senate Journal*, 1795 session, p. 5; Isaac Shelby to John Grant, 1795, Shelby MSS, UC; *House Journal*, 1795 session, p. 16; *Session Laws*, 1795 session, Chapt. XV.

53. List of omissions in the court and revenue laws, Shelby MSS, LC; list of objections to court law, which includes a reference to the high allowance given to quarter sessions, in Shelby's handwriting, Governors MSS, Section 1, Box 1, Jacket 1; compare with veto message, *House Journal*, June 1792 session, p. 33; "Censor," *Kentucky Gazette*, 11 August, 17 November 1792; Marshall, *History of Kentucky*, 2: 189.

54. Shelby's patronage papers, found in Governors MSS; Shelby MSS, LC; Shelby MSS, UC; Shelby MSS, FC; Shelby Memorandum book, 1792-1794, Shelby MSS, LC; Shelby Memorandum book, 1795, Shelby MSS, UC; Executive Journal, KHS. See also "A Farmer," *Kentucky Gazette*, 22 September 1792.

55. John Edwards to [?], and James Brown to Isaac Shelby, 15 August 1792, both in Shelby MSS, LC; see also "Truth," *Kentucky Gazette*, 28 July 1792; John Waller, ibid., 18 August 1792.

56. Patronage papers, see above, note 54.

57. Ibid., especially Charles Ewing and Philemon Waters to Isaac Shelby, 18 December 1794, Governors MSS, Section 1, Box 1, Jacket 4,

58. Ibid.; see William Buckner et al. to Isaac Shelby, 15 October 1793, Governors MSS, Section 1, Box 1, Jacket 3; John Hall et al. to Shelby, 14 April 1795, ibid., Jacket

6; Green Clay et al. to Shelby, 17 December 1793, ibid., Jacket 3; Shelby to William Casey, [1793], Draper 16 DD 30; Benjamin Letcher to Shelby, 12 March 1794, Richard C. Anderson et al. to Shelby, 6 April 1795, Shelby MSS, LC.

59. Edmund Searcy to John Breckinridge, 6 May 1793, Breckinridge MSS; Woodford County Court Order Books, UK. The disappointed candidate may have been mollified when the acting sheriff appointed him deputy in 1794.

60. Patronage papers, see above, note 54; see especially Benjamin Harrison to Isaac Shelby, 19 September 1792, Shelby MSS, LC.

61. Humphrey Marshall to Isaac Shelby, 20 June 1792, Harry Innes to Shelby, 17 February 1794, Shelby MSS, LC; see also Benjamin Harrison to Shelby, 19 September 1792, ibid.

62. *Kentucky Gazette*, 28 May, 26 November 1796; *House Journal*, 1796 session, p. 83; James Blair to John Breckinridge, 10 December 1796, Breckinridge MSS; Talbert, *Benjamin Logan*, pp. 285-91.

63. Garrard's patronage papers, found in Governors MSS; Executive Journal, KHS; Addresses of the governor, *House Journal*, see especially 1796 session, pp. 29-30; *Session Laws*, February 1797 session, [Chapt. LIX]; "A Voter in Woodford," 6 April 1800, draft in Breckinridge MSS.

64. *House Journal*, January 1798 session, pp. 96, 100; ibid., November 1798 session, pp. 69, 75.

65. Patronage papers, Governors MSS; Executive Journal, KHS; *Palladium*, 10 July 1800.

66. John Grant to James Garrard, 15 May 1798, David Davis to Henry Lee, 26 March 1798, Governors MSS, Section 1, Box 2, Jacket 14; patronage papers, Governors MSS; Executive Journal, KHS.

67. Philemon Thomas to James Garrard, 8 May, 30 June 1798, Governors MSS, Section 1, Box 3, Jacket 17; Clift, *"Corn Stalk" Militia*.

Chapter 5

1. "Coriolanus," *Kentucky Gazette*, 25 August 1792; fragment of memorandum and resolution, 28 July 1792, and undated fragment, "To the People," both in William Calk Papers, UK; *House Journal*, November 1792 session, p. 27, mentions a Madison County protest against laws of the June session; see also ibid., pp. 19, 38, 46, 68, 103, 183.

2. Reuben Searcy, *Kentucky Gazette*, 16 March 1793, 27 September 1794; see also ibid., 22 February, 2 August 1794.

3. "NOTICE," ibid., 20 April 1793; Reuben Searcy, ibid., 22 February, 1 March 1794; see also "Peasant," ibid., 27 April 1793; "Patrician," ibid.; "A plain Republican," ibid., 8 June, 10 August, 19 October 1793.

4. Eugene P. Link, *Democratic-Republican Societies, 1790-1800* (New York, 1942), pp. 6-13.

5. *Kentucky Gazette*, 24, 31 August, 14 September 1793; the first notice of the Bourbon branch was in ibid., 2 November 1793; Committee of Correspondence for Scott County, "To the Corresponding Committee of Kentucky for the Meeting of Fayette in Lexington," 9 January 1794, Innes MSS.

6. Link, *Democratic-Republican Societies*, pp. 125-51.

7. *To the President and Congress of the United States of America*, 6 January 1794, Breckinridge MSS; John Breckinridge, *To the Inhabitants of the United States West of the Allegany and Apalachian Mountains*, 13 December 1793, ibid.; E. Merton Coulter, "The Efforts of the Democratic Societies of the West to Open the Navigation of the Mississippi," *Mississippi Valley Historical Review* 11 (1924): 376-86.

8. *Kentucky Gazette*, 24, 31 August, 16 November 1793, 9 August 1794; Chairman John Breckinridge was himself still a townsman, since he had not yet removed to his plantation; "a petition drawn for the Democratic Society," November 1793, draft in Breckinridge MSS; "An old fashioned Republican," *Kentucky Gazette*, 8 February 1794, draft in Breckinridge MSS; "At a meeting of the Inhabitants of Fayette County at Lexington the 28th of August 1795 to consider of the treaty," draft in ibid.; "Iscarus," draft in ibid.

9. Scott County Committee of Correspondence, "To the Corresponding Committee of Kentucky," 9 January 1794, Innes MSS.

10. *Kentucky Gazette*, 2 November 1793, 12 April, 12 July, 9 August 1794; Bourbon County Tax Lists, KHS; Marshall, *History of Kentucky*, 2: 123.

11. *Kentucky Gazette*, 2 November 1793, 31 May, 12 July, 9 August 1794; "A Farmer," ibid., 1, 8 March 1794.

12. "Moses," ibid., 23 August 1794.

13. "A Farmer," ibid., 1, 8 March 1794; William Henry, ibid., 12 April, 4, 11 October 1794; "Fools will be Medling," ibid., 18 October 1794.

14. "A Farmer," ibid., 1, 8 March 1794; William Henry, ibid., 12 April 1794.

15. *House Journal*, 1793 session, pp. 36, 64, 76; ibid., 1794 session, pp. 47, 58.

16. *Senate Journal*, 1794 session, p. 37; William Henry, *Kentucky Gazette*, 11 October 1794; "Fools will be Medling," ibid., 18 October 1794.

17. Coulter, "Efforts of the Democratic Societies"; Link, *Democratic-Republican Societies*, p. 133. There were a number of popular meetings, including one in Bourbon County, but proceedings were limited to the outcry against Jay and Marshall: see *Kentucky Gazette*, 19, 26 September, 3, 10, 17, 24, 31 October, 7, 14 November 1795; *House Journal*, 1795 session, p. 9.

18. *House Journal*, 1795 session, pp. 13, 34-36, 39, 66, 70.

19. Marshall, *History of Kentucky*, 2: 219; Kentucky, *Constitution* (1792), Art. XI, Sect. 1; *House Journal*, February 1797 session, pp. 5, 7, 10, 19; *Session Laws*, February 1797 session, Chapt. [LXXIII].

20. *Session Laws*, February 1797 session, Chapt. [LXXIII]; *Kentucky Gazette*, 5 April 1797.

21. *House Journal*, January 1798 session, pp. 20-21.

22. Ibid., especially p. 42; *Kentucky Gazette*, 14, 21 February, 7, 14 March 1798.

23. *House Journal*, January 1798 session, pp. 82-83, 88.

24. *Senate Journal*, January 1798 session, pp. 45-46, 50; copy of tabulations in Governors MSS, Section 1, Box 2, Jacket 8.

25. *House Journal*, January 1798 session, pp. 101, 104; *Senate Journal*, January 1798 session, pp. 63, 68-69.

26. *House Journal*, January 1798 session, p. 102; *Senate Journal*, January 1798 session, p. 69; *Kentucky Gazette*, 14, 21 February, 14 March 1798; *Mirror*, 24 February, 24 March 1798. The public had been forewarned that the second convention referendum was expected to fail in the Senate: *Kentucky Gazette*, 31 January 1798.

27. *Kentucky Gazette*, 14 March 1798; *Mirror*, 24 March 1798; "Gracchus," *Shall we have a Convention?*, [April 1798], Broadside Collection, LC; see also "Junius," *To the Electors of Franklin County*, 1 May 1798, ibid.; "A Republican," *Shall the Free Men of Kentucky Secure their Rights?* [1798], ibid.; "To the Independent Electors," *Stewart's Kentucky Herald*, 10 April 1798; "A Voter," ibid., 17 April 1798; "A Customer," *Kentucky Gazette*, 18 April 1798.

28. "Gracchus," *Shall we have a Convention?*, [April 1798], Broadside Collection, LC; "Keiling," *A Convention if You Please*, [April 1798], ibid.; "A Republican," *Stewart's Kentucky Herald*, 10 April 1798; "A Voter," ibid., 17 April 1798; "Scaevola," *Kentucky Gazette*, 25 April 1798.

29. "A Republican," *Stewart's Kentucky Herald*, 10 April 1798; "To the Independent Electors," ibid.; "A Voter," ibid., 17 April 1798; "Scaevola," *Kentucky Gazette*, 25 April 1798; "Cassius," ibid., 2 May 1798.

30. Marshall, *History of Kentucky*, 2: 247; David Rice to James Todd, 26 April 1797, Manuscript Collection, Pennsylvania Abolition Society MSS; Samuel Brown to John Brown, 12 January 1798, Brown MSS; Bernard Mayo, *Henry Clay: Spokesman of the New West* (Boston, 1937), pp. 66-67.

31. *A Political Creed*, [April 1798], Broadside Collection, LC; "An Impartial Citizen," *Stewart's Kentucky Herald*, 24 April 1798.

32. "Algernon Sidney," *NO CONVENTION*, [1798], Broadside Collection, LC. Authorship has been attributed to John Breckinridge (Martin, *Anti-Slavery in Kentucky*, pp. 26-27, and Harrison, *John Breckinridge*, p. 98), but the opinions were so different from those he expressed elsewhere that the attribution may be incorrect.

33. "A Friend to Order," *Stewart's Kentucky Herald*, 1 May 1798, draft in Breckinridge MSS; "Attend!," *Kentucky Gazette*, 2 May 1798, draft in Breckinridge MSS.

34. *At a meeting . . .* , 28 April 1798, Broadside Collection, LC.

35. John Breckinridge to Isaac Shelby, 11 March 1798, Breckinridge MSS; George Nicholas to Shelby, 27 December 1798, Shelby MSS, LC; "Algernon Sidney," *NO CONVENTION*, [1798], Broadside Collection, LC; *A Political Creed*, [April 1798], ibid.; "A Friend to Order," *Stewart's Kentucky Herald*, 1 May 1798.

36. Returns found in Governors MSS, Section 1, Box 2, Jacket 9. These figures do not include Mason County for which a return was published, *Kentucky Gazette*, 12 September 1798; revised to include them, the totals are 17,477 voters and 9,681 in favor of a convention.

37. Charles Smith, Jr., to John Breckinridge, 29 April 1798, Breckinridge MSS; Benjamin Howard to Breckinridge, 15 August 1798, ibid.; "To the Citizens of Fayette," *Stewart's Kentucky Herald*, 24 April 1798; election returns, ibid., 8 May 1798.

38. Marshall, *History of Kentucky*, 2: 234; Samuel Hopkins to Thomas Hart, 8 April 1799, Samuel Hopkins Papers, KHS.

39. James M. Smith, "The Grass Roots Origins of the Kentucky Resolutions," *William and Mary Quarterly*, 3d ser., 27 (1970): 222-28.

40. Ibid.; drafts of Clarke and Woodford County Resolutions, August 1798, in Breckinridge MSS; toasts reported in *Guardian of Freedom*, 10, 17 July 1798; resolutions in *Kentucky Gazette*, 11 July, 1, 8, 15, 29 August, 5, 12 September 1798; *Stewart's Kentucky Herald*, 3 July, 4, 18 September 1798. Humphrey Marshall ruefully admitted Kentuckians were "never more unanimous": Marshall, *History of Kentucky*, 2: 251; petitions from Fayette and Mason counties in Adams Family Papers (microfilm), Massachusetts Historical Society.

41. *Kentucky Gazette*, 28 November 1798; *Mirror*, 7 December 1798; Mayo, *Henry Clay*, pp. 73-75.

42. Samuel Brown to John Brown, 12 January 1798, Brown MSS, describes the two as working together. They were on opposite sides in the contested governor's election in 1796 and in the *Kenton* v. *McConnell* land case ("A Citizen," *Kentucky Gazette*, 11 June 1796; "A Fundamentalist," 1 July 1796, draft in Breckinridge MSS, endorsed as refutation of Nicholas; memorial to assembly, November 1794, draft in ibid.).

43. Samuel Brown to John Brown, 12 January 1798, Brown MSS; George Nicholas to John Breckinridge, 17 June 1798, Breckinridge MSS.

44. Marshall, *History of Kentucky*, 2: 281; *Kentucky Gazette*, 1, 8, 15, 29 August, 5, 12 September 1798; *Stewart's Kentucky Herald*, 3 July, 4, 18 September 1798; five of the nine men elected chairmen were justices or past justices, one was county clerk.

45. Nicholas thought he himself was popular enough to get a near unanimous vote: George Nicholas to Isaac Shelby, 27 December 1798, Shelby MSS, LC; Caleb Wallace to John Breckinridge, 13 November 1798, Breckinridge MSS; Harrison, *John Breckinridge*, p. 101; Smith, "The Grass Roots Origins of the Kentucky Resolutions," passim.

46. *House Journal*, November 1798 session, pp. 6-8, 12-16; Smith, "The Grass Roots Origins of the Kentucky Resolutions," especially p. 239.

47. *House Journal*, November 1798 session, passim, especially pp. 55-56.

48. Ibid.

49. Senate debate published in *Palladium*, 18 December 1798; *Mirror*, 28 December 1798; Orval W. Baylor, *John Pope, Kentuckian: His Life and Times, 1770-1845* (Cynthiana, Ky., 1943), especially pp. xii, 18.

50. *Palladium*, 18 December 1798.

51. Ibid.; see also *House Journal*, November 1798 session, p. 55: only ten voted to reapportion before the convention.

52. *Palladium*, 18 December 1798; James Garrard to John Brown, 1 January 1799, Brown MSS; *House Journal*, November 1798 session, p. 74. The motive is conjectural; alternatively, there may have been an unknown agreement between members of the Senate.

53. George Nicholas to Isaac Shelby, 27 December 1798, Shelby MSS, LC; *Session Laws*, November 1798 session, Chapt. LXIX.

54. George Nicholas to Isaac Shelby, 27 December 1798, Shelby MSS, LC.

55. Ibid.; correspondence with five prospective candidates in Breckinridge MSS.

56. George Nicholas to Isaac Shelby, 27 December 1798, Shelby MSS, LC; ibid., 29 January 1799, Shelby MSS, FC.

57. George Nicholas to John Breckinridge, 20 January 1799, Breckinridge MSS.

58. Ibid.; *Kentucky Gazette*, 24, 31 January 1799; "To the Editors of the *Mirror*," *Mirror*, 8 March 1799.

59. George Nicholas to John Breckinridge, 20 January 1799, Breckinridge MSS; Nicholas to Isaac Shelby, 29 January 1799, Shelby MSS, FC; *Kentucky Gazette*, 31 January 1799.

60. George Nicholas to John Breckinridge, [Spring 1799], Breckinridge MSS; *Kentucky Gazette*, 31 January 1799; *Palladium*, 28 March 1799; Fayette County Will Books, UK; U.S., Congress, *Biographical Directory of the American Congress, 1774-1961* (Washington, D.C., 1961), p. 1714; W. H. Perrin, *History of Fayette County*,

Kentucky (Chicago, 1882), p. 775; Green, *Historic Families of Kentucky*, pp. 39-42.

61. "Don Quixotte," 17 March 1799, draft in Breckinridge MSS; "Progress of Humanity," *Mirror*, 1 February 1799; "Another Voter in Fayette," *Kentucky Gazette*, 21 February 1799; "A Layman," ibid., 14 March, 18 April 1799; "A Friend to the Committee Plan," ibid., 28 March 1799; "Aristoblus," ibid., 4 April 1799; "Massa Sammy," *Mirror*, 5 April 1799; "A Committee Man," *Palladium*, 11, 25 April, 9 May 1799; "Sacred Advances," *Mirror*, 3, 17 May 1799.

62. Conover, *Concerning the Forefathers*, p. 268; "Memorandum of sums paid Col. Patterson, May 1799," Draper 3 MM 96; Fayette County Tax List, KHS.

63. "Memorandum," Draper 3 MM 96; "Gustavas Vasa," *Stewart's Kentucky Herald*, 12 February 1799; "A Voter in Fayette," *Kentucky Gazette*, 14 February, 7 March 1799; "Emancipo," *Mirror*, 22 February, 1, 8, 22, 29 March, 17 May 1799; "Scaevola," *Kentucky Gazette*, 28 February 1799; "Philanthropos," *Mirror*, 15 March 1799; "Spectator," *Kentucky Gazette*, 21 March, 4 April 1799; "An Emancipator," ibid., 21 March 1799; "Franklin," *To the People of Kentucky*, [April 1799], Broadside Collection, LC; "Gelon," *Kentucky Gazette*, 25 April 1799.

64. *Mirror*, 26 April 1799; "Mr. Swopes publication," [1799], Draper 3 MM 95.

65. "Wilberforce," *Mirror*, 22 March 1799; George Nicholas, *Kentucky Gazette*, 11 April 1799; Nicholas, *To the Freemen of Kentucky*, 30 March 1799, Broadside Collection, LC.

66. Those raising the suffrage issue are Hampden, *The Universal Right of Suffrage Is in Danger from the Bryan's Station Ticket*, [1799], Broadside Collection, UC; "Scaevola," *Kentucky Gazette*, 28 February 1799; "A Voter who does not wish to be a committee Man," *Stewart's Kentucky Herald*, 12 March 1799; "The Bag," *Kentucky Gazette*, 18 April 1799; "An Independent Elector," ibid., 2 May 1799. See also "A Slave Holder," *Kentucky Gazette*, 7 March 1799; William E. Boswell to John Breckinridge, 12 May 1799, Breckinridge MSS.

67. "Spectator," *Kentucky Gazette*, 14 March 1799; "The Bag," ibid., 18 April 1799.

68. *Kentucky Gazette*, 28 March 1799; "The Bag," ibid., 18 April 1799; Fayette County Tax List, KHS. Conservative criticism of this group in "A Committee Man," *Palladium*, 11 April 1799; "Camillus," *Kentucky Gazette*, 11 April 1799; "A Voter," ibid., 25 April 1799.

69. "Camillus," *Kentucky Gazette*, 11 April 1799; "A Voter," ibid., 25 April 1799.

70. *Stewart's Kentucky Herald*, 26 February 1799; *Kentucky Gazette*, 7 March, 11 April 1799; correspondence with prospective candidates in Breckinridge MSS; George Nicholas to Isaac Shelby, 27 December 1798, Shelby MSS, LC; Marshall, *History of Kentucky*, 2: 292.

71. John McIntire to John Breckinridge, 10 February 1799, Breckinridge MSS; David Rice to Reverend [Walch], 11 December 1799, in Autograph Letters to the Reverend James Blyth, Shane Collection; Bishop, *History of the Church*, pp. 80-81; Purviance, *Biography of Elder David Purviance*, p. 34; notice of Scott County meeting, *Kentucky Gazette*, 4 April 1799; names are same as in the Sessional Record of the Miller's Run . . . Churches, 1792-1803, UK.

72. "Emancipo," *Mirror*, 22 February, 1, 8, 22, 29 March 1799; Drake, *Pioneer*

Life in Kentucky, p. 209; Miles W. Conway, *Mirror*, 26 April 1799; Jilston Payne to John Breckinridge, 12 April 1799, Breckinridge MSS; Ninian Edwards to [Benjamin Edwards], 17 October 1799, Ninian Edwards Papers, Chicago Historical Society (hereafter Edwards MSS).

73. "Cogitativus," *Mirror*, 1 February 1799; "Another Reader," *Kentucky Gazette*, 2 May 1799, Extra; this was a response to "One of Your Readers," ibid., 21, 28 March 1799, who had inserted "A Fragment of an Ancient Chronicle," solely concerned with slavery.

74. David Meade to Judge Prentis, 4 September 1799, Webb-Prentis Papers, Department of Research and Record, Colonial Williamsburg, Inc. (hereafter Webb-Prentis MSS); William Lewis to John Breckinridge, 18 July 1799, Samuel Hopkins to Breckinridge, 15 July 1799, Breckinridge MSS. Hopkins expressed satisfaction at the results, even though he reported that the voters did "me the unspeakable favor of rejecting my services as a Conventionist." See also John McIntire to Breckinridge, 10 February 1799, Benjamin Helm to Breckinridge, 17 February 1799, Jilston Payne to Breckinridge, 12 April 1799, William E. Boswell to Breckinridge, 12 May 1799, ibid.; Payne and Boswell were elected; Fayette County election returns, *Kentucky Gazette*, 9 May 1799; Purviance, *Biography of Elder David Purviance*, p. 34.

Chapter 6

1. *Palladium*, 15, 29 August, 12 September 1799; "A Friend to Fair Play," ibid., 1 May 1800; "A Freeman," ibid.; petitions to Governor Garrard for a pardon in Governors MSS, Section 1, Box 2, Jacket 13. Garrard declined to intervene and Field was executed; the petitions were published by Garrard's opponents during the 1800 election campaign, *Sundry Letters and Petitions Addressed to His Excellency James Garrard, Esq. Governor of Kentucky: Relative to the Case of Henry Field* (N.p., [1800]).

2. Humphrey Marshall said it took effect "without even an emotion, much less commotion": Marshall, *History of Kentucky*, 2: 327.

3. Ibid., pp. 293-94. The assumption that John Breckinridge was not so dominant in 1799 as George Nicholas had been in 1792 is based upon contemporary reactions to the two men; an interview with a contemporary fifty years later is illuminating: "Dr. R.J.B. [Robert J. Breckinridge] wrote the account of his father, in Collin's Ky; Nicholas died while that convention was in session, or just before it. Nicholas was the great man in Ky. then. The acc[ount] the Dr. gives of Jno. B. [John Breckinridge] is very improper – a ridiculous account, and ought never to have been put in the book at all": Joseph Ficklin interview, Draper 16 CC 283.

4. J. Howard to John Breckinridge, 10 July 1799, David Logan to Breckinridge, 17 July 1799, John Hume to Breckinridge, 17 July 1799, Breckinridge MSS. The only suggestion of any appeal for eastern advice was a long letter from John Taylor to Harry Innes, 25 April 1799, Innes MSS, evidently in response to a request from Innes. "Breckinridge Resolutions," [June 1799], Breckinridge MSS; they were written by John Breckinridge, with notations by Nicholas and at least one other. Resolution No. 18 was cut out, but an undated sheet on county representation in ibid., with papers of July 1799, seems to be the missing section.

5. "To the Members of Convention . . .," *Kentucky Gazette*, 11 July 1799;

"Somebrious," *Palladium*, 20 June 1799; "Epaminondas," *Stewart's Kentucky Herald*, 25 June 1799; "Notice," *Kentucky Gazette*, 18 July 1799. The fifty-eight delegates are those actually elected: see *Journal of the Convention, Begun and Held at the Capitol in the Town of Frankfort, on Monday the Twenty-Second Day of July, in the Year of Our Lord One Thousand, Seven Hundred and Ninety-Nine* (Frankfort, 1799), p. 4 (hereafter *Journal of the Convention, 1799*). They include Henry Crist of Bullitt County, who apparently never attended the convention, and Jonathan Forbis of Lincoln County, who left midway in the proceedings. Although a consideration of voting blocs will not include these two men, this profile of the delegates does.

6. Marshall, *History of Kentucky*, 2: 332; William A. Pusey, "Three Kentucky Pioneers: James, Patrick, and William Brown," *Filson Club Quarterly* 4 (1930): 165-83, says Brown freed slaves after the convention; Hardin County Tax List, KHS, shows him owning five slaves in 1794, none in 1796 or thereafter. This profile of the 1799 delegates is based upon the same sources as that of the 1792 convention, see note 23 in Chapter 2.

7. Bracken County Deed Books, UK; "Diary of Captain Philip Buckner, with notes by William Buckner McGroarty," *William and Mary Quarterly*, 2d ser., 6 (1926): 173-207; interview with Benjamin Allen, Draper 11 CC 69; List of county officials in Kentucky counties, 1792-1799, see Appendix for sources; Ninian Edwards to [Benjamin Edwards], 17 October 1799, Edwards MSS; Clift, *"Corn Stalk" Militia*.

8. Minutes of the East Hickman Baptist Church, 1 March, 6 April 1799, Southern Baptist Theological Seminary, Louisville; Robert B. Semple, *A History of the Rise and Progress of the Baptists in Virginia*, (Richmond, 1810), p. 319; Benedict, *A General History of the Baptist Denomination*, 2: 234; Spencer, *Kentucky Baptists*, 1: 79-81, 386; Martin J. Spaulding, *Sketches of the Early Catholic Missions of Kentucky*, (Louisville, [1844]), pp. 25-27.

9. Harrison, *John Breckinridge*; William H. Whitsitt, *Life and Times of Judge Caleb Wallace*, Filson Club Publications No. 4 (Louisville, 1888); Collins, *Historical Sketches*, 2: 80; U.S., Congress, *Biographical Directory*, p. 1714; Weist, "Harry Innes," *DAB* 5: 485-86.

10. George Nicholas to Isaac Shelby, 27 December 1798, Shelby MSS, LC; Green, *Historic Families of Kentucky*, pp. 143-47; *Biographical Encyclopaedia*, p. 69.

11. Judge Henry Pirtle, "Biographical Sketch of John Rowan," written in 1843, Filson Club; Nelson County Tax List, KHS. Rowan's richly decorated mansion in Bardstown is the one made famous by the song "My Old Kentucky Home."

12. Spencer, *Kentucky Baptists*, 1: 231; *House Journal*, January 1798 session, p. 13; *Senate Journal*, January 1798 session, p. 24; Forrest Calico, *History of Garrard County, Kentucky, and Its Churches* (New York, 1947), pp. 295, 303.

13. Joseph H. Parks, *Felix Grundy: Champion of Democracy* (University, La., 1940), especially pp. 10, 56; notes on convention debates by John Breckinridge, Breckinridge MSS (hereafter "Breckinridge Notes").

14. List of members of Kentucky House of Representatives, 1792-1799, and List of members of Kentucky Senate, 1792-1799, see Appendix for sources; List of leaders in Kentucky House of Representatives, 1792-1798, see Appendix for note on methodology. Delegates who had been leaders in at least one legislative session were John Adair, John Breckinridge, Green Clay, Thomas Clay, Robert Johnson, Benjamin Logan, John McDowell, John Rowan, Richard Taylor, Samuel Taylor, and Philemon Thomas.

15. "An old acquaintance & school fellow" to Alexander S. Bullitt, 10 October 1797, Bullitt MSS.

16. State officeholders listed in Collins, *Historical Sketches;* congressional service listed in U.S., Congress, *Biographical Directory*.

17. Collins, *Historical Sketches;* U.S., Congress, *Biographical Directory*.

18. *Kentucky Gazette*, 1 August 1799, Extra.

19. *Journal of the Convention, 1799*, especially pp. 3-6.

20. Ibid., passim; "Breckinridge Notes," Breckinridge MSS: the notes end on 2 August. Secretary of State Harry Toulmin published an advertisement, proposing to publish the debates if he could obtain enough subscribers, but the project was apparently never carried out: *Mirror*, 15 February, 1 March 1799; *Kentucky Gazette*, 25 July 1799, Extra.

21. Spaulding, *Sketches of the Catholic Missions*, p. 26; "Breckinridge Notes," Breckinridge MSS.

22. "Breckinridge Notes," especially 23 July, 1 August, Breckinridge MSS.

23. Ibid., passim.

24. Ibid.; William G. Leger, "The Public Life of John Adair" (Ph.D. diss., University of Kentucky, 1953), pp. 64-72.

25. *Journal of the Convention, 1799*, pp. 3, 8.

26. David Truman, *The Congressional Party: A Case Study* (New York, 1959); Patricia Watlington, "The Partisan Spirit: Kentucky Politics, 1779-1792" (Ph.D. diss., Yale University, 1964), pp. 271-303, 316-23.

27. *Journal of the Convention, 1799*, passim; "Breckinridge Notes," Breckinridge MSS.

28. Rudolph J. Rummel, *Applied Factor Analysis* (Evanston, Ill., 1970) and "Understanding Factor Analysis," *Journal of Conflict Resolution* 11 (1967): 444-80. For further note on methodology, see Appendix.

29. Rummel, "Understanding Factor Analysis," pp. 453-54.

30. Nearly all analysts of this convention and of early Kentucky politics assume such a split, although sometimes defining it as radical/moderate: Barnhart, *Valley of Democracy*, pp. 66-105; E. Merton Coulter, "Early Frontier Democracy in the First Kentucky Constitution," *Political Science Quarterly* 39 (1924): 665-77; Pratt Byrd, "The Kentucky Frontier in 1792," *Filson Club Quarterly* 25 (1951): 181-203, 286-94; Thomas P. Abernethy, *Three Virginia Frontiers* (Baton Rouge, La., 1940), pp. 95-96; Leger, "John Adair," pp. 56-67; Ellis, *Jeffersonian Crisis*, pp. 123-56. Ellis is probably on solid ground, since his study focuses upon one issue with fairly clear-cut ideological cleavage.

31. Samuel Hopkins to John Breckinridge, 15 July 1799, Breckinridge MSS; David Meade to Judge Prentis, 4 September 1799, Webb-Prentis MSS; Kentucky, *Constitution* (1799), Art. VII.

32. *Journal of the Convention, 1799*, pp. 36, 47; Kentucky, *Constitution* (1792), Art. IX, Sect. 1, Art. XII, Sect. 1; ibid. (1799), Art. VII, Sect. 1, Art. X, Sect. 1.

33. Kentucky, *Constitution* (1792), Art. IX, Sect. 1; *Session Laws*, 1794 session, Chapt. XXVII; "Breckinridge Resolutions," Breckinridge MSS; *Journal of the Convention, 1799*, pp. 46-47.

34. *Journal of the Convention, 1799*, pp. 46-47; Gray, *History of Agriculture*, 2: 848-50; Harrison, *John Breckinridge*, pp. 108-9, 122; Samuel McDowell to Arthur Campbell, 22 June 1796, Draper 9 DD 61; Davis, *Problem of Slavery*, p. 119. Harry

Innes, a rich antislavery judge, is the only delegate in the minority who does not fit into either category.

35. Kentucky County Tax Lists, KHS, demonstrate that most of the delegates were increasing their slaveholdings. One delegate had just purchased a stud horse, other stock, and a black man and woman, see James Duncan bill of sale, December 1798, exhibited in the Duncan Tavern, Paris, Ky.

36. *Journal of the Convention, 1799*, pp. 46-47; Davis, *Problem of Slavery*, p. 119.

37. "Breckinridge Resolutions," Breckinridge MSS.

38. *Journal of the Convention, 1799*, pp. 39, 42-44.

39. "Breckinridge Resolutions," Breckinridge MSS; Kentucky, *Constitution* (1792), Art. II, Sect. 8; ibid. (1799), Art. III, Sects. 9, 31.

40. *Journal of the Convention, 1799*, p. 39; Marshall, *History of Kentucky*, 2: 237.

41. "Breckinridge Notes," 30 July, Breckinridge MSS; "Rusticus," *Kentucky Gazette*, 19 July 1806.

42. *Journal of the Convention, 1799*, pp. 24, 28, 41; Kentucky, *Constitution* (1799), Art. II, Sect. 26, Art. III, Sect. 31; county court order books, UK; "Rusticus," *Kentucky Gazette*, 19 July 1806; Marshall, *History of Kentucky*, 2: 352, 373. One writer predicted as early as 1800 that the office would be farmed out because he thought justices would be unwilling to take on the duties of sheriff: William Littell, *Palladium*, 18 November 1800. The practice became one of the most noxious features of the government, see Fields, "Making Kentucky's Third Constitution," p. 173.

43. *Journal of the Convention, 1799*, pp. 15, 42-43.

44. "Breckinridge Resolutions," Breckinridge MSS; *Journal of the Convention, 1799*, pp. 17, 39; Clift, *"Corn Stalk" Militia;* Kentucky, *Constitution* (1799), Art. III, Sects. 29, 30.

45. "Breckinridge Resolutions," Breckinridge MSS; Kentucky, *Constitution* (1792), Art. V, Sect. 6; ibid. (1799), Art. IV, Sect. 6.

46. "Breckinridge Notes," 30 July, Breckinridge MSS.

47. Ibid.; *Journal of the Convention, 1799*, pp. 43-44.

48. "Breckinridge Notes," 27 July, Breckinridge MSS; Kentucky, *Constitution* (1792), Art. I, Sect. 27; ibid. (1799), Art. VI, Sect. 3.

49. George Nicholas to Isaac Shelby, 29 January 1799, Shelby MSS, FC; John Breckinridge to Shelby, 11 March 1798, Breckinridge MSS.

50. "Breckinridge Resolutions," Breckinridge MSS.

51. "Breckinridge Notes," 24 July, ibid. Actually, as Bailey must have known, Logan sent two representatives. Both Bailey and Breckinridge refer to the 6-to-1 ratio, perhaps anticipating that it would be established in the 1799 reapportionment. If that is the explanation, it did not work out in fact: the ratio then established was four representatives for Fayette, two for Logan.

52. Ibid., 23, 24 July; *Journal of the Convention, 1799*, p. 10.

53. *Journal of the Convention, 1799*, p. 40.

54. Ibid., p. 46.

55. Ibid.

56. "Breckinridge Resolutions," Breckinridge MSS; Kentucky, *Constitution* (1799), Art. II, Sect. 5.

57. *Kentucky Gazette*, 31 January 1799.

58. "Breckinridge Resolutions," Breckinridge MSS.

59. "Breckinridge Notes," 24 July, ibid.

60. Ibid., 24, 25 July.

61. Ibid.

62. "Considerations on the Mode of Chusing Senate," Bullitt MSS, is a prepared speech with no notation of where Bullitt gave it; "Breckinridge Notes," 25 July, Breckinridge MSS, indicate that Bullitt addressed the convention and it seems reasonable to assume that this was his text. Senator William Henry of Scott County is not the Bourbon County committeeman of the same name.

63. "Breckinridge Resolutions," Breckinridge MSS; "Breckinridge Notes," 25 July, ibid.

64. "Breckinridge Notes," 25 July, ibid.

65. Ibid.

66. Ibid., 24, 26 July; *Journal of the Convention, 1799*, pp. 40-41.

67. *Journal of the Convention, 1799*, pp. 41-42.

68. "Breckinridge Notes," 30 July, Breckinridge MSS.

69. Ibid., 29 July.

70. Ibid.

71. Ibid.; see also "Breckinridge Resolutions," ibid.

72. "Breckinridge Notes," 29 July, ibid.; Kentucky, *Constitution* (1799), Art. IV, Sect. 12.

73. "Breckinridge Notes," 27, 29, 30 July, Breckinridge MSS.

74. Kentucky, *Constitution* (1799), Art. III, Sect. 6; "A Voter in Woodford," draft in Breckinridge MSS; "A Freeman," *Palladium*, 1 May 1800; ibid., 30 December 1800; *Kentucky Gazette*, 3 January 1804; Mark Hardin to Lyman Draper, 22 January 1863, Draper 4 CC 153-55.

75. "Breckinridge Notes," 30 July, 1 August, Breckinridge MSS.

76. Ibid.

77. Ibid.

78. Ibid., 27, 30 July, 1 August; *Journal of the Convention, 1799*, pp. 37-38.

79. "Breckinridge Notes," 30 July, 1 August, Breckinridge MSS.

80. *Journal of the Convention, 1799*, p. 17; "Hibernian Visitor," *Kentucky Gazette*, 3 April 1804; Marshall, *History of Kentucky*, 2: 350, describes the court as "part brass and part clay"; Ninian Edwards to [Benjamin Edwards], 17 October 1799, Edwards MSS; Parks, *Felix Grundy*, pp. 14-17.

81. "Breckinridge Notes," 27 July, 1, 2 August, Breckinridge MSS; Kentucky, *Constitution* (1792), Art. V, Sect. 2.

82. *The Address of George Muter and Benjamin Sebastian.*

83. "Breckinridge Notes," 1 August, Breckinridge MSS.

84. Comparison of votes, *House Journal*, 1794 session, pp. 80-82, and *Senate Journal*, 1794 session, p. 53, with *Journal of the Convention, 1799*, pp. 41-42. See Hubbard Taylor to James Madison, 3 February 1795, Madison MSS, for the part John Breckinridge played.

85. *House Journal*, 1794 session, pp. 80-82; *Senate Journal*, 1794 session, p. 53.

86. "Breckinridge Notes," 1, 2 August, Breckinridge MSS.

87. Ibid.

88. Ibid., 2 August; compare with "Breckinridge Resolutions," ibid.

89. *Journal of the Convention, 1799*, pp. 41-42.

90. Arndt M. Stickles, *The Critical Court Struggle in Kentucky, 1819-1829* (Bloomington, Ind., 1929); Thomas D. Clark, *A History of Kentucky* (New York, 1937), pp. 198-210.

91. George Nicholas to Isaac Shelby, 29 January 1799, Shelby MSS, FC.

92. "Breckinridge Resolutions," Breckinridge MSS.

93. *Journal of the Convention, 1799*, pp. 44-45, 47-48; Kentucky, *Constitution* (1799), Art. IX, Sect. 1.

94. *Journal of the Convention, 1799*, pp. 48-50.

95. Returns in Governors MSS, Section 1, Box 2, Jacket 19.

96. Samuel Hopkins to John Breckinridge, 5 September 1799, Breckinridge to Thomas Jefferson (copy), 9 December 1799, Breckinridge MSS; see also George Rogers Clark to Jonathan Clarke, 8 January 1800, Draper 2 L 53.

97. Marshall, *History of Kentucky*, 2: 330-32; Ninian Edwards to [Benjamin Edwards], 17 October 1799, Edwards MSS; Butler, *History of the Commonwealth*, p. 291.

98. David Rice to Reverend [Walch], 11 December 1799, in Autograph Letters to the Reverend James Blyth, Shane Collection; "A Voter in Woodford," 6 April 1800, draft in Breckinridge MSS; "A Voter," *Palladium*, 13 March 1800; Fields, "Making Kentucky's Third Constitution," pp. 188-89; Martin, *Anti-Slavery in Kentucky*, p. 33.

Epilogue

1. Thorpe, *Federal and State Constitutions*, vols. 1-7, passim.

2. "Rusticus," *Kentucky Gazette*, 19 July 1806; Marshall, *History of Kentucky*, 2: 352, 373. The same decline was occurring elsewhere: Beeman, *Old Dominion and the New Nation*, pp. 30-32.

3. Fields, "Making Kentucky's Third Constitution," p. 173; Ireland, *County Courts in Antebellum Kentucky*, pp. 153-59.

4. Thorpe, *Federal and State Constitutions*, passim. Northern states used the original formulation of Virginia, as slightly altered by Pennsylvania. The only northern state to use Kentucky's phrase "all free men, when they form a social compact, are equal" was Connecticut (1818), which deleted the word "free."

5. Fields, "Making Kentucky's Third Constitution," pp. 19-26; Ireland, *County Courts in Antebellum Kentucky*, pp. 153-59.

APPENDIX

A Note on Sources and Methodology

HISTORIANS have rarely studied early Kentucky, probably in part because sources are widely scattered, and many are no longer extant. For this study, it was necessary to collect data on the people active in state and local government and on the structure of the Kentucky economy. In order to supplement the meager narrative and manuscript material available on the 1799 convention, statistical techniques have also been applied to data concerning the convention.

List of county officials in Kentucky counties before statehood, 1780-1792. County court order books, UK, are complete for seven of the original counties: Bourbon, Lincoln, Madison, Mason, Mercer, Nelson, and Woodford. The records of Jefferson County are only partial and have been supplemented by a list of county court justices in 1792 (including date of commission and also including men earlier commissioned but not serving in 1792), found in the Governors MSS, Section 1, Box 1, Jacket 1, KHS. Fayette County records are entirely lost, and the only available list is that found in ibid. It does not include a record of those previously named but not serving.

List of Kentucky delegates to Virginia House of Delegates, 1776-1791. Compiled from Swem and Williams, *Register of the General Assembly.*

List of delegates to Kentucky statehood conventions, 1784-1790. The roster of delegates is complete for the first, second, third, fifth, sixth, seventh, and eighth conventions. For the ninth, the list is based primarily upon a roll-call vote with only last names given; thus the list is incomplete and delegates only tentatively identified. Sources are scattered: (1st) "Journal of the First Kentucky Convention," ed. Thomas P. Abernethy, *Journal of Southern History* 1 (1935): 67-78; (2d) Collins, *Historical Sketches*, 1: 354; (3d) Marshall, *History of Kentucky*, 1: 207; (5th) Collins, *Historical Sketches*, 1: 354; (6th) ibid., pp. 354-55; (7th) Journal of the Conventions held in Danville, Kentucky, 1788, 1789, 1790, and 1792, copied in August

1873, by W. G. Lord at the Office of R. H. Collins, Covington, Ky., p. 15, Durrett, UC; (8th) ibid., and manuscript journal, KHS; (9th) ibid.

List of county officials in Kentucky counties, 1792-1799. County court compilations from Executive Journals, KHS. The journals provide a fairly adequate roster of appointments, with date of commission, but frequently fail to mention termination. For this information, the Executive Journals were supplemented by Governors MSS, KHS, and Shelby MSS, LC, where letters of resignation may be found. Journal of the Treasurer, KHS, records the dates quarter sessions justices were paid for their services.

List of sheriffs in Kentucky counties, 1792-1799. The governor usually noted appointments in the Executive Journals, KHS. Election returns were often published, although returns were not usually complete for all counties. For 1792, *Kentucky Gazette*, 5, 12, 19 May 1792; for 1795, ibid., 9, 16, 23 May 1795; for 1798, *Guardian of Freedom*, 8, 15, 22 May 1798. There were a few notations in the Executive Journal, in which it is not clear whether the individuals were elected or appointed.

List of members of the Kentucky Senate, 1792-1799. Senate Journals have been used where available: June 1792 session, 1793 session [incomplete], 1794 session, 1795 session, January 1798 session. *Journals* have been supplemented by *Kentucky Gazette*, 21 May 1796, and *Palladium*, 13 November 1798.

List of members of Kentucky House of Representatives, 1792-1799. The *House Journals* are extant for all years through 1799, and the list of members has been taken from them. The *Journals* have been supplemented, particularly for 1797-1798 for which the *Journal* roster is not complete, by election returns, Governors MSS, Section 1, Box 2, Jacket 8, KHS; *Kentucky Gazette*, 6 May 1797; *Mirror*, 30 December 1797.

Legislative service after 1799 has been determined from Collins, *Historical Sketches*, vol. 2, passim, in which he lists fairly complete rosters of delegates. For 1800, a year for which the *House Journal* is not extant, Collins's list has been supplemented by the record of House proceedings published in *Palladium*, 4, 11, 18, 25 November, 2, 9, 16, 23, 30 December 1800, with roll-call votes recorded therein.

List of leaders in Kentucky House of Representatives, 1792-1798. Leadership was computed according to the methodology employed by Greene, "Foundations of Political Power," pp. 485-506. Zemsky's method, *Merchants, Farmers, and River Gods*, pp. 287-94, is less appropriate since Massachusetts had no standing committees.

Two ways of determining leadership may be employed. One is to count the number of committee assignments; the other is to assign point values for particular kinds of committees as Greene did. I have computed the legislative leadership both ways; although I refer in the text mainly to the latter method, in nearly every case the first method produced the same results. I followed Greene's point values in every case: 15 points for chairman of a standing committee, 5 points for member of a standing committee, 5 points for chairman of a select committee, 3 points for member of a select committee, 3 points for chairman of an ad hoc committee, 2 points for member of an ad hoc committee. Kentucky did not employ interim committees sitting between legislative sessions, so this category of Greene's was not required.

List of trustees of Kentucky academies, 1798. Rosters found in *Public Session Laws*, January 1798 session, Chapt. LI; *Private Session Laws*, January 1798 session, Chapt. XXXI; *Session Laws*, November 1798 session, Chapts. XIX, LXXII.

Landholdings and Slaveholdings in Kentucky, 1792 and 1800. These figures were compiled from available Kentucky County Tax Lists, KHS.

The 1792 records seem to be complete for Bourbon, Fayette, Mason, Madison, and Nelson counties. Jefferson (including the area that became Shelby County), Lincoln (including the area that became Logan County), and Woodford counties are incomplete, the last because the area that became Scott County is covered in badly blurred records. Mercer County records are completely missing.

The United States Census records for Kentucky are not extant for either the 1790 or 1800 census; in United States Bureau of the Census, *A Century of Population Growth*, p. 135, it was estimated that 17 percent of the householders held slaves, but this was only an extrapolation based upon the presumed similarity of Kentucky to North Carolina.

Landholding and slaveholding figures for 1800 were taken from the records of that year if available and complete; if not, I have used 1799 records (Bracken, Cumberland [partial], Fayette, and Warren counties); if neither 1799 or 1800 is available, I have used 1801 (Franklin and Scott counties). There are no available records for Floyd County before 1830.

Voting blocs in the 1799 Convention. The actual votes have been recorded from the roll-call votes, *Journal of the Convention, 1799.* The percentages are of the votes when both delegates actually voted.

Only high percentages are recorded on the chart so that voting blocs may be more easily identified. I have arbitrarily raised the figure Watlington preferred in "The Partisan Spirit," 67 or even 60 percent, for several reasons. A number of the votes in the convention were one-sided, such as the 53 to 3 acceptance of the constitution. Thus a substantial proportion of the convention delegates voted with each other 60 percent of the time. Also, a 60 percent cutoff would mean that two delegates who had opposed each other on ten issues could be placed in the same bloc. Such inclusion obscures the real differences the two delegates demonstrated. Since this analysis attempts to delineate differences, major and minor, within the convention, a higher cutoff point of 75 percent seemed more useful.

One delegate, Charles Smith of Bourbon County, is not included on the chart because he did not vote 75 percent of the time with any other delegate.

Factor analysis of the 1799 Convention. The same twenty-six roll-call votes were used as input in the factor analysis. The first output is a correlation matrix, giving the correlation of each of the twenty-six votes (issues) with each other vote. This correlation matrix is then analyzed or rotated to obtain the "best fit." The correlation matrix shows the correlation of only two votes, just as the voting of two delegates has been correlated in the Voting Chart; the factor analysis identifies a group of issues which were intercorrelated.

A factor analysis merely identifies clusters of intercorrelated issues. The historian must then attempt to identify the reason for the correlation, the underlying factor. In some cases it is impossible to do so and in all cases the labeling of the underlying factor must be considered tentative. Thus, I have assumed that the four issues intercorrelated in Factor 9 were related to democracy, but this is only my hypothesis.

BIBLIOGRAPHICAL ESSAY

OFFICIAL RECORDS of county and state government formed the skeleton of this study. Much of the material regarding county government has been microfilmed by the University of Kentucky Library, including valuable county court order books; the Kentucky Historical Society holds a complete file of county tax lists. The Governors Papers at the Historical Society include many of the patronage papers, although some important Isaac Shelby papers are in Shelby manuscript collections in the Library of Congress, the University of Chicago, and the Filson Club. The Historical Society also holds the *Journals of the General Assembly* and the *Session Laws;* they have been microfilmed as a part of the Early State Records Project of the Library of Congress and the University of North Carolina, which also includes the *Journal of the Convention, Begun and Held at the Capitol in the Town of Frankfort, on Monday the Twenty-Second Day of July, in the Year of Our Lord One Thousand, Seven Hundred and Ninety-Nine* (Frankfort, 1799). The *Journal of the First Constitutional Convention of Kentucky, Held in Danville, Kentucky, April 2 to 19, 1792* has been published in a modern edition (Lexington, 1942).

The legislative and convention journals include no minutes of debates, and none of the records, except for some correspondence in the Governors Papers, contains any descriptive or narrative material to fill out the skeleton. A major source of such material is the correspondence of contemporary observers, located in the manuscript collections of the recipients. The most important collections are those of the Breckinridge Family, James Madison, Harry Innes, and Thomas Jefferson in the Library of Congress; John Mason Brown at Yale University; the Bullitt Family at the Filson Club; William Fleming at Washington and Lee University; and the Fleming-Christian papers (Hugh Blair Grigsby Collection) at the Virginia Historical Society. The most cogent description and analysis of Kentucky politics came from George Nicholas, whose letters are scattered in the above collections, as well as in smaller collections at the University of Virginia, the Kentucky Historical Society, the Library of Congress, the University of Kentucky, and the Filson Club. The important George Nicholas Papers at the University of Chicago primarily consist of speeches and material he prepared for the 1792 constitutional convention.

A wealth of material upon the trans-Appalachian frontier is in the Lyman C. Draper Collection at the Wisconsin Historical Society (cataloged and microfilmed), including official documents, correspondence, memoirs, and interviews transcribed in the mid-1800s. The John D. Shane Collection in the Presbyterian Historical Society contains additional such material. The interviews are particularly important because there are few memoirs which describe early Kentucky social and political life with any detail. Two memoirs which were useful are Daniel Drake, *Pioneer Life in Kentucky, 1785-1800*, ed. by Emmet F. Horine (New York, 1948), and Harry Toulmin, *The Western Country in 1793: Reports on Kentucky and Virginia*, ed. by Marion Tinling and Godfrey Davis (San Marino, Calif., 1948). Religious memoirs were disappointingly thin upon secular affairs, even those of David Rice, contained in Robert H. Bishop, *An Outline of the History of the Church in the State of Kentucky* (Lexington, 1824); however, Levi Purviance, *The Biography of Elder David Purviance, with his Memoirs* (Dayton, Ohio, 1848) and *Autobiography of Rev. James B. Finley or Pioneer Life in the West*, ed. by W. P. Strickland (Cincinnati, 1853), were informative.

Humphrey Marshall, *The History of Kentucky. Exhibiting an Account of the Modern Discovery, Settlement, Progressive Improvement, Civil and Military Transactions, and the Present State of the Country*, 2d ed., 2 vols. (Frankfort, 1824), is an extremely valuable narrative source. Since Marshall was a fierce Federalist partisan and an active participant in the events he described, allowance must be made for his biases. Nonetheless, he had access to original documents when he wrote his account, and he was an acute observer; his assessment of events is usually borne out, though not his judgments of individuals who had incurred his animosity. Richard H. Collins, *Collins' Historical Sketches of Kentucky, History of Kentucky by the Late Lewis Collins, Revised, Enlarged Four-fold, and Brought Down to the Year 1874*, 2 vols. (Covington, Ky., 1874), is also useful for the primary source material it includes, but its historical coverage and accuracy are very spotty.

Newspapers in the 1790s did not report local politics, but they printed letters by pseudonymous authors representing all shades of political opinion. Consequently their weekly or biweekly issues provide the best continuous source of information about political conflict. The *Kentucky Gazette* is most important, since it began publishing in 1787, but the convention controversy in the latter 1790s was covered in the Lexington *Stewart's Kentucky Herald*, the Frankfort *Guardian of Freedom* and *Palladium*, and the Washington *Mirror*. During the late 1790s, broadsides were employed for the first time; the best collections are in the Library of Congress and the University of

Chicago. Polemical pamphlets published by active partisans offer valuable insight into particular episodes: "Philanthropos" [David Rice] explored the most important antislavery arguments during the 1792 convention prelim- inaries in *Slavery Inconsistent with Justice and Good Policy* (Lexington, 1792); *The Address of George Muter and Benjamin Sebastian, Two of the Judges of the Court of Appeals, To the Free Men of Kentucky* (Lexington, 1795) exposes the relationships between the legislature, the judiciary, and public opinion in the aftermath of a controversial judicial decision; many of the details of land speculation and politics in the mid-1790s were bared in *Observations and Documents, Relative to a Calumny, Circulated by John Brown, a Member of the Senate of the United States, from Kentucky, to the Prejudice of Elisha I. Hall, of Frederick County, Virginia* (N.p., [1802]) and James Brown, *An Address to the Public, Accompanied by Documents, Ex- posing the Misrepresentations, Calumnies and Falsehoods, Contained in the Pamphlet of Elisha I. Hall, of Frederick County, Virginia* (Lexington, [1803]); and *Sundry Letters and Petitions Addressed to His Excellency James Garrard, Esq. Governor of Kentucky; Relative to the Case of Henry Field* [N.p., 1800] suggests some of the controversy which revolved around Ken- tucky's second executive.

Apart from comments in the correspondence mentioned above and in the Draper Collection interviews, the most important sources for the anti- slavery movement are records of churches and church associations where the issue surfaced. The most extensive collections of such records are at the Uni- versity of Kentucky (especially the Transylvania Presbytery records and the Sessional Record of Miller's Run, Dry Run, Davis Fork, and McConnell's Run Presbyterian churches) and at the Southern Baptist Theological Sem- inary (especially the East Hickman Baptist Church Minutes). The relation- ship of Kentucky antislavery with the East is suggested in the Pennsylvania Abolition Society Papers at the Pennsylvania Historical Society, and in the Shane Collection at the Presbyterian Historical Society, particularly the James H. Dickey Papers; the relationship of Kentucky and Ohio antislavery emerges from Minutes of the Associate Presbytery of Miami at Wooster Col- lege; Henry Howe, *Historical Collections of Ohio in three Volumes. An En- cyclopedia of the State* (Columbus, 1891); and Charlotte R. Conover, *Con- cerning the Forefathers; Being a Memoir, with Personal Narrative and Let- ters of Two Pioneers, Col. Robert Patterson and Col. John Johnston* (Day- ton, Ohio, 1902).

Collective and individual biographies were compiled from county and state records; articles and genealogical data published in the *Kentucky His- torical Society Register*, the *Filson Club Quarterly, Kentucky Ancestors, William and Mary Quarterly*, and the *Virginia Magazine of History and Bi- ography;* published registers of officeholders; biographical encyclopaedias; county and local histories; histories of religious denominations; and individual biographies. The most helpful political biographies were Lowell H. Harrison, *John Breckinridge: Jeffersonian Republican*, Filson Club Publications, 2d ser., No. 2 (Louisville, 1969); Joseph H. Parks, *Felix Grundy: Champion of Democracy* (University, La., 1940); William G. Leger, "The Public Life of John Adair," (Ph.D. diss., University of Kentucky, 1953); and Bernard Mayo, *Henry Clay: Spokesman of the New West* (Boston, 1937). Also useful were Richard H. Caldemeyer, "The Career of George Nicholas" (Ph.D. diss., Indiana University, 1951), and Charles G. Talbert, *Benjamin Logan: Kentucky Frontiersman* (Lexington, 1962).

The most helpful secondary works dealing with Kentucky were Patricia S. Watlington, *The Partisan Spirit, Kentucky Politics, 1779-1792*, Institute of Early American History and Culture (New York, 1972); Thomas P. Abernethy, *Three Virginia Frontiers* (Baton Rouge, La., 1940); Robert M. Ireland, *The County Courts in Antebellum Kentucky* (Lexington, 1972); Asa E. Martin, *The Anti-Slavery Movement in Kentucky Prior to 1850*, Filson Club Publications No. 29 (Louisville, 1918); John D. Barnhart, *Valley of Democracy: The Frontier versus the Plantation in the Ohio Valley, 1775-1818* (Bloomington, Ind., 1953). Although I disagree with Barnhart's Turnerian frame of reference, I have found his focus upon the comparative development of political institutions suggestive and his biographical approach useful. The most valuable book in providing a national context for Kentucky's political development was Gordon S. Wood, *The Creation of the American Republic, 1776-1787*, Institute of Early American History and Culture (Chapel Hill, N.C., 1969): others were Robert A. Rutland, *The Birth of the Bill of Rights, 1776-1791*, Institute of Early American History and Culture (Chapel Hill, N.C., 1955); Richard R. Beeman, *The Old Dominion and the New Nation, 1788-1801* (Lexington, Ky., 1972); Fletcher M. Green, *Constitutional Development in the South Atlantic States, 1776-1860* (Chapel Hill, N.C., 1930); Richard E. Ellis, *The Jeffersonian Crisis: Courts and Politics in the Young Republic* (New York, 1971); and Eugene P. Link, *Democratic-Republican Societies, 1790-1800* (New York, 1942). Winthrop D. Jordan, *White over Black: American Attitudes toward the Negro, 1550-1812* (Chapel Hill, N.C., 1968), and David B. Davis, *The Problem of Slavery in the Age of Revolution, 1770-1823* (Ithaca, 1975), provide encyclopaedic detail upon antislavery and proslavery thought.

INDEX

"A.B.C." (1791-1792), 18
Abell, Robert, 127
abolition societies, 65; in Kentucky, 67-68, 108. *See also* education
Adair, John, 158; in 1799 constitutional convention, 131-33, 196 n.14; on ballot voting, 143; on Senate, 149; on election of executive, 151
Adams, John, President, 111
agriculture, 65; slavery and, 20, 37, 64, 139; loan office to aid, 35; domestic manufactures and, 36; tobacco culture, 38, 64, 139; in southern Kentucky, 50, 64; stockbreeding, 50, 139; in the Bluegrass, 139
"Algernon Sidney" (1798), 108, 192 n. 32
Alien and Sedition Acts, 87, 90, 97, 131; John Breckinridge leads opposition to, 50, 110, 112-13; Kentucky protests, 110-13, 192 n. 40; and local politics, 112-13, 119-20
Allen, John, 127
American Revolution, 24, 99; effects of, on constitutionalism, 1-2; effects of, on migration, 1-2; effects of, on deferential politics, 2-3; officers of, in Kentucky, 4, 21, 131; local committees in, 15; effects of, on slavery, 36
"Another Reader" (1799), 122-23
antislavery, 9, 66-68; relationship of, to county committees, 19-20, 176 n. 19; arguments for, 19, 39-41, 67,

107, 119-20; as political issue, 19-20, 36-43, 45, 65-67, 107-12, 118-23, 126-27; status of advocates of, 20, 23-24, 43 Table 2, 44, 94-95, 118, 121, 126 Table 9; relationship of, to organized religion, 21, 38-39, 44-45, 66-67; origins and sources of, 36-39, 44-45; and national movement, 36-37, 67; and migration, 38, 40, 44-45, 62, 68; divisions among advocates of, 39-40, 181 n.79; and 1792 constitutional provision, 40, 67, 119; and gradual emancipation, 40, 107, 119; and manumission, 40, 66; and racial prejudice, 40-41, 123; and removal plan, 40-41, 67; and slave importation, 40, 65-66, 164; and Bill of Rights, 42, 138; and constitutional convention campaign, 67-68, 107, 109-10, 112, 118-23, 164; legacy of, 164-66
anti-statehood fight, 7-9; efforts at popular mobilization, 7, 9; linked with county committees, 15; Samuel Taylor, leader of, 24, 101-2
Appalachian Mountains, migration across, 2
appointment of local officials, 2, 29; alternative means of, 16, 30; problems in, 30, 61-62; mode of, 30-31, 81, 89-94, 151-52
appointment of militia officers, 31, 93-96, 142. *See also* militia
appointment of state officials, 2, 29; alternative means of, 16, 30; mode of, 31, 89-90, 152

Pinckney, Charles, 42
platforms. *See* instructions
Political Club of Danville, 10-11;
members of, in 1792 convention,
23-24; opposes tobacco culture,
38
political parties. *See* Democratic
Republican party; Federalist party
Pope, John, 114-15
Presbyterian Church, 45, 85, 118;
differences with Baptists, 3-4;
ministers in 1792 convention, 21;
antislavery within, 45, 66-67; Scott
County group of, 122
Price, John, 126-27, 150
Priestley, James, 128
Princeton College, 24
printer, public, 90, 152
property rights: Bill of Rights to
protect, 17; as defense of slavery, 17,
36-37, 40-41, 108-9, 118-19;
importance of, to encourage
immigration, 26, 41
proslavery: arguments for, 19, 41-43;
constitutional package, 42-43, 136,
138, 166; status of advocates of, 43-
44, 43 Table 2, 126 Table 9;
strengthening of, 62, 63 Table 6, 64-
65, 64 Table 7, 68; and slave
importation, 65-66; and second
constitutional convention campaign,
108-9, 118-21. *See also* antislavery;
slavery in Kentucky

quarter sessions courts, 73, 98, 154;
jurisdiction of, 72, 82-83; eligibility
for assembly of, 77, 78 Table 8, 79,
83, 141; members in 1799
convention, 126. *See also* Kentucky,
judiciary of

"A Real Friend to the People"
(Samuel Taylor) (1789), 24
religion, 117; importance of, on
frontier, 21; ministers in 1792
convention, 21; relation to
antislavery, 38-39, 45, 66-67; church
migration to Ohio, 68; and defense
of slavery, 118; ministers in 1799
convention, 126-27; eligibility of
ministers to office, 136, 153
religious liberty, 13, 38-39

representation. *See* apportionment,
House of Representatives;
apportionment, Senate
representation, concept of, 3, 7, 18,
122
republicanism: concept of, 3, 17;
fitted to needs of Kentucky, 11;
George Nicholas's application of, to
Kentucky, 26-34; second convention
and, 124, 127, 130-33, 146-53, 155-
59; of 1792 and 1799 constitutions,
163-67
revenues, 83-84; taxation provision in
constitution for, 35-36, 74; land
used for, 51, 53
Rice, David, 45, 107; in 1792
convention, 23-24, 40-42; author of
pamphlet, 24, 39; and antislavery
after 1792, 66-68, 122; on 1799
constitution, 161
Richmond, Va., 9, 86
"Rogue's Harbor," 62
Roman Catholic Church, 127
Rowan, John, 87; in 1799 convention,
128, 132, 196 n.11, 196 n.14; on
separation of powers, 157; in 1820s,
159

Saint Domingue, 40
Sandford, Thomas, 95
"Scaevola" (1798), 107
Scotch-Irish, migration of, 3
Scott County, 88; correspondence
committee of Kentucky Democratic
Society in, 99-100; Presbyterian
church group in, 122
Searcy, Reuben, 98
Sebastian, Benjamin, 82; in 1792
convention, 21-22
Second Great Awakening, 45
sectionalism, 53, 58-59
separation of powers, 2, 82-83, 89-90,
102, 109, 122; defense of, 17; in
1799 convention, 130-33, 139, 146-
53, 155-59; in 1799 constitution,
164. *See also* Kentucky, executive of;
Kentucky, judiciary of, independence of; Kentucky, Senate of
Shelby, Isaac, 61, 95; in 1792
convention, 23; as governor, 71, 79,
84, 90-94, 153; use of veto by, 77,
90-91; appointment power of, 91-94,